Lecture Notes in Computer Science 3437

Commenced Publication in 1973
Founding and Former Series Editors:
Gerhard Goos, Juris Hartmanis, and Jan van Leeuwen

T0232837

Thomas Gschwind   Cecilia Mascolo (Eds.)

Software Engineering and Middleware

4th International Workshop, SEM 2004
Linz, Austria, September 20-21, 2004
Revised Selected Papers

 Springer

Volume Editors

Thomas Gschwind
IBM Research, Zurich Research Laboratory
Säumerstrasse 4, 8803 Rüschlikon, Switzerland
E-mail: thomasg at ieee.org

Cecilia Mascolo
University College of London, Department of Computer Science
Gower Street, London WC1E 6BT, UK
E-mail: c.mascolo at cs.ucl.ac.uk

Library of Congress Control Number: 2005923878

CR Subject Classification (1998): D.2, C.2.4, D.3.4

ISSN	0302-9743
ISBN-10	3-540-25328-9 Springer Berlin Heidelberg New York
ISBN-13	978-3-540-25328-0 Springer Berlin Heidelberg New York

Springer is a part of Springer Science+Business Media

springeronline.com

© Springer-Verlag Berlin Heidelberg 2005
Printed in Germany

Typesetting: Camera-ready by author, data conversion by Scientific Publishing Services, Chennai, India
Printed on acid-free paper   SPIN: 11407386   06/3142   5 4 3 2 1 0

Preface

Middleware provides an integration framework for multiple and potentially diverse computing platforms. It allows developers to engineer distributed applications more easily, providing abstractions and primitives to handle distribution and coordination.

Middleware is constantly facing new challenges. Today's advances in computing, including development of pervasive applications, exacerbates the diversity problem, introducing variations not only in terms of performance, but also in terms of environments and device characteristics. Software engineers are therefore challenged both in the area of the development of new and scalable middleware systems, where open, heterogeneous, component-based platforms should provide richer functionality and services, and in the area of application development, where tools to simplify the use of middleware solutions are necessary.

Software Engineering and Middleware is the premier workshop for the research and practice community of software engineering working in both areas to present and discuss new ideas in this field. SEM 2004 was the fourth international workshop on software engineering and middleware of the EDO/SEM workshop series. Previous workshops of this series were successfully held in 2002, 2000 and 1999. Most of the proceedings have been published by Springer in the Lecture Notes in Computer Science series.

The program consisted of a keynote given by Prof. Gustavo Alonso and 16 technical paper presentations. The technical papers were carefully selected from a total of 44 submitted papers. Each paper was thoroughly peer reviewed by at least three members of the Program Committee and consensus on acceptance was achieved by means of an electronic PC discussion. Among the accepted papers, the Program Committee selected the paper "Formally Designing an Event-Based Application for Mobile Collaboration: A Case Study," by Pascal Fenkam and Mehdi Jazayeri, for the Best Paper Award, and the paper "Towards the Development of Ubiquitous Middleware Product Lines," by Sven Apel and Klemens Böhm, for the Best Student Paper Award.

The organizers would like to express their appreciation to a large number of people without whom this event would not have been possible: the authors of submitted papers; the Steering Committee, the Program Committee, and the external referees for their careful reviews and active participation in the paper selection process; and Michael Fischer who managed the electronic submission and reviewing service. We would also like to thank Paul Gruenbacher, in his role as General Chair of ASE, and Stefan Tai and George Spanoudakis, in their roles as ASE Workshops Chairs; they simplified our task considerably by scheduling our work and providing us with templates and instructions. Especially, we would like to thank the Steering Committee for giving us the opportunity to lead this instance of the SEM workshop, and for their invaluable advice.

Finally, we are extremely grateful to IBM for the continuous support given to the workshop: this has allowed us to offer prizes and to sponsor students' participation.

November 2004   Thomas Gschwind and Cecilia Mascolo
                                                      Program Co-chairs
                                                          SEM 2004

Organization

This year's Software Engineering and Middleware Workshop (SEM 2004) was held on September 20-21, 2004, in Linz, Austria, as a co-located event of the International Conference on Automated Software Engineering 2004. SEM 2004 was the fourth international workshop on software engineering and middleware of the EDO/SEM workshop series.

Executive Committee

General Chair	Gerti Kappel (Technische Universität Wien, Austria)
Program Co-chairs	Thomas Gschwind (IBM Research, Switzerland)
	Cecilia Mascolo (University College London, UK)
Web Chair	Michael Fischer (Technische Universität Wien, Austria)
Steering Committee	Alberto Coen-Porisini (Università dell'Insubria, Italy)
	Premkumar Devanbu (University of California, Davis, USA)
	Wolfgang Emmerich (University College London, UK)
	Volker Gruhn (Universität Leipzig, Germany)
	Stefan Tai (IBM Research, USA)
	André van der Hoek (University of California, Irvine, USA)

Program Committee

Judith Bishop (University of Pretoria, South Africa)
Gordon Blair (Lancaster University, UK)
Licia Capra (University College London, UK)
Antonio Carzaniga (University of Colorado at Boulder, USA)
Jun Han (Swinburne University of Technology, Australia)
Katsuro Inoue (Osaka University, Japan)
Paola Inverardi (Università dell'Aquila, Italy)
Valerie Issarny (INRIA, France)
Arno Jacobson (University of Toronto, Canada)
Mehdi Jazayeri (Technische Universität Wien, Austria)
Doug Lea (State University of New York at Oswego, USA)
Amy Murphy (University of Rochester, USA)
Koichiro Ochimizu (Japan Institute of Technology, Japan)
Gian Pietro Picco (Politecnico di Milano, Italy)

Isabelle Rouvellou (IBM Watson Research, USA)
Steve Vinoski (IONA, USA)
Eric Wohlstadter (University of British Columbia, Canada)

External Referees

Celeste Campo
Mauro Caporuscio
Alan Colman
Yan Jin
Heiko Ludwig
Johann Oberleitner
Patrizio Pelliccione

Francoise Sailhan
Masato Suzuki
Massimo Tivoli
Jian Yin
Stefanos Zachariadis

Sponsoring Institutions

International Business Machines (IBM), Armonk, NY, USA

Table of Contents

Keynote

Middleware Services

Ubiquitous Computing

Building Distributed Applications

Dynamic Software Adaptation: Middleware for Pervasive Computing

Gustavo Alonso

Information and Communication Systems Group,
Institute for Pervasive Computing,
Department of Computer Science,
ETH Zürich

Abstract. The many different application scenarios found in pervasive and ubiquitous computing have one aspect in common: software will be confronted with continuously changing execution environments. To guarantee seamless service, protocols, infrastructure, and applications will have to be able to adapt to changes in, e.g., networks, system configuration, available resources, varying policies, etc. In other words, adaptation will have to be a key feature of any mobile software system. In this talk I will discuss the problems encountered when designing middleware for pervasive computing and the role that software engineering could play in solving those problems. I will mostly focus on dynamic software adaptation and how it can be used to great effect to provide much more flexible software platforms. The talk will revolve around the work done on the PROSE system, a modified Java Virtual Machine that uses dynamic Aspect Oriented Programming to extend a running application with new functionality as dictated by the context where such an application runs. The extensions are code fragments that transparently adapt the underlying application. The extensions can be used to modified every aspect of the software hierarchy, e.g., they can be use both to replace a routing protocol as well as to change an application's behavior. In the talk, I will discuss the advantage of such an approach as well as the many challenges it poses in terms of software development and maintenance, security, software modularity, and even the accepted perception of what constitutes a software application.

Biography

Gustavo Alonso is professor in the Department of Computer Science at the Swiss Federal Institute of Technology in Zurich (ETHZ). Gustavo Alonso is from Madrid, Spain, where he completed in 1989 his undergraduate studies in Telecommunications Engineering at the Madrid Technical University (UPM-ETSIT). As a Fulbright student, he did his graduate studies in computer science (M.S. 1992, Ph.D. 1994) in the University of California at Santa Barbara. After graduating, he was a visiting scientist in the IBM Almaden Research Laboratory in San Jose, California, where he worked within the Exotica project in areas

T. Gschwind and C. Mascolo (Eds.): SEM 2004, LNCS 3437, pp. 1–2, 2005.

such as workflow management and transaction processing. In September 1995 he joined ETH where he has since then lead several projects in databases, workflow management, replication, and advanced applications. Currently, Gustavo Alonso leads the Information and Communication Systems Research Group. The research interests of the group include Web Services, grid and cluster computing, databases, workflow management, scientific applications of database and workflow technology (for geographic, astronomical, and biochemical data), pervasive computing and dynamic aspect oriented programming. Gustavo Alonso is co-author of a recently published book on Web Services (Springer Verlag, Berlin 2004, ISBN 3-540-44008-9) and has participated in numerous conferences, panels and projects related to the topic. He also regularly works as an independent consultant in areas like enterprise application integration, Web Services, and middleware.

Here's Your Lego^{TM} Security Kit: How to Give Developers All Protection Mechanisms They Will Ever Need

Konstantin Beznosov

Department of Electrical and Computer Engineering, University of British Columbia
beznosov@ece.ubc.ca

Abstract. By presenting a protection architecture for ASP.NET Web services, this paper demonstrates the feasibility of creating middleware mechanisms in the form of composable, flexible, and extensible building blocks. Like Lego^{TM} constructor parts, such blocks enable the reduction of the effort of constructing, extending, and adjusting the application properties and middleware services in response to requirements or environment changes.

1 Introduction

The main premise of this paper is that the developers and owners of distributed applications need and can be provided with three things: 1) Lego^{TM}-like reusable and versatile building blocks, 2) middleware architectures and tools for composing useful customized solutions out of such blocks, and 3) the means of creating their own inexpensive and error-proof building blocks. They could then create custom distributed applications suitable to their needs and environments, while avoiding costly reinvention and reconstruction of generic and, more often than not, quite complex functionality common across applications. And we are not referring to the business logic, which could arguably be included in the list. The focus is on the nonfunctional properties and services (fault tolerance, performance, security, etc.) of distributed applications.

The above needs have been determined from the author's experience of working for end-user, consulting, and vendor organizations. Working on the end-user side showed that no vendor could ever satisfy all requirements for customizing their solutions to our needs and constraints. Vendors' customization mechanisms required too much effort and expertise from in-house developers. Experience as a consultant, product developer and architect gave convincing evidence that this problem was common to many end-user organizations.

To demonstrate that useful building blocks, architectures, and extension means can indeed be provided for customizing nonfunctional properties of distributed applications without demanding seasoned expertise in the subject matter from application developers, we present an *authentication and authorization (A &A)* architecture for ASP.NET Web services. This architecture, we believe, features all three desired characteristics. It builds on the results of several years of applied research and practical

T. Gschwind and C. Mascolo (Eds.): SEM 2004, LNCS 3437, pp. 3 – 18, 2005.

experience, giving the hope that similar architectures can be developed for easy customization of other properties and services for distributed applications.

The paper is organized as follows: section 2 provides background and discusses related work; Section 3 explains technical motivations for the architecture and gives its overview; Section 4 highlights those design decisions that made the architecture easy to customize; discussion is in Section 5; and we conclude with Section 6.

2 Background and Related Work

Research on composition and customization for middleware has been largely focused on three areas: core functionality; domain-specific properties and characteristics; and middleware services. Research in core functionality concentrates on data (un)marshaling, invocation dispatching, object life-cycle, data transport, etc. (TAO [1], Quarterware [2], COMERA [3], Spring [4]). Examples from the work in domain-specific properties and characteristics are real-time [5], load-balancing [6], QoS [7, 8], performance and consistency [9]. Our work is on composable and customizable A&A mechanisms and belongs to middleware services research, which concentrates on such services as event notification [10], transactions and concurrency [11, 12], and security.

Work on customizable security mechanisms in middleware has been conducted at least since DCE [13]. A wider known example is CORBA, which has a Security Service [14] architecture that enables customization by supporting interceptors as well as making authorization and audit decision objects, security context and some other elements replaceable. However, because the granularity of CORBA Security replaceable parts is too coarse it takes too much effort to customize the service. This drawback can also be viewed as low degree of *composability*. Besides DCE and CORBA, other examples of architectures with replaceable security logic but low degree of composability are more modern JAAS [15], Java Authorization Contract for Containers architecture [16], and Legion [17]. Our approach achieves fine granularity of the replaceable parts and therefore a higher degree of composability.

What our approach (intentionally) leaves unanswered is how to express A&A policies and map them into a composition of A&A building blocks. Andersen et al. [18] approach the problem from the other end and propose "programmable security" approach that uses Obol language to "program" middleware security protocols without addressing the issue of translating such programs into compositions of specific elements of the middleware security architecture.

Design of the authorization mechanism described in this paper is largely based on the Resource Access Decision (RAD) architecture [19, 20], which we follow more in the spirit than in detail—rather as an architectural style. Briefly reviewed in Appendix A, RAD is one of the first attempts to compose and customize authorization logic out of simpler parts.

Although, neither RAD nor this work address the issue of conflicts that could arise as a result of authorization logic composition, several solutions have been proposed elsewhere. Jajodia et al. [21] have proposed an access control model in which inconsistencies among authorizations can be resolved using rules. The framework for access control policy enforcement developed by Siewe et al. [22] allows multiple policies to be enforced through policies composition. It provides a way to specify complex policies and to reason about their properties.

3 Architecture Motivation and Overview

The ASP.NET container is a popular hosting environment for Web services built and run on Microsoft Windows and .NET platforms. However, the ASP.NET security architecture [23], as provided out-of-the-box is not sufficiently flexible and extensible to be adequate for enterprise applications. As we describe in [24], ASP.NET supports limited authentication and group/user-based authorization, both bound to Microsoft proprietary technologies. If an application needs to be protected with enterprise A&A services, the developers have two options: The first, is to develop home-grown container security extensions, which are hard for average application developers to get right. The second option is to program the security logic into the Web service business logic, but the resulting application is costly to evolve and support. In both cases, the development of security-specific parts by average application developers is commonly believed to result in high vulnerability rates due to security-related bugs that are hard to avoid and catch.

Due to its flexibility and extensibility, the protection architecture described in this paper makes ASP.NET easier to integrate with organizational security infrastructure with a reduced effort on the side of Web service developers. The architecture is flexible because it allows configuring of machine-wide authentication and authorization functions, and overriding them for a subtree of the Web services (up to an individual Web service application) in the directory-based ASP.NET hierarchy. Its extensibility is revealed through the support of wide variety of A&A logic, as long as the logic can be programmed as a .NET class and/or accessed (possibly via a proxy) through a predefined .NET API. Furthermore, one can reuse other instances of such logic by combining authorization decisions from them according to predefined or custom rules.

4 The Architecture

The architecture details are described elsewhere [25]. This section focuses mainly on those features of the architecture that enable the composition of more complex A&A functionality from basic, reusable, building blocks. There are five features:

1. the separation of A&A enforcement logic from the decision logic,
2. the employment of the RAD architecture style, which makes creation of custom authorization decision logic easier and avoids the need for a general-purpose policy evaluation engine,
3. flexible configuration-driven construction of the authorization decision information,
4. fine-grained replaceable modules that enable support for a wide range of A&A functionalities, and
5. the support for the scalability, extensibility, and reusability in the configuration part of the architecture.

While most of these features have been already reported individually in the literature, the novelty of our approach is in achieving new characteristics of middleware protection mechanisms by exploiting and combining these features.

4.1 Separation of Enforcement and Decision Logic

To integrate with ASP.NET run-time, the architecture takes advantage of the ASP.NET interception mechanism, *SOAP Extension* [26], intended for additional processing of SOAP messages. Although this mechanism is specific to ASP.NET, other modern middleware technologies (e.g., CORBA, EJB, RMI) can intercept requests or even individual messages [27-30]. Hence, the reliance on the existence of an interception point in the request invocation chain does not limit our approach or makes it specific to ASP.NET.

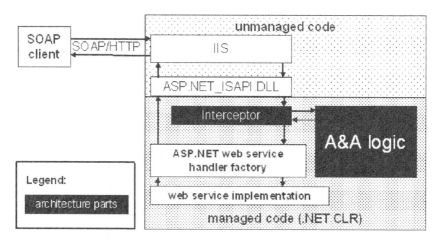

Fig. 1. General organization of the architecture into an interceptor

As shown in Figure 1, our custom version of SOAP Extension module (labeled "interceptor") performs initial extraction, formatting, and other preparation of HTTP requests and contained in them SOAP messages, passing the data to the decision A&A logic, and enforcing authorization decisions. Through the separation of the enforcement and decision functions, we were able to make the enforcement policy neutral and common to all Web services, while allowing the latter to be customizable to each application. The customizable functionalities are authentication and authorization.

Authentication is commonly divided into two phases: retrieving authentication data and validating it. *CredentialsRetriever* objects specialize in retrieving authentication data, whereas validation follows lazy strategy and is left to the authorization phase. Each retriever implementation is responsible for extracting particular data types from appropriate locations. Authentication data and retrievers are represented in a uniform fashion as implementations of *Credential* and *CredentialsRetreiver* interfaces accordingly. This extensibility enables support for diverse authentication policies. For instance, in the same ASP.NET container, one application might use only HTTP basic authentication with username and password (HTTP-BA) over SSL, whereas another could require client SSL certificate and a security token in the SOAP message header to be present for successful authentication.

4.2 Employment of the RAD Architectural Style

The structure of the authorization-related elements of the architecture follows RAD style, which enables the composition of more complex authorization policies out of simpler ones. A brief overview of RAD is provided in Appendix A.

An authorization decision is reached in a three-step process made by evaluators, combinator, and interceptor. Initial decisions are made by zero or more predefined or custom authorization modules referred as *Policy Evaluators* (PEs). The strength of RAD architectural style is in the support of fairly sophisticated authorization policies (see [31] for an example) without the need for complex authorization engines. The support is achieved by combining run-time decisions from several simple PEs into one at the second step, performed by a *Decision Combinator* (DC).

Similarly to PEs, common variations of combination logic are provided in pre-built DCs with the ability for developers to "plug in" custom implementations. To appreciate the power of DC&PEs approach, consider a composition of "All Permits Required" DC with a role-based access control (RBAC) [32] PE. If an application owner decides to further restrict access to a particular range of IP addresses, he or she can do so by adding a PE that authorizes IP addresses, instead of modifying fairly complex logic of the RBAC PE. The result is shown in Figure 2. Support for policies in which PEs might have different priorities, is enabled through the use of PE names so that a DC can discriminate between them.

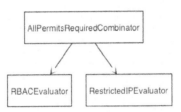

Fig. 2. Resulted configuration after adding the PE, which restricts access based on the sender's IP address

The authorization process continues to its third stage in order to achieve *fail-safe defaults*, in the cases when a DC experiences a failure, and, due to a design or implementation error, does not come to a binary decision, During this stage, the interceptor, which originally delegated the process to the corresponding DC, renders any decision, except "permit," received from the DC to "deny" and thus reaches an authorization verdict. If access has been denied, the corresponding exception is thrown to the ASP.NET run-time, which translates it into an appropriate SOAP exception message.

4.3   Adaptable Information for Authorization Decisions

Besides credentials, PEs are supplied with other request-related information, which is constructed into a *permission*. Thus, the authorization process determines whether a permission should be granted to a subject given its credentials. It is the adaptable construction of the permission that furthers the composability and customizability of the architecture. A permission is constructed out of four distinct elements, as shown in Figure 3. Examples are provided in Table 1 at the end of this subsection.

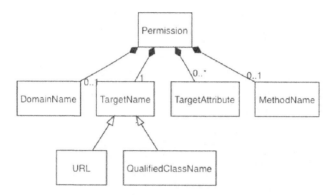

Fig. 3. Elements of the permission generated by the default permission factory

1. *TargetName:* the name of the target Web service can be represented by either the URL or the .NET class name of the service implementation. By using the .NET class name instead of the URL, all instances of a Web service application can share the same authorization policy rules.
2. *DomainName:* the use of the domain classifier is borrowed from CORBA Security [14] architecture, whose policy domains support different security requirements for implementations of same interfaces. In our architecture, optional domains allow discrimination between those same implementations of a Web service that have different access control requirements. Another intended purpose of domains is to allow a logical grouping of several Web services, perhaps so that they can share an authorization server or its policy database.
3. *TargetAttributes:* further differentiation among Web service instances is achieved through an optional list of name-value pairs holding target attributes. For example, a Web service representing a university course could have the course Id as one of its attributes. The use of target attributes reduces the need for mixing authorization and other security logic with business logic. These application-specific attributes and the mechanism for obtaining them are directly based on our prior work on Attribute Function (AF) [33, 34], overview of which is provided in Appendix B.
4. *MethodName:* since ASP.NET supports only RPC semantics, acceptable SOAP messages have to specify the method of the corresponding .NET server class.

Table 1 shows examples of permissions. The construction of permissions is done by a default permission factory, which can be replaced by a custom implementation possibly producing permissions of other format and content.

Table 1. Examples of permissions

Permission Example	Explanation
http://foobank.com/bar.asmx	Only the URL is used
com.foobank.ws.Sbar/m1	Class and method names
D1/com.foobank.ws.Sbar /m1	Same but in domain "D1"
com.foobank.ws.Sbar/owner=smith	Class name and attribute
D1/com.foobank.ws.Sbar/owner=smith/m1	Domain, class, attribute, method

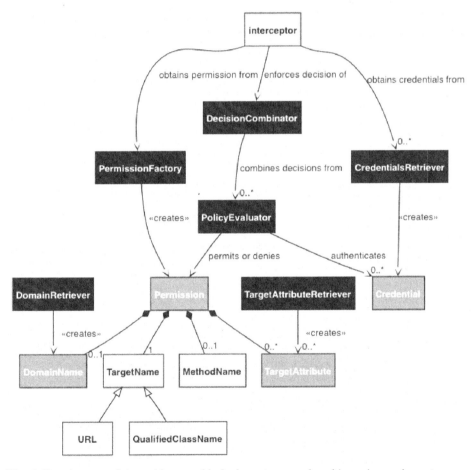

Fig. 4. Key elements of the architecture: black elements are replaceable, and grey elements are modifiable by their creators

4.4 Fine-Grained Replaceability

The flexibility and extensibility of the architecture is achieved in part by designing most of its elements to be replaceable. Any of the black boxes in Figure 4 can be replaced by a version that comes with the implementation or by a version produced by application developers or owners.

Custom versions of the grey boxes are subject to the control by those modules that create them. Other architectures, e.g., CORBA Security, also make some of their parts replaceable. The novelty of our approach is the level of replaceable parts' granularity. In CORBA Security, for instance, authorization logic has to be replaced as a whole, whereas in our architecture, one can selectively replace specific PEs and/or a DC. Additionally, each Web service in the same container can be protected by a different set of replaceable elements, which is not the case with CORBA Security implementations.

To demonstrate the ability of our architecture to be customized through different compositions of black-box implementations we provide examples of implementing two different policies.

4.4.1 Example 1: University Course Web Service
Consider a simplified hypothetical application that enables online access to university courses as Web services. Let us assume that the following is a relevant to the example fragment of the application security policy to be enforced:

Policy 1:

1. All users should authenticate using HTTP-BA.
2. **Anybody** can *lookup course descriptions.*
3. **Registration clerks** can *list students* registered for the course and *(un)register* students.
4. The **course instructor** can *list registered students* as well as *manage course assignments* and *course material.*
5. **Registered students** can *download assignments* and *course material,* as well as *submit assignments.*

Given that each course is represented by a separate instance of a Web service, the following is a configuration of our architecture that enables the enforcement of Policy 1.

Configuration 1:

- An HTTP-BA *CredentialRetriever* CR_1 extracts the user name and password from the HTTP request that carried the corresponding SOAP request.
- A custom *TargetAttributeRetriever* provides the course number in a form of an attribute, e.g. CourseId=EECE412.
- The default *PermissionFactory* is configured to compose permissions with the qualified class name of the .NET class, as a *TargetName*, the corresponding method name, and the attributes provided by the custom retriever. For example: 'ca.ubc.CourseManagment.SimpleCourse/CourseId=EECE412/GetDescription'. No domain name is used in this configuration.

- A prebuilt *PolicyEvaluator* PE$_1$ grants permissions to any request on publicly accessible methods. In the case of Policy 1, there is one public method, GetCourseDescription.
- A custom *PolicyEvaluator* PE$_2$ is programmed and configured to make authorization decisions according to the rules informally described as follows:

   1. Permit users in role 'registration clerk' to access methods 'ListStudents', 'RegisterStudent' and 'UnregisterStudent'.
   2. Permit users in role 'instructor' whose attribute 'CourseTaught' contains the course listed in Permission.TargetAttributes.CourseId to list registered students, manage course assignments and material.
   3. Permit users in role 'student' whose attribute 'RegisteredCourses' contains the course listed in Permission.TargetAttributes.CourseId to list registered students, manage course assignments and material.

   Note that user roles and other attributes are retrieved by the PE during or after it validates the credential received from HTTP-BA *CredentialRetriever*. This step is not discussed since it is very specific to the particular student and employee databases used by the university and is irrelevant here.

- A pre-built *DecisionCombinator* of type *Permit Overrides*, which grants access if either PE grants access.

4.4.2 Example 2: Human Resource Web Service for International Organization

Now consider a multinational company that has its divisions in Japan, Canada, Austria, and Russia. Each division has its own department of human resources (HR). The company rolls out a Web service application in all of its divisions to provide online access to employee information. Each division has one or more Web services providing HR information of that division. The company establishes the following security policy for accessing this application.

Policy 2:

1. Only users within the *company's intranet* or those who access the service over SSL and have valid X.509 certificates issued by the company should be able to access the application.
2. **Anybody** in the company can *look up* any employee and *get essential information* about her/him (e.g., contact information, title, and names of the manager and supervised employees).
3. **Employees of HR** departments can *modify contact information* and *review salary information* of any employee from the same division.
4. **Managers of HR** departments can *modify any information* about the employees of the same department.

Configuration 2:

- Same *CredentialsRetriever* CR$_1$ as in Example 1.
- Another *CredentialRetriever* CR$_2$ obtains an SSL client certificate from the corresponding HTTPS connection.

- A prebuilt simple *DomainRetriever* that always returns same statically config-ured domain name. The domain name designates the division for which HR in-formation is served by the Web service instance, e.g., 'Japan'.
- The default *PermissionFactory* is configured to compose permissions with the domain name, qualified class name of the .NET class, as a target name, and the corresponding method name. No target attributes are used in this case. For ex-ample: 'Japan/com.mega-foo.EmployeeInfo/GetContactInfo'.
- Same prebuilt *PolicyEvaluator* PE_1 as in Example 1. In the case of Policy 2, there are four public methods: FindEmployee, GetEmployeeInformation, GetEmployeeManager, GetSupervisedEmployees.
- A prebuilt *PolicyEvaluator* PE_3 that permits access to any request made from a machine with an IP address in the range of the company's intranet addresses.
- A custom-built *PolicyEvaluator* PE_4 that permits access to any request made by a user with valid X.509 certificate issued by the company. This certificate, if avail-able, is retrieved by CR_2.
- A generic RBAC *PolicyEvaluator* PE_5 that permits invocation of different meth-ods based on the role of the user:
    1. Any user with role 'hr employee' can invoke methods that modify contact in-formation and review salary.
    2. Any user with role 'hr manager' can invoke methods permitted to users with role 'hr employee' as well as methods that modify employee's salary, title, and names of the manager and supervised employees.
- A custom-built *PolicyEvaluator* PE_6 that permits access to any authenticated user, whose attribute 'Division' has the same value as the domain in the per-mission.
- A custom-built *DecisionCombinator*, which grants access according to the fol-lowing formula: $(PE_3 \vee PE_4) \wedge (PE_1 \vee (PE_5 \wedge PE_6))$. That is, a request is permit-ted only to intranet users or those with valid company's certificate $(PE_3 \vee PE_4)$, provided that either the requested method is public (PE_1) or an authorized HR person is accessing a record of the employee from same division $(PE_5 \wedge PE_6)$.

The high degree of the architecture composability allows reusing two prebuilt (1 & 3) and one generic (RBAC) PE (5) out of five. Among the other two, PE_4 is simple to build using certificate validation tools and libraries, and PE_6 requires marginal effort. The DC can be implemented in one 'if' structure.

4.5 Configuration Scalability, Extensibility, and Reuse

Extensible and scalable configuration turned out to be critical in order for our archi-tecture to support the composition of more complex A&A functionality from basic, reusable, building blocks, and, at the same time, carry low administration or run-time overhead. We developed a simple hierarchical language for defining and configuring various elements of the A&A decision logic as well as the protection policies com-posed of them. The relationships among these elements and the policies are shown in Figure 5.

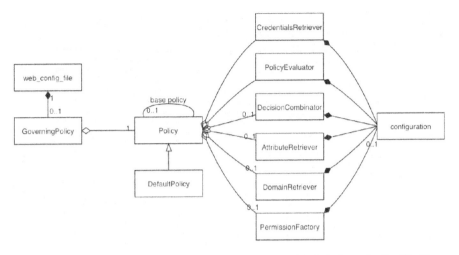

Fig. 5. Simplified model of the configuration elements with default cardinality "0..*"

A protection policy can simply be viewed as a collection of specific credential retrievers; Pes; DC; target and domain and target attribute retrievers; as well as a permission factory, which is defined in other sections of the configuration. Since all these
elements are defined independently of the policies and have unique names, they can
be referenced by more than one policy. *Governing Policy* (GP) specifies which particular policy is used for controlling access to a Web service. Thus, multiple policies
can be prepackaged and used for quickly switching the behavior of the protection
mechanisms from one predefined mode to another.

Illustrated in Figure 6, the hierarchal nature of web.config parsing semantics enables a high degree of scalability without losing a fine level of granularity in the control over subsets of (or individual) Web services. The GP defined in the web.config of
the ASP.NET root determines the protection of all those Web services, for which no
web.config file between the service and the root directory overrides it.

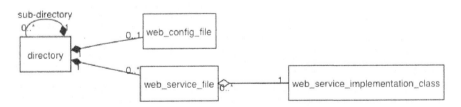

Fig. 6. The association among Web services, their implementations, directories and configuration files

The configuration extensibility and reusability is achieved through two design decisions: First, any web.config file down in the ASP.NET directory hierarchy can override GP, or define any new element, including new policies as long as the name of

this element has not been used in an ascendent web.config.[1] Second, to reduce the amount of effort required for creating policy variations, we also introduced single inheritance mechanism for policy definitions. This way, a policy could reuse most of another policy's definition and override just few elements.

5 Discussion

Besides the practical value for developers and owners of Web services hosted by ASP.NET containers, the work on the A&A architecture demonstrated two points worth of discussion: First, the architecture of protection mechanisms for distributed applications can be designed as a collection of easy-to-create building blocks with multiple places for extending and altering the overall behavior. Hopefully, this work will encourage middleware and software engineering communities to look into the feasibility of similar designs for other mechanisms and services.

Second, there is an alternative to complex, almost universal (and therefore expensive to build and administer) general-purpose authorization engines. This alternative is lightweight, simple to construct, and provides an inexpensive way to run authorization modules, each of which is dedicated to evaluating very specific subset of authorization rules. The decisions from these modules are combined with yet other lightweight specialized modules. As a result, for every distinct authorization policy, a specialized version of the authorization engine is composed out of such modules.

What are the benefit(s), if any, of avoiding general-purpose authorization languages and engines for run-time decisions? We can identify several. To start, no matter how completely a language is supported by an authorization engine, there will always a case that it does not support. Even though most modern authorization languages and engines come with extension points, we are not aware of any instance that would enable simple and efficient synthesis of authorization run-time logic out of existing and new logic.

Composing run-time authorization logic from lightweight specialized modules also enables "pay-for-what-you-use" implementations. The run-time and the administrative overheads become proportional to the complexity of the policies enforced and not to the complexity of all the possible policies supported. Last, but not least, the learning curve for administering, as well as the effort for testing authorization logic composed out of simple modules is again believed to be proportional to the complexity of the enforced policy. By avoiding large generic decision engines and replacing them with the architectures and tools for composing customized engines, developers can better meet the goals for short times to market and for developing solutions useful in a wide range of application domains.

Our approach is not in conflict with the principle of designing a system with security in mind from the beginning. The design of distributed applications still has to take into account the security requirements as well as the capability of the security mechanisms and the underlying middleware technology. For instance, unless each employee record in Example 2 is designed to correspond to a separate distributed object, it would be impossible to allow employees to change their own contact information

---

[1] By "ascendent web.config" we mean a web.config file located down in the directory hierarchy.

without mixing authorization and application logic. What our approach aims at is reducing the effort required to create and adjust adequate A&A controls in the presence of changes to security policies.

5.1 What About AOSD?

The two points discussed above also apply to the aspect-oriented software development (AOSD) methods. Even though AOSD is mostly about dealing with crosscutting concerns that cannot be cleanly modularized, the question of designing decision logic remains. The approach of Lego™-like building blocks combined with a flexible and extensible base for composition, as well as the means of creating new blocks can be employed for designing whatever parts of the aspect in question that the AOSD techniques and tools are able to decouple from the business logic. This also pertains to the choice between large generic policy engines and those composable from specialized light-weight modules.

It is not surprising that the reverse is also applicable, i.e., the implementations of the architectures like the one presented in this paper could benefit from AOSD techniques. An example can be found in [35] which proposes an AOSD-based approach for improving the flexibility and extensibility of security systems at finer levels of granularity than what OO techniques can offer.

6 Conclusions

In this paper, we presented a flexible and extensible authentication and authorization architecture for protecting ASP.NET Web services. While presenting the architecture, we demonstrate the feasibility and benefits of a) the use of lightweight building blocks along with the means for composing them into specialized solutions as well as adding new blocks with custom logic, and b) composing run-time logic for authorization decisions from small encapsulated units of specialized logic. The architecture has been implemented in an actual security solution.

References

1. Schmidt, D.C. and C. Cleeland, *Applying patterns to develop extensible ORB middleware.* IEEE Communications Magazine, 1999. **37**(4): p. 54-63.
2. Singhai, A., A. Sane, and R.H. Campbell. *Quarterware for middleware.* in *18th International Conference on Distributed Computing Systems.* 1998. Amsterdam, Netherlands: IEEE Computer Society.
3. Wang, Y.-M. and W.-J. Lee. *COMERA: COM extensible remoting architecture.* in *Proceedings of COOTS: 4th USENIX Conference on Object-Oriented Technologies and Systems, 27-30 April 1998.* 1998. Sante Fe, NM, USA: USENIX Assoc.
4. Hamilton, G., M.L. Powell, and J.G. Mitchell, *Subcontract; A flexible base for distributed programming.* Operating Systems Review (ACM): Proceedings of the 14th ACM Symposium on Operating Systems Principles, Dec 5-8 1993, 1993. **27**(5): p. 69-79.

5. Balasubramanian, K., et al. *Towards composable distributed real-time and embedded software.* in *WORDS 2003: 8th International Workshop on Object-oriented Real-Time Dependable Systems, 15-17 Jan. 2003.* 2003. Guadalajara, Mexico: IEEE.

6. Othman, O., C. O'Ryan, and D.C. Schmidt, *Designing an adaptive CORBA load balancing service using TAO.* IEEE Distributed Systems Online, 2001. **2**(4).

7. Nahrstedt, K., et al., *QoS-aware middleware for ubiquitous and heterogeneous environments.* IEEE Communications Magazine, 2001. **39**(11): p. 140-8.

8. Venkatasubramanian, N., *Safe 'composability' of middleware services.* Communications of the ACM, 2002. **45**(6): p. 49-52.

9. Krishnamurthy, S., W.H. Sanders, and M. Cukier, *An Adaptive Quality of Service Aware Middleware for Replicated Services.* IEEE Transactions on Parallel and Distributed Systems, 2003. **14**(11): p. 1112-1125.

10. Crowcroft, J., et al., *Channel islands in a reflective ocean: large-scale event distribution in heterogeneous networks.* IEEE Communications Magazine. **40**(9): p. 112-15.

11. Yang, J. and G.E. Kaiser, *JPernLite: extensible transaction services for the WWW.* IEEE Transactions on Knowledge and Data Engineering, 1999. **11**(4): p. 639-657.

12. Houston, I., et al., *The CORBA Activity Service Framework for supporting extended transactions.* Software - Practice and Experience, 2003. **33**(4): p. 351-73.

13. Gittler, F. and A.C. Hopkins, *The DCE Security Service.* Hewlett-Packard Journal, 1995. **46**(6): p. 41-48.

14. OMG, *CORBAservices: Common Object Services Specification, Security Service Specification v1.8.* 2002, Object Management Group, document formal/2002-03-11.

15. Sun, *Java Authentication and Authorization Service (JAAS).* 2001, Sun Microsystems.

16. Sun, *Java Authorization Contract for Containers.* 2002.

17. Chapin, S.J., et al., *New model of security for metasystems.* Future Generation Computer Systems, 1999. **15**(5): p. 713-722.

18. Andersen, A., et al. *Security and middleware.* in *WORDS 2003: 8th International Workshop on Object-oriented Real-Time Dependable Systems, 15-17 Jan. 2003.* 2003. Guadalajara, Mexico: IEEE.

19. Beznosov, K., et al. *A Resource Access Decision Service for CORBA-based Distributed Systems.* in *Annual Computer Security Applications Conference.* 1999. Phoenix, Arizona, USA: IEEE Computer Society.

20. OMG, *Resource Access Decision Facility.* 2001, Object Management Group.

21. Jajodia, S., et al., *Flexible support for multiple access control policies.* ACM Transactions on Database Systems, 2001. **26**(2): p. 214-60.

22. Siewe, F., A. Cau, and H. Zedan. *A compositional framework for access control policies enforcement.* in *Proceedings of the 2003 ACM Workshop on Formal Methods in Security Engineering, FMSE'03, Oct 30 2003.* 2003. Washington, DC, United States: Association for Computing Machinery.

23. Microsoft, *Building Secure ASP.NET Applications: Authentication, Authorization, and Secure Communication.* 2002: Microsoft Press.

24. Hartman, B., et al., *Mastering Web Services Security.* 1st ed. 2003, New York: John Wiley & Sons, Inc.

25. Beznosov, K. *Protecting ASP.NET Web Services: Experience Report.* in *preparation.* 2004.

26. Microsoft, *Altering the SOAP Message Using SOAP Extensions.* 2002.

27. Fleury, M. and F. Reverbel. *The JBoss extensible server.* in *ACM/IFIP/USENIX International Middleware Conference.* 2003. Rio de Janeiro, Brazil: Springer-Verlag.

28. Wang, N., et al., *Evaluating meta-programming mechanisms for ORB middleware*, in *IEEE Communications Magazine*. 2001. p. 102-113.
29. Baldoni, R., C. Marchetti, and L. Verde, *CORBA request portable interceptors: analysis and applications*. Concurrency and Computation Practice & Experience, 2003. **15**(6): p. 551-579.
30. Narasimhan, N., L.E. Moser, and P.M. Melliar-Smith, *Interceptors for Java Remote Method Invocation*. Concurrency Computation Practice and Experience, 2001. **13**(8-9): p. 755-774.
31. Barkley, J., K. Beznosov, and J. Uppal. *Supporting Relationships in Access Control Using Role Based Access Control*. in *Fourth ACM Role-based Access Control Workshop*. 1999. Fairfax, Virginia, USA.
32. Sandhu, R., et al., *Role-Based Access Control Models*. IEEE Computer, 1996. **29**(2): p. 38-47.
33. Beznosov, K. *Object Security Attributes: Enabling Application-specific Access Control in Middleware*. in *4th International Symposium on Distributed Objects & Applications (DOA)*. 2002. Irvine, California, USA: Springer-Verlag.
34. OMG, *Security Domain Membership Management Service, Final Submission*. 2001, Object Management Group.
35. Gao, S., et al. *Applying Aspect-Orientation in Designing Security Systems: A Case Study*. in *The Sixteenth International Conference on Software Engineering and Knowledge Engineering*. 2004. Banff, Alberta, Canada.

Appendix A. Overview of Resource Access Decision Architecture

With the RAD architecture, an application requests an authorization decision from a RAD authorization service and enforces the decision. A RAD service is composed of the following components (Figure 7): The *AccessDecisionObject* (ADO) serves as the interface to RAD clients and coordinates the interactions between other RAD components. Zero or more *PolicyEvaluators* (PEs) perform evaluation decisions based on certain access control policies that govern the access to a protected resource. The *DecisionCombinator* (DC) combines the results of the evaluations made by potentially multiple PEs into a final authorization decision by applying certain combination policies. The *PolicyEvaluatorLocator* (PEL), for a given access request to a protected resource, keeps track of and provides references to a DC and potentially several PEs, which are collectively responsible for making the authorization decision to the request. The *DynamicAttributeService* (DAS) collects and provides dynamic attributes about the client in the context of the intended access operation on the given resource associated with the provided resource name.

Figure 7 shows interactions among components of authorization service:

1. The authorization service receives a request via the ADO interface.
2. The ADO obtains object references to those *PEs* associated with the resource name in question and an object reference for the responsible *DC*.
3. The ADO obtains dynamic attributes of the principal (client) in the context of the resource name and the intended access operation.

4. The ADO delegates an instance of *DC* for polling the *PEs* (selected in Step 2).
5. The *DC* obtains decisions from *PEs* and combines them according to its policy.
6. The decision is forwarded to the ADO, which returns it to the application.

Further details on RAD architecture could be found in [19, 20].

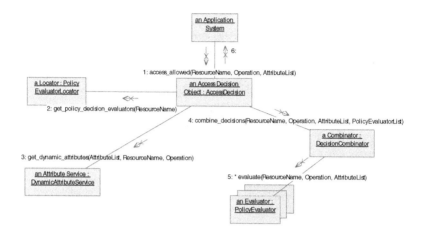

Fig. 7. RAD interaction diagram

Appendix B. Overview of Attribute Function Architecture

The concept of the Attribute Function (AF), as an addition to the traditional decision and enforcement functions, has been proposed in [33]. Its application to CORBA was developed as well [34].

AF has simple syntax: it accepts (middleware-specific) data that are necessary for identifying the state of the target object and returns a set of application-specific attributes of that object. The target object state is necessary for retrieving such object metadata. Since the semantics of object attributes is very specific to the application being protected, AF is provided by the application and not by the middleware or security layers.

The introduction of the AF in the security mechanism design for distributed applications is expected to enable the use of application-specific factors in security policy decisions without coupling enforcement and decision functions with the application.

Integration of a Text Search Engine with a Java Messaging Service

Justin Almquist[1], Ian Gorton[2], and Jereme Haack[1]

[1] Information Sciences and Engineering, Pacific Northwest National Lab,
Richland, WA 99352, USA
[2] Empirical Software Engineering Group, National ICT Australia,
Australian Technology Park, Eveleigh, NSW 1430, Australia

Abstract. Large-scale information processing applications must rapidly search through high volume streams of structured and unstructured textual data to locate useful information. Content-based messaging systems (CBMSs) provide a powerful technology platform for building such stream handling systems. CBMSs make it possible to efficiently execute queries on messages in streams to extract those that contain content of interest. In this paper, we describe efforts to augment an experimental CBMS with the ability to perform efficient free-text search operations. The design of the CBMS platform, based upon a Java Messaging Service, is described, and an empirical evaluation is presented to demonstrate the performance implications of a range of queries varying in complexity.

1 Introduction

Efficiently finding useful data in the ever-growing sources of digital information is a highly challenging research problem. Many applications must search for messages or packets of information located, for example, in network protocol traffic or email messages. Such applications are typically known as data stream processing applications.

Processing continuous data streams [1] poses some unique problems. A streams processing environment must assume that the messages it receives are transient, and cannot all be stored for rapid post-processing. Although some approaches attempt to offer rich query languages for long-running continuous queries on streams [2], these systems are still essentially research prototypes.

Content-based messaging systems (CBMSs) have proven practical technology platforms for building data stream processing applications. A CBMS employs some mechanism for querying the content of an individual message and extracting messages from the stream that satisfy one or more query. Systems such as Elvin [3], Gryphon [4], XMLBlaster [5] and Siena [6] all achieve similar forms of content-based message notification on textual data arriving in message streams. The querying capabilities of these systems do however vary considerably, but in general most utilize a relatively simple query language.

In addition, some commercial, standards-based technologies also can provide content-based messaging. Implementations of the CORBA Notification Service

T. Gschwind and C. Mascolo (Eds.): SEM 2004, LNCS 3437, pp. 19–30, 2005.
© Springer-Verlag Berlin Heidelberg 2005

specification and Java Messaging Service (JMS) API include the ability to select or filter messages using a query language based on SQL-92. These technologies have multiple implementations, including open source, and are widely utilized and deployed in applications.

In [9], we describe our efforts to improve the performance of an open source JMS implementation to provide scalable performance when multiple simultaneous queries must be evaluated against each message in a stream. Algorithms similar to those described in [4, 6, 10] are empirically demonstrated to provide greater than order of magnitude performance improvement and significantly improved scalability when compared to the original JMS implementation.

In practice however, the query language supported by the JMS has proven too simple to be of great utility in application environments. Therefore, this paper describes the extension of our JMS-based CBMS to integrate with an off-the-shelf high performance text search engine. We describe the approach taken to extending the JMS query capability and utilizing the text processing engine. An empirical evaluation of the performance of the resulting platform clearly shows the feasibility of the approach. Further performance analysis factors out the influence of the underlying JMS implementation, and the results display potential for achieving even greater performance from a CBMS platform built from a combination of a JMS and text search engine.

2   A JMS-Based Content-Based Message System

The JMS is a mandatory part of the Java 2 Enterprise Edition (J2EE) platform. The JMS specification defines a set of Java interfaces and associated semantics for an asynchronous publish-subscribe messaging system. Individual vendors implement the JMS by building a JMS *provider* that supports the JMS interfaces. This can be done by wrapping an existing messaging technology such as MQSeries, or by implementing the JMS semantics in Java.

JMS subscribers can specify which messages they wish to receive from a topic based on a *message selector*. The JMS provider ensures that only messages that match the criteria in the message selector are delivered to the subscriber. Message selectors are defined by a subscriber on a per topic basis. The selector language is based on a subset of the SQL92 conditional expression syntax. This includes basic conditional and logical expressions, as well as more sophisticated operators such as LIKE.

[9] describes how we extended the open source JBoss JMS implementation to form a CBMS that can efficiently process multiple streams of data. In summary, the extensions are briefly described below.

Figure 1 depicts the basic architecture for the CBMS platform. The roles of the four key subsystems are as follows:

Data Source Adapter: The *Data Source Adapter* (DSA) subsystem has several responsibilities. It first inputs messages from the data source in their native format, and transforms them in to a well-defined XML message. In addition, it generates a data signature for the message, which is encapsulated in a Java object. A data signature is a mathematical representation of the textual message, and can be used by the CBMS

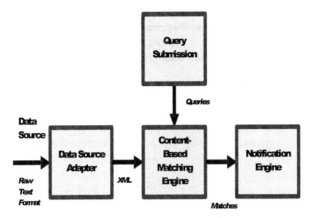

Fig. 1. Overview of CBMS Architecture

engine to efficiently satisfy queries on the message's content. Finally, it publishes the XML message and associated signature to the CBM engine on a defined topic.

CBM Engine: The CBM engine receives messages published by one or more DSA's, with one topic per data source. It also receives queries from the *Query Submission* component. Multiple queries can be registered with a single topic, and hence each message published on a topic must be evaluated against every query. Messages that match one or more queries are sent to the notification engine.

Query Submission: The *Query Submission* subsystem is responsible for managing the set of queries across the topics handled by the CBM engine. It comprises a base API and a set of user tools for submitting, browsing, deleting and optimizing queries.

Notification Engine: This receives messages that match user queries and delivers them to the respective users. Users may specify a delivery mechanism, such as email, store in a database, and so on. The *Notification Engine* therefore manages all aspects of notification and message delivery, freeing the CBM subsystem from this responsibility. Additionally, the Notification Engine is responsible for persisting matched messages. This allows relations between users, queries, and messages to be established such that end users can determine which queries caused certain messages to be matched and saved.

The core CBM engine comprises the modified JBoss JMS. The JMS was modified internally to exploit new algorithms for rapidly evaluating message selectors (queries). The algorithms basically break down each message selector (query) in to a set of individual elements, which are termed *cachable units*. When a selector is evaluated against the message content, the result of each cacheable unit is stored in a cache data structure, which maps a cacheable unit to a Boolean result.

As each message is tested against all the other registered selectors, the cache is accessed in order to locate any shared selector elements that have already been evaluated. When a cacheable unit is associated with a result for this message, its result is simply used in evaluating the current selector. Hence, the commonality

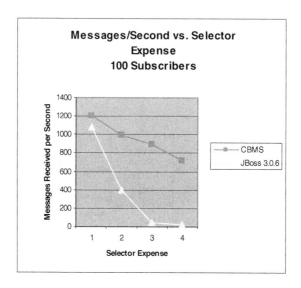

Fig. 2. CBMS message throughput with 100 Subscribers and increasing complexity in message selector evaluation

between selectors is exploited to reduce the number of queries that must be satisfied, and produce greater message throughput. Figure 2 illustrates the improved performance that the CBMS platform achieves. These are more results are fully explained in [9].

3   Extending the JMS Query Language

3.1   The Need for Powerful Text Search

In discussions with potential users of the CBMS platform, it became clear that existing commercial technologies, while slower, expensive and heavyweight, offered much greater flexibility and power in free-text search queries. We therefore decided to investigate how the CBMS platform could incorporate a richer query language in order to increase the relevance of messages delivered to users. At the same time, it remained imperative that the query language did not degrade significantly the performance and scalability gains already achieved.   After investigating the capabilities of existing technologies in the user's application domain, our goal became to extend the current JMS query language with greater free-text searching capabilities.

High performance text searching engines are highly specialized technologies, and hence writing our own was not a sensible option. An investigation of available technologies led us to decide to integrate the open source Lucene[1] full-featured text search engine into the CBMS. Lucene supports a simple API, is extensible, has small

---

[1] (http://jakarta.apache.org/lucene/docs/index.html)

heap and index size requirements, and claims high performance and scalability. It also has the following extensive text query features[2]:

- *Terms* - A Single Term is a single word such as "test" or "hello". A Phrase is a group of words surrounded by double quotes such as "test hello".
- *Wildcard Searches* – Using the '?' will match a single character, such as "te?t". Using the '*' will match multiple characters, such as "test*".
- *Fuzzy Searches* - The fuzzy search features uses the tilde, "~" symbol at the end of a Single word Term. For example, a query with "roam~" would return terms like foam and roams.
- *Proximity Searches* - Lucene supports finding words that are within a specific distance away from each other.
- *Boolean Operators* – The traditional Boolean operators of "AND", "OR", and "NOT are supported, as well as the "+" (required) and "-" (prohibit) operators.

3.2 Messaging with Lucene

In order to investigate the implications of integrating Lucene into the CBMS, we decided to initially extend the query language supported by the JMS standard. The JMS specification's keywords were consequently extended with a new keyword, INCLUDES. Extending the specification is attractive, as it allows the CBMS to still meet the JMS specification, but at the same time extends the JMS functionality for applications that require advanced query behavior.

To simplify the implementation, only queries using the INCLUDES keyword would result in a call to the Lucene API. Hence the internals of the query processing implementation of the CBMS were left unchanged, and the overheads of utilizing Lucene were only incurred when necessary.

Integrating Lucene also required design decisions to be made regarding Lucene's usage. The single largest impact on performance when using a text search engine is the indexing of the source data. In normal modes of application, indexing is an expensive process that requires analyzing many documents and writing the results of the analysis to a disk-based index. Lucene incorporates a high performance indexing mechanism; however any indexing scheme that would have to write files to disk would be prohibitively slow and non-scalable.

Thus, it was determined to use memory based indexes instead of disk-based. This exploited the same optimized indexing and avoided the overhead of disk I/O. This design is especially appropriate since an index is created for every message, and can be discarded when the message has been fully processed.

Another key design decision in exploiting the Lucene engine is the ability to index a message once and run multiple sub-queries against the index. A complex query that is typical in the CBMS application environment would comprise many grouped sub-queries such as:

```
(body INCLUDES "flour") AND (body INCLUDES "sugar") AND
(body INCLUDES "peanuts")
```

---

[2] (http://jakarta.apache.org/lucene/docs/queryparsersyntax.html)

Using Lucene, in our solution the message is indexed once, which is expensive, and then each subsequent sub-query searches the index, which incurs a minimal cost. This should lead to complex queries having approximately the same performance as simple queries, which is an extremely desirable property for the CBMS.

One area that was not explored was that of the analyzer performance. Indexing and subsequent searching in Lucene utilizes a class that implements a *StandardAnalyzer* interface. Since analyzers are involved in all expensive operations (indexing and searching) it is imperative that they are optimized. However, lack of time prevented the further testing of different analyzers to measure performance differences.

4 Performance Analysis of Text Queries

4.1 Test Case Description

In order to verify that the use of text search engine does not impact performance and scalability of the CBMS, a series of performance tests were carried out. The same test suite used to verify the improved JMS query engine [9] was used to measure and quantify the performance impact of using the Lucene search engine. Our goal was to demonstrate that the Lucene based text queries execute at least as fast as the original JBoss implementation while providing expanded querying capabilities. Hence we designed and executed 2 sets of equivalent tests to compare the performance of the JBoss JMS executing LIKE queries with the CBMS features that exploited Lucene, namely the INCLUDE queries.

The test suite creates multiple instances of publishers to simulate increasing message loads. The same message is posted to the JMS topic that all subscribers listen, thus creating an environment with known input data. For each message, subscribers specify message selectors of varying complexity. For the JBoss JMS tests, the selectors utilize the keyword LIKE along with wildcard indicators ("%"). The Lucene engine in the CBMS is tested by selectors utilizing the INCLUDES keyword, as well as the Lucene wildcard characters ("*").

To explore the impact of the cost of evaluating individual selectors, the series of tests uses selectors of varying complexity. At one extreme, very simple selectors that are inexpensive to evaluate were tested. Subsequent tests used progressively more complex selectors to examine the effects of their evaluation on the JBoss JMS and CBMS with Lucene. These are explained below.

For the JBoss JMS tests, the least expensive is a query that runs against a small text field, such as the subject field of an email. An example simple selector is:

```
Subject LIKE "%question%"
```

This simple selector is labeled *selector expense level 1* in the presentation of the performance results.

A slightly more expensive query is one that operates against a larger text field, such as the body of the message. An example selector for this case is as follows:

```
Body LIKE "%question%"
```

This type of selector is labeled *selector expense level 2* in the results.

A third level of selector expense involves searching within a much larger text field, but where the match is near the end of the text. The length of the text greatly influences the speed at which wildcards can execute, thus making the field larger will cause the operation to be much more expensive to execute. An example selector for this case, and *labeled selector expense level 3* in the results is:

```
Body LIKE "%garlic%"
```

The fourth most expensive operator for the test suite is one that searches a large block of text using two sub-queries with wildcards to locate certain words. This operation is more expensive because both wildcard expressions must search the entire block of text to determine if a match is made. An example selector for this case, which is labeled *selector expense level 4* in the results is:

```
Body LIKE "%garlic%" AND
Body LIKE "%question%"
```

The fifth selector level increases the number of sub-queries to three, which will require all three words to be found in the large block of text. An example for *selector level 5* is:

```
Body LIKE "%garlic%" AND
Body LIKE "%question%" AND
Body LIKE "%afternoon%"
```

The most expensive selector level is a query that finds many words in a given text block. This type of complex query is expected to be typical in the environment the CBM is being constructed for. An example for *Selector level 6* is:

```
Body LIKE "%garlic%" AND
Body LIKE "%question%" AND
Body LIKE "%afternoon%" AND
Body LIKE "%freezing%"
```

Equivalent queries were also constructed for the CBMS with Lucene, utilizing the INCLUDE keyword instead of LIKE. Hence, when the two sets of queries are executed on identical data, the same set of results is produced.

The performance tests were run on hardware with the following configuration:

- **Publisher/Subscriber Node:** Pentium III 1.3 GHz with 768MB of RAM running Windows XP and Java 1.3.1
- **CBMS/JBoss Server:** Quad 2GHz Pentiums running Windows 2000 Server and Java 1.3.1

To alleviate clock synchronization issues in the performance measurement, all publishers and all subscribers were run on the same machine. Additionally, the publishers and subscribers were run within the same Java Virtual Machine, but on different threads.   The CPU utilization was low however, and did not influence tests results. For all test cases, there were 10 publishers publishing at the maximum sustainable throughput rate [8], which ensures messages do not build up in the JMS queues and degrade performance. The number of subscribers is listed for each test case.

Since the focus of the CBMS engine is to handle large amounts of streaming data, it is assumed that speed should be favored over reliability when it comes to message delivery. Consequently, all messages were published with a *delivery mode* of NON_PERSISTENT, which indicates that the JMS provider does not need to persistently store the message to ensure delivery in the case of server failure. Moreover, this also eliminates any decreases in performance due to disk access and allows the test to concentrate solely on the message selector processing algorithm.

4.2 Results

Figures 3 and 4 show the performance results for increasing numbers of subscribers. For these cases, 100% of the messages sent by the publishers match the selector for each subscriber, thus all messages are sent out to subscribers.

In Figure 3, for the least inexpensive selector, the CBMS and JBoss have little difference in respective throughput. However, as selectors increase in complexity, the performance of JBoss degrades rapidly from 384 messages per second with the simplest selector to 28 messages per second for the most complex selector. Thus, JBoss' performance drops by approximately 93%. Alternatively, the CBMS with the Lucene engine peaks at 385.6 messages per second for the simplest selector, and slows to 174.48 messages per second for the most complex, which represents only a 55% drop in performance.

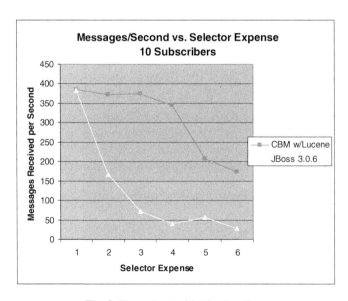

Fig. 3. Throughput with 10 subscribers

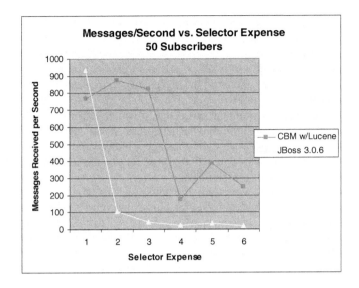

Fig. 4. Throughput with 50 subscribers

As the number of subscribers increases (Figure 4), the CBMS with Lucene clearly outperforms the original JBoss. Moreover, the original JBoss engine is completely unable to handle increasingly complex selectors and degrades 98% while the CBMS with Lucene drops in performance by only 67%.

These test results clearly demonstrate that the introduction of the Lucene search engine as the selector matching engine does not negatively impact the performance of the original JBoss implementation. Rather, Lucene performs better than the original JBoss implementation in terms of throughput and scalability. Thus, the original goal of increasing query expressiveness in order to improve message matching has been achieved with no penalties in terms of performance or scalability.

4.3 Analysis

The original JBoss wildcard engine is implemented by a regular expression package. Essentially, the selector is converted to a regular expression and then passed on to the regular expression library to be handled. However, regular expressions are quite expensive to calculate and this limitation clearly shows as the complexity of the selector increases.

Conversely, the CBMS with Lucene performance does not degrade so severely as the selector complexity increases. This is due to the fact that the matching engine uses Lucene to create an index for each message. Then, each sub-query against that message is run against the original index. The cost of searching against an index is much less than the cost of evaluating a regular expression. Thus, the performance of CBMS with Lucene is dominated by the cost of creating the index for each message.

Therefore, the benefit of utilizing Lucene for complex selectors combined with the earlier selector caching algorithms make for a fast, scalable platform for content-based matching.

5 Analyzing Lucene Performance

Another test suite was developed to measure the differences between Lucene and the CBMS with Lucene. The aim was to assess the maximum performance that might be achievable with Lucene, and quantify the overheads introduced by the underlying JBoss JMS platform.

To this end, one test environment was setup in which text messages are handled by the CBMS utilizing JMS publishers and subscribers (as described earlier). A second test environment simply delivered messages to a Java program that called the Lucene engine. The latter hence aimed to illustrate the performance potential of Lucene without any influence from the JMS.

The same input messages were used for both environments. Likewise, the same selectors were setup for the content based matching algorithms, with varying selector complexities.

Table 1 shows the selectors used.

Table 1. Selector Complexities

```
Selector 1    subject INCLUDES 'atheism'
Selector 2    body INCLUDES 'might'
Selector 3    body INCLUDES 'angry'
              body INCLUDES 'might' AND
Selector 4    body INCLUDES 'angry'
              body INCLUDES 'might' AND
              body INCLUDES 'angry' AND
Selector 5    body INCLUDES 'important'
              body INCLUDES 'strange' AND
              body INCLUDES 'important' AND
              body INCLUDES 'might' AND
Selector 6    body INCLUDES 'angry'
```

Both tests were executed on the same hardware platform[3], and all test components were executed on the same machine. Figure 5 shows the results obtained.

The results starkly illustrate the JMS implementation overhead. For this set of test data and queries, the Lucene search engine is able to process 694.52 messages per second at the lowest selector complexity, while the CBMS with Lucene is only able to sustain 184.52 messages per second. This represents a 73% performance degradation.

At the time of writing, we have not had time to investigate thoroughly the cause of the overheads in the JBoss JMS. However, in associated tests with other JMS platforms, greater JMS message throughput has been observed. Hence we have a good degree of confidence that a faster JMS implementation is possible, and that such an implementation may be able to fully exploit the performance potential of the Lucene engine.

---

[3] Pentium IV 3 GHz with 1GB of RAM running Windows XP and Java 1.3.1.

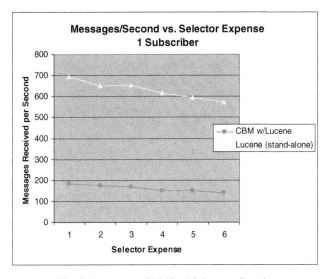

Fig. 5. Lucene vs. CBMS with Lucene Results

6 Further Work and Conclusions

By introducing new algorithms in to a JMS implementation that exploit commonality in message selectors, this project has clearly demonstrated the performance and scalability gains that can be achieved. This is an extremely positive result that shows how standard JMS implementations can be improved to make them faster for content-based messaging.

In this paper, we have demonstrated the feasibility of further integrating a full-featured text search engine, Lucene, with a JMS implementation. Empirical testing shows that Lucene can provide excellent, scalable performance. This gives us confidence that we can go on to implement a CBMS based upon the messaging features of a JMS combined with extensions of the JMS query capability to exploit powerful full-text searching.

We are continuing to explore content-based matching with JMS infrastructures. To this end, we are performing a set of experiments that attempt to factor out the transport cost of a particular JMS. This will enable us to directly compare the costs of our content-based text matching engine with those of several JMS implementations. We also intend to scale our CBMS platform to run across a cluster of machines to ensure a large number of subscriptions can be handled.

Acknowledgements

This work has been funded by PNNL's Energy Sciences & Technology Directorate Lab Directed Research & Development Program.

National ICT Australia is funded through the Australian Government's *Backing Australia's Ability* initiative, in part through the Australian Research Council.

References

[1] Babcock, Brian; Babu, Shivnath; Datar, Mayur; Motwani, Rajeev; Widom, Jennifer. Models and Issues in Data Stream Systems, Proceedings of 21st ACM Symposium on Principles of Database Systems (PODS 2002)

[2] R. Motwani, J. Widom, A. Arasu, B. Babcock, S. Babu, M. Datar, G. Manku, C. Olston, J. Rosenstein, and R. Varma. Query Processing, Resource Management, and Approximation in a Data Stream Management System, *In Proc. of the 2003 Conference on Innovative Data Systems Research (CIDR), January 2003*

[3] Bill Segall and David Arnold, "Elvin has left the building: A publish/subscribe notification service with quenching," *Proceedings AUUG Technical Conference (AUUG'97)*, pp. 243-255 (September 1997).

[4] M.K.Aguilera,R.E.Strom,D.C.Sturman,M.Astley,andT.D.Chandra. Matching events in a content-based subscription system. In Eighteenth ACM Symposium on Principles of Distributed Computing (PODC '99), pages 53--61, Atlanta, Georgia, May 4--6 1999.

[5] Marcel Ruff, *White Paper xmlBlaster: Message Oriented Middleware (MOM)*, http://www.xmlblaster.org/xmlBlaster/doc/whitepaper/whitepaper.html 2000.

[6] A. Carzaniga, D.S. Rosenblum, and A.L. Wolf ,"Design and Evaluation of a Wide-Area Event Notification Service". *ACM Transactions on Computer Systems*, 19(3):332-383, Aug 2001.

[7] A. Carzaniga, D.S. Rosenblum, and A.L. Wolf , "Achieving Expressiveness and Scalability in an Internet-Scale Event Notification Service". *19th ACM Symposium on Principles of Distributed Computing (PODC 2000)*, Portland OR. July, 2000.

[8] P. Tran, P. Greenfield, I. Gorton, Behavior and Performance of Message-Oriented Middleware Systems, *Proceedings, 22nd Int'l Conf on Dist. Computing Systems Workshops*, Vienna 2-5 Jul 2002. Pages 645-650, IEEE

[9] I.Gorton, Justin Almquist, Nick Cramer, Jereme Haack, Mark Hoza, An Efficient, Scalable Content-Based Messaging System, in Procs The 7th IEEE International Enterprise Distributed Object Computing Conference, (EDOC 2003), pages 278-285, Brisbane Sept 2003

[10] Francoise Fabret, H.-Arrno Jacobsen, Francois Llirbat, Joao Pereira, Kenneth Ross, Dennis Shasha, Filtering Algorithms and Implementation for Very Fast Publish/Subscribe Systems. ACM SIGMOD 2001 Conference, Santa Barbara, pages 115-126, CA. May, 2001.

A Common Conceptual Basis for Analyzing Transaction Service Configurations

Sten Loecher

Department of Computer Science, Dresden University of Technology
Sten.Loecher@inf.tu-dresden.de

Abstract. Transaction management services play an important role in modern component technologies, such as Enterprise JavaBeans. They are provided as middleware service by the container, which requires configuration information to apply them properly to the application. In our work, we follow a model-driven transaction service configuration approach to allow transaction design early in the software engineering process. An important element of our approach is a common conceptual basis for describing, analyzing, and comparing transaction service configurations. It also supports the notion of contract with regard to transactional logic, which is a prerequisite for the reliable composition of components to component-based applications. In this paper, we present our approach to model-driven service configuration and introduce a common set of concepts for describing transaction service configurations.

1   Introduction

Modern component technologies, such as Enterprise JavaBeans (EJB)[5], that are used to build server-side business applications combine two fundamental software engineering paradigms. On the one hand, component-based engineering[19] is used to structure and manage application-specific logic. On the other hand, application-independent middleware services are added to the applications by a conceptually rather aspect-oriented engineering approach.Such middleware services are provided by the container, which is the runtime environment of component-based applications and requires configuration information to apply the services properly. The focus of our work is on transaction management services, which are used to provide fault tolerance to applications and which enable the isolated execution of concurrent processes that share resources.

An important point about middleware services is standardization, which is required to allow interoperability between technically heterogeneous applications. Current transaction processing standards, such as the Object Transaction Service[14], usually define a number of interfaces with respect to a reference architecture that must be implemented or invoked by the involved components to provide respectively access the service. However, as the level of abstraction in software engineering raises to enable interoperability not just among applications but also among engineering tools and to promote the reuse of design artifacts, models become first-class entities in the engineering process. This development towards model-driven development is currently boosted by the Model-Driven Architecture (MDA)[8, 12] initiative, which tries to establish model-driven development

T. Gschwind and C. Mascolo (Eds.): SEM 2004, LNCS 3437, pp. 31–46, 2005.

based on modeling-standards defined by the Object Management Group (OMG), e.g., the Unified Modeling Language (UML)[15].

In our work, we follow a model-driven approach to transaction service configuration [10, 9]. Our objective is to develop a conceptual framework that allows the management and integration of various schemas for declarative configuration of transaction services, i.e., we focus on container-managed transactions exclusively. We want to support existing schemas, such as the EJB single attribute schema[5] or the NT&CT attribute schema[16], but also new schemas that we have designed. The purpose of the framework is to allow the transaction designer to choose from different configuration schemas, to compare configurations of different types, and to analyze different types of configurations based on a common set of tools. An important part of the framework is therefore a set of common modeling concepts for describing transaction service configurations. This common set of modeling concepts will be presented in this paper by means of a metamodel.

The contribution of our work is twofold. On the one hand, we contribute to the development of model-driven software engineering with respect to the domain of transaction design. We propose a set of modeling concepts for describing transaction service configurations, which is common in a sense of being independent of specific transaction models and transaction processing technologies. This allows platform-independent transaction design an reuse of configurations across different technologies. The definition of the modeling concepts and their semantics is based on standards defined by the Object Management Group (OMG) and therefore integrates with the MDA. On the other hand, the proposed modeling concepts support the notion of contract[1], which is an important prerequisite for the reliable composition of component-based applications from components. A component contract must contain essential information for reasoning about the behavior of component compositions. We think that the proposed modeling concepts are well suited for this purpose. An important point about our work is that it does not reinvent transaction processing theory but bridges the gap between transaction processing theory and software engineering practice by transferring existing knowledge to a new problem domain.

In Sect. 2, the approach to model-driven transaction service configuration is introduced and a tool that supports the approach is presented. After a discussion of some preliminary issues, we propose in Sect. 3 a set of common concepts to model transaction service configurations. Finally, Sect. 4 discusses related work and Section 5 concludes by summarizing the paper and provides information about current and future work.

2   Model-Driven Transaction Service Configuration

To apply transaction services properly to the application, the container requires information. A transaction service configuration must describe the required transaction demarcation, dependencies between transactions, and the behavior in case of failures. The transaction designer can provide this information by associating pre-defined configuration attributes to the provided operations of components. This *declarative configuration approach* allows simple and efficient specification of transaction services required by applications and supports clear separation of concerns with respect to application-

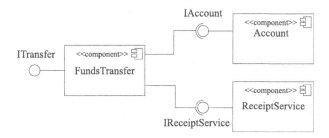

Fig. 1. Example application

specific and application-independent logic[11]. It therefore *provides the foundation for our model-driven configuration approach.*

Figure 1 shows a simple example to illustrate the declarative configuration approach. It comprises three components that implement funds transfer between two accounts. For this, component FundsTransfer provides an operation transfer via interface ITransfer. This operation is responsible for calling the debit and credit operations provided by interface IAccount of component Account. After successful funds transfer, the transfer operation calls operation printReceipt, which is implemented by component ReceiptService and provided by interface IReceiptService, to issue a receipt via a printing device. A configuration using the pre-defined attributes of EJB, for example, would be specified as follows:

```
<container-transaction>
    <method>
        <ejb-name>FundsTransfer</ejb-name>
        <method-name>transfer</method-name>
    </method>
    <trans-attribute>RequiresNew</trans-attribute>
</container-transaction>
```

The example shows part of a deployment descriptor, which is an XML file and holds the configuration information that is read and interpreted by the container at runtime. The transfer operation of component FundsTransfer must be invoked within a new transaction, which has been declared using the pre-defined configuration attribute RequiresNew. The debit and credit operations of interface IAccount must be accordingly configured, e.g., using the configuration attribute Mandatory, which declares that the operations must be invoked from within a transaction. Finally, operation printReceipt may be configured using attribute NotSupported to declare that the ReceiptService component does not support transactions, because printed receipts cannot be backed out by the system.

The association of configuration attributes to operations, as illustrated in the example, is in fact transaction design. To allow this design to be performed early in the software engineering process, we follow a model-driven configuration approach. This allows analysis of configurations and adaptation of transaction designs to required functional as well as non-functional properties, such as absence of deadlocks and high concurrency. The model-driven configuration approach comprises the following three major steps:

1. Assembling an application respectively business logic model from a set of selected component specifications by the application designer. The component specifications provide information about provided and required interfaces as well as specifications relating these interfaces to each other. For the purpose of our work, we do not require a complete formal specification of the behavior of components but only information that is necessary for analyzing transactional logic in subsequent steps, e.g., the messages sent by components as well as their temporal ordering.
2. Configuration of the application model by the transaction designer using configuration models, which capture the properties of configuration schemas and are associated to elements of the application logic. The configuration model supported by EJB, for example, simply comprises six configuration attributes.
3. The mapping of the application as well as configuration models to specific platforms by tools. In other words, the assembling of the application and the configuration of the application must be performed according to the models.

As indicated in the first two steps of the model-driven development procedure, different types of models are required for the approach. For describing the business logic, an application model is used. The description of transaction services required by the application is based on configuration models. An important point about configuration models is their multiplicity. Our work is based on the *assumption that multiple types of configuration models are required.* This is due to the various transaction models that must be supported and the preferences of the different developers that participate in the transactions design process. A detailed discussion about that subject can be found in [9].

For analyzing and comparing transaction configurations, we have introduced a third type of model: the integrated model. Figure 2 illustrates the complete picture of the modeling framework. The application and the configuration model are merged and transformed to the integrated model, which is depicted by the hollow arrow pointing to the right. The integrated model comprises business as well as transaction logic. The transaction logic is based on a small set of common concepts that integrate seamlessly with the modeling concepts for the business logic and are independent of particular transaction models and transaction processing technologies. The arrows pointing to the business as well as configuration model represent the transformation of an integrated model back into the respective models to update for example the configuration model after modifications of the integrated model. Having an integrated model results in a number of advantages for the modeling approach:

- The integrated model serves as basis for defining the meaning of configurations. Defining the meaning, i.e., semantics, for each individual configuration model type is expensive. Instead, a number of rather simple transformation rules from configuration models to the integrated model defines the meaning of configurations implicitly.
- The integrated model provides a uniform foundation for analyzing configurations. New configuration models can be easily integrated into the framework by defining a number of transformation rules.
- The integrated model provides the foundation for the comparison of different configurations and different configuration types based on a common set of modeling concepts. For example, to compare two configurations of different type, the respective

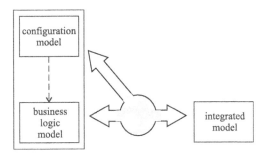

Fig. 2. Types of models in the approach

integrated models must be compared with respect to similarity of model elements. In case of dissimilarities further investigations and reasoning may be required.

An important point about our work is that we use metamodeling for designing the introduced types of models. On the one hand, this is required to closely relate our work to the MDA. On the other hand, the use of metamodeling enables the rapid development of tool support. We have already developed a prototype to investigate the applicability of our approach. Figure 3 sketches the architecture of the prototype.

The main component of the prototype is a meta data repository, which is responsible for managing metamodels and models. It is based on the Meta Data Repository (MDR) distributed with the NetBeans development environment project[1]. Different sets of interfaces, which are depicted by double circles in Fig. 3, enable to access business models (`IBusinessLogic`), configuration models (`IConfiguration`), and integrated models (`IIntegratedModel`).

A parser is used to create business as well as configuration models within the repository. We currently use a proprietary XML-based input format for the parser since it enables efficient prototyping. However, other kinds of user interfaces are conceivable, e.g., the coupling of the prototype to graphical user interfaces.

Transformations between the different types of models are specified by a notation similar to that proposed in [8] and implemented directly in Java. The transformations access the models via reflective interfaces (`IReflective`). It was originally planned to use a QVT[2] engine for this purpose. However, available prototypes are not yet mature enough to be used in our work.

One goal is to couple several analysis tools that use the integrated model as common basis. Such analysis tools may perform static as well as dynamic analysis. Currently, the prototype comprises a code generator that produces Promela scripts, which are the input for the SPIN[3] software model checker. That way, we can simulate as well as model check configurations, analyze their properties, and use this information to improve the transaction design.

---

[1] http://www.netbeans.org
[2] Queries, Views, and Transformations. A standard yet to be defined by the OMG.
[3] http://spinroot.com

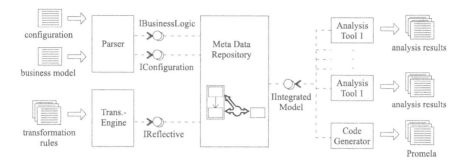

Fig. 3. Prototype architecture

3   Integrated Model Concepts

This section explains the conceptual foundation for integrated models, i.e., a metamodel is presented and its interpretation is defined. The proposed metamodel is based on two existing works. On the one hand, we use the results of the study in [7] for the business logic specific part of the metamodel. It defines a core language for describing static as well as dynamic properties of an application that we have extended with concepts to describe component-based applications. On the other hand, we use ACTA[3, 2] as starting point for integrating transaction logic specific modeling concepts to the metamodel. ACTA is a formal framework for describing transaction models and reasoning about them. We have decided to use ACTA as starting point for designing the transaction specific part, because it identifies concepts to describe transaction properties independently from specific transaction models and implementation technology, which aligns with our goal of platform independent modeling in the early phases of the software engineering process.

We do not elaborate on the business logic specific part of the metamodel in this paper, because it is discussed in detail in [7]. Instead we focus on the concepts for describing transaction logic. Section 3.1 provides more details on the ACTA framework and introduces the approach to metamodeling that we use in our work. The transaction logic specific part of the metamodel is presented in Sect. 3.2. Section 3.3 finally defines the interpretation of the metamodel more precisely.

3.1   Preliminaries

ACTA. ACTA[3, 2] is a formal framework based on first-order logic for describing transaction models and reasoning about them. It is based on a small set of fundamental concepts such as events that are classified into significant and object events, a history of events, the specification of effects of transactions on other transactions, and the specification of effects of transactions on objects:

Events: A basic building block of ACTA are events, which are classified into significant and object events. Significant events are invocations of transaction management primitives that are used to initiate or terminate transactions, e.g., *Begin*, *Commit*, and *Abort*. Object events are invocations of operations on objects. Objects are abstract entities that represent shared entities in a database. Each object has a type which determines the operations that can be invoked on the object.

History: A history of events represents the concurrent execution of a set of transactions. It contains all events that are associated with transactions and indicates a partial order in which these events occur. Constraints over the history are used to specify the effects between transactions and the effects of transactions on objects.

Effects on Transactions: The effects of transactions on other transactions are captured by dependencies, which are constraints over the temporal ordering of the significant events of two transactions. For example, the nested transaction model[13] uses two kinds of transactions, namely root and subtransactions. Two types of dependencies are required to describe the dependencies between those two kinds of transactions, namely commit dependencies and weak-abort dependencies, which have been specified for two transactions t_i and t_j in [2] as follows:

- A *Commit Dependency* (t_j CD t_i) specifies, that if both transactions commit, then the commitment of t_i precedes the commitment of t_j.
- A *Weak-Abort Dependency* (t_j WD t_i) specifies, that if t_j commits and t_i aborts then the commitment of t_j precedes the abortion of t_i in the history.

We will use the two presented dependencies in the rest of the paper for illustration. Other types of dependencies exist within other transaction models and have been defined for example in [2].

Effects on Objects: The effects of transactions on objects are specified by two sets, namely the *view* and the *conflict set* of a transaction. The view of a transaction basically specifies the state of objects that is visible to a transaction at a point in time. The conflict set specifies the operations for which conflicts have to be determined during execution of a transaction. These two sets model the isolation property of transactions independently from specific synchronization mechanisms. The view and conflict set are usually expressed as predicates over the history, the current set of dependencies between transactions and the transactions itself.

Besides the discussed concepts, an important artifact of the ACTA framework is the concept of *delegation*. In ACTA, each operation is assigned a commit and abort operation, which must be called by the responsible transaction to make the operation results visible to other transactions in the system. Basically, a transaction is responsible for committing or aborting an operation if the operation was invoked within the scope of the transaction. Delegation allows to pass those responsibilities between transactions and therefore enables the description of different kinds of transaction termination semantics. In the nested transaction model, for example, the commit of a subtransaction results in delegation of subtransaction responsibilities to the parent of the subtransaction whereas the commit of a root transaction requires the root transaction to commit or abort all operations it is responsible for.

Modeling Approach. We use the MMF approach[4] to define metamodels and their semantics, which aims at providing a facility that allows the definition of modeling languages and their semantics in a way that is accessible to tool builders and those who use the UML[15] as modeling language. For this, all models are based on UML notation. To define a language and its semantics, the MMF approach requires to:

1. Define an abstract and concrete syntax of the language by UML models. Whereas the abstract syntax is a computer-centric representation of the language concepts, the concrete syntax is a human-centric representation model.
2. Define a semantic domain, i.e., the things that are denoted by the abstract syntax. The semantic domain itself is also a UML model.
3. Define a display mapping to relate concrete and abstract syntax as well as a semantic mapping to give the modeling language, i.e., the abstract syntax, a meaning.

The approach is denotational with respect to traditional language engineering. However, the use of commonly comprehensible notations for defining the syntax, domain, and mappings makes it attractive for practically oriented software engineers and tool developers.

We define in Section 3.2 the abstract syntax of the language that describes the transactional logic of the integrated model. *We do not define a concrete syntax in this paper, because we want to focus on the concepts rather than the notation. Besides that, the integrated model is a computer-centric model primarily used by analysis tools, which anyway do not require a human-centric representation of the model.* Section 3.3 then defines the semantic domain and discusses the semantic mapping from the concepts presented in Sect. 3.2.

Working Example. Figure 4 shows a UML instance diagram[4]. It is an example for an integrated model and will be used in the following sections. We assume that the `FundsTransfer` component from the example in Sect. 2 is deployed to a container that provides nested transactions, which is different from the example in Sect. 2 but more suitable for explaining the modeling concepts in the next section. The model reflects the fact that the `transfer` operation will be invoked within a root transaction, which is denoted by the modeled dependencies and will be explained in the next section. The instances of `Operation`, `CompoundAction`, and `FeatureRef` are part of the business logic. An `Operation` is a dynamic feature of an object. Coherent actions are modeled by compound actions, i.e., the call to three operations in the example. A `FeatureRef` references a feature of an object, such as an operation. The reader should be aware that the example is simplified, i.e., parameters and details of the business logic have been omitted for reasons of clarity.

3.2   Model Concepts

Figure 5 shows the metamodel of the transaction logic specific part of integrated models. The metamodel primarily comprises two categories of metaclasses for describing transactional logic:

---

[4] Boxes represent instances of model classes. Instances my have a name, which is written underlined within the box and separated by a colon from the type of the instance. Lines depict links, which are instances of associations between model classes. Link ends correspond to association ends and are accordingly named. For reasons of clarity `provider`, `dependant`, and `receiver` are abbreviated by `prov`, `dep`, and `rec` within the figure.

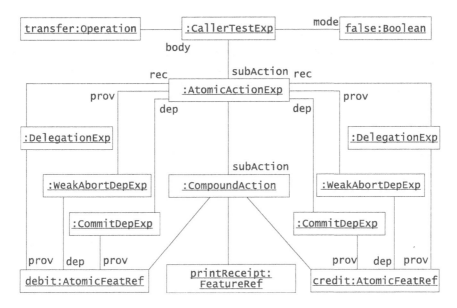

Fig. 4. Example instance of an integrated model

1. Metaclasses that result from mapping ACTA concepts to the context of our work, i.e., by integrating them into the metamodel provided in [7]. These metaclasses are `AtomicActionExp`, `DependencyExp`, and `DelegationExp`.
2. Metaclasses that have been added to support component-based engineering more adequately and to allow conditional control over transaction propagation. These metaclasses are `AtomicFeatRef` and `CallerTestExp`.

These metaclasses are based on the concepts `ActionExpression` and `FeatureRef` defined in [7]. An action expression defines the fundamental construct that models the evaluation of the state of an object or the change of its state over time. A `FeatureRef` is a special action expression that models the reference or call to a feature of an object.

An important point is, that the mapping of ACTA concepts was not straightforward. Since we wanted to design a minimal set of modeling concepts that results in compact integrated models, we decided to include only those modeling concepts into the metamodel that are required to declare transaction demarcation, internal transaction structure, and effects of transactions on other transactions. The specification of effects of transactions on objects directly in the integrated model would have added to much complexity. These effects are therefore expressed by means of profiles applied to the semantic domain of the modeling concepts, which will be explained in the next section. In the following, the metaclasses are explained in more detail:

AtomicActionExp: Atomic action expressions declare actions that are performed atomically and isolated from other actions, i.e., they declare demarcation borders of transactions. An important point about the resulting transaction, which we denote atomic action in our work, is that it is bound to an individual component. The propagation of atomic actions across different component instances must be explicitly declared using `AtomicFeatRef`. The business logic that is executed within an atomic action is defined by association end `subAction`. In the example, this is the compound action that defines the call to `debit`, `credit`, and `printReceipt`. If an atomic action establishes dependencies to the atomic action of the invoking operation and requires the delegation of responsibilities to it, this is modeled by the association ends `dep2Caller` and `del2Caller`. In the example no such dependencies and delegations are defined, since the atomic action expression models a root transaction of the nested transaction model, which only declares dependencies to subtransactions.

AtomicFeatRef: Atomic feature references are abstract interfaces to the atomic actions of called operations respectively referenced features. They explicitly declare the requirement that the referenced feature must be executed within an atomic action. They are abstract in a sense of hiding the details of the atomic action within the referenced feature, such as the dependencies established by this atomic action. In the example, the `transfer` operation requires the `debit` and `credit` operations to be executed within atomic actions.

DependencyExp: Dependency expressions define dependencies between atomic actions. `DependencyExp` denotes the general concept of dependency. Actual dependencies between atomic actions are modeled by specializations of this class, such as `CommitDepExp` and `WeakAbortDepExp`, which model commit dependencies and weak-abort dependencies, respectively. The association ends `provider` and `dependant` are used to specify the respective action expressions between which the dependency is declared. Dependency expressions can be used in two ways. On the one hand, they are used to express dependencies between two atomic action expressions that belong to the same component. On the other hand, they are used to express dependencies to atomic actions of either calling operations or referenced features. If dependencies are not expressed between two atomic action expressions, either the dependant or the provider is undefined or refers to an atomic feature reference[5]. In the example model, four dependencies have been declared, which model the fact that the `AtomicActionExp` specifies a root transaction in the nested transaction model and `debit` and `credit` are executed within atomic actions that are required to behave like subtransactions. In the nested transaction model, a root transaction is commit dependent to its subtransactions and subtransactions are weak-abort dependant to their parent transaction. For modeling these facts, the respective dependencies have been added to the model between the atomic action expression and the atomic feature references.

DelegationExp: Delegation expressions are used to declare the delegation of responsibilities to commit or abort individual action executions. The association ends `provider` and `receiver` specify the provider and receiver of the responsibilities, respectively. In the example, two delegation expressions have been defined between the feature references to `debit` and `credit` and the atomic action expression to model the fact that

---

[5] In UML models, such facts are usually defined by well-formedness rules using the Object Constraint Language (OCL). We omit these rules in the paper for reasons of brevity.

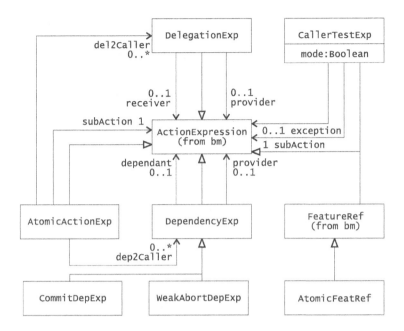

Fig. 5. Metamodel for transaction logic of integrated models

upon commit of the atomic actions of the feature references, the responsibilities are delegated to the atomic action of `transfer`.

CallerTestExp: Caller test expressions are required to determine the properties of an operation call with respect to transactional logic. A caller test expression has a `mode` which determines the further processing of either the `subaction` or the `exception`. If the evaluation of the `CallerTestExp` is positive, the `subAction` is executed, otherwise the `exception` will be performed. In the example, a caller test expression is used to determine if the `transfer` operation has been called from an operation running an atomic action. The mode `false` specifies that the `subaction` will be executed only if this is not the case. An exception has not been declared for the example, i.e, the exceptional behavior has been left unspecified.

The introduced metamodel provides a small set of concepts that is sufficient to describe transaction configurations. The concepts are platform-independent in a sense of abstraction from concrete transaction models, concurrency control mechanisms, and technology-specific mechanisms, such as propagation policies. In our work, we have already elaborated rules for mapping configuration models of current technologies, such as EJB[5], to the integrated model but also of research prototypes, such as the one presented in [16].

3.3   Interpretation of Model Concepts

This section defines the correct interpretation of the presented modeling concepts. We first provide an overview about the semantic mapping and subsequently explain the

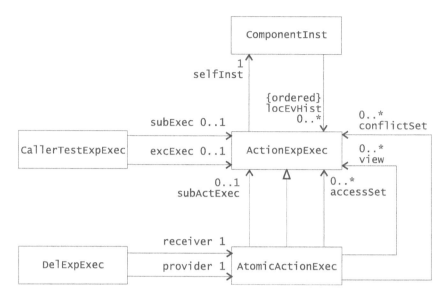

Fig. 6. View one on the semantic domain

concepts of the semantic domain individually. Since an exhaustive presentation would go beyond the scope of this paper, we will focus on primary issues and simplify the description accordingly.

The following table summarizes the mapping of modeling concepts to elements of the semantic domain:

model concept	domain concept
ActionExpression	ActionExpExec
AtomicActionExp	AtomicActionExec
DependencyExp	DepExpExec
DelegationExp	DelExpExec
CallerTestExp	CallerTestExpExec
AtomicFeatRef	AtomicFeatRefExec

The left column of the table denotes the modeling concepts, whereas the right column specifies the respective instance. For example, it defines that ActionExpExec is an instance of ActionExpression. Since all model concepts are specializations of ActionExpression, we use the ending Exec to denote the execution of such an expression in the domain model.

For reasons of clarity, we have split the illustration of the domain model on two figures. Figure 6 and 7 show different views respectively details of the domain model. The individual domain concepts are explained in the following.

ActionExpExec: A concept that is central to the semantic domain is ActionExpExec, which models an executable unit that evaluates or changes the state of an object (see

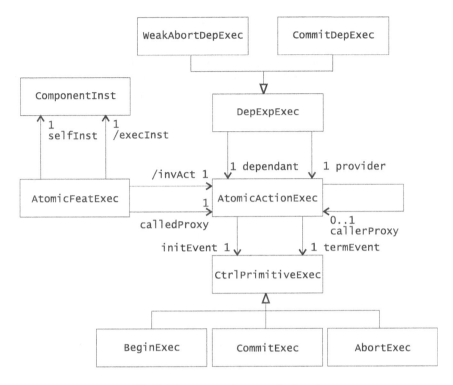

Fig. 7. View two on the semantic domain

Fig. 6). It is executed by a component instance (`ComponentInst`), which is modeled by the association end `selfInst`. An important concept of the semantic domain are local event histories. Each component instance is associated to a local event history (`locEvHist`), which contains the events performed by a component instance. Local event histories are a result from mapping event histories from ACTA into our semantic domain. An event is presented by an `ActionExpExec` in our work, which seamlessly integrates with the concept of local states of [7], i.e., the event of executing an action expression results in a new state of a component instance.

AtomicActionExec: A specialization of `ActionExpExec` is `AtomicActionExec`, which models a unit that is executed atomically and isolated from other atomic actions. To be more precise, the unit that is executed isolated and atomically is defined by all actions that are contained within the subtree defined by association end `subActExec` and executed by the `selfInst` of the atomic action, which is depicted in Fig. 6. An `AtomicActionExec` in fact corresponds to a transaction in the ACTA framework.

Each `AtomicActionExec` is associated to a `view` and `conflictSet`. As introduced in Sect. 3.1, these two sets model the synchronization behavior. In Sect. 3.2, it has been stipulated that the synchronization behavior is not directly modeled in the integrated model. Instead, profiles attached to the semantic domain are used to specify this aspect. A profile basically comprises a number of invariants that specify the properties of `view` and `conflictSet` more precisely and is bound to individual components, i.e., profiles are part of component descriptions. *This in fact restricts a component instance to support only one type of transaction model at a time.* We think that this restriction is appropriate, since a components instance is the unit of management for the container. The following OCL constraint gives an example for the specification of `view` and `conflictSet` for traditional atomic transactions:

```
context AtomicActionExec
inv: view = self.selfInst.locEvHist
inv: conflictSet = ActionExpExec.allInstances->select(aae|
                        not (aae.isSubAction(self))
                        and (aae.inProgress() = true))
```

The invariants specify that an atomic action can see the current state of the component instance that executes it, but conflicts have to be determined for all action executions that are not performed within the scope of the atomic action. The operations `isSubAction` and `inProgress` determine if an action execution is contained within the subtree associated by `subActExec` of the atomic action and if an action execution is currently in progress, respectively.

DepExpExec: An atomic action also results in significant events that model the initiation an termination of atomic actions, modeled by `CtrlPrimitiveExec` (see Fig. 7). They allow, for example, to express dependencies between atomic actions by `DepExpExec` respectively specializations of it. The precise meaning of particular dependencies is expressed by OCL constraints, for example:

```
context CommitDepExec
inv: let i = self.dependant.termEvent,
         j = self.provider.termEvent in
    (j.oclIsTypeOf(CommitExec))
  implies
    (i.oclIsKindOf(CommitExec) implies j.pred->includes(i))
```

The invariant specifies that in the case both atomic actions commit, the commit of the `provider` must precede the commit of the `dependant`.

DelExpExec: A `DelExpExec` results in delegation of responsibilities to commit individual actions of one atomic action (`provider`) to another (`receiver`). The actions an atomic action is responsible for are contained within the `accessSet` of `AtomicActionExec`. That means, the execution of a delegation expression results in the assignment of the `accessSet` of the `provider` to the `accessSet` of the `receiver`.

CallerTestExpExec: A `CallerTestExpExec` evaluates whether an atomic action has been invoked from within the scope of another atomic action and results in a subaction execution (`subExec`) or in throwing an exception (`excExec`). The evaluation of the invocation property is performed by evaluating the existence of a `callerProxy`, depicted in Fig. 7.

AtomicFeatExec: The communication between two linked components with respect to transactional logic is modeled by `AtomicFeatExec`, which is the execution of an `AtomicFeatRef`. `AtomicFeatExec` establishes a link (`invAct`) between the referencing (`selfInst`) and the referenced (`execInst`) component instance (see Fig. 7). The link is used to synchronize two proxy actions (`callerProxy` and `calledProxy`) with its original actions in the linked component instance. Proxy actions mirror the behavior of the original actions by inserting corresponding events in the local event history of component. That way, we abstract from technology specific communication concepts, such as polling and callbacks, and provide a more general description of the behavior.

4   Related Work

As already discussed extensively, our work is closely related to the study in [7] and ACTA[2, 3]. We use the study in [7] as basis for our work and have transferred concepts from ACTA to it. Our work is also closely related to the MDA approach[8, 12] in general and initiatives for model-driven domain engineering in particular, such as the COSMIC project[6]. However, whereas [6] focuses on the general model-driven configuration approach, our focuses in particular on details of transaction service configuration. There exist also numerous approaches to formal modeling of transaction configurations to enable analysis of configurations. One example is the formal definition of the EJB transaction attributes in [18]. Whereas such formalizations solve the problem for specific platforms, we aim at providing a common platform-independent modeling basis. In [17] an extensible framework for transaction service configurations is proposed. This is also a goal of our work. However, the approach chosen in [17] does not support model-driven service configuration.

5   Summary and Outlook

In this paper, we have presented a model-driven transaction service configuration approach. An important part of the approach is an integrated model that describes business as well as transaction logic and provides a common, i.e., platform-independent, foundation for analysis of transaction configurations. We have presented a metamodel for the transaction logic specific part and defined its interpretation based on the MMF approach to language engineering.

The presented work contributes to the discussion about model-driven development, especially in the context of MDA and within the domain of transaction modeling. To provide a common basis for describing and analyzing transaction configurations, we have transferred existing concepts from transaction processing theory to the software engineering domain. Furthermore, we think that integrated models express exactly those information with regard to transaction logic that is required to describe contracts between components.

We have already developed a prototype that supports our model-driven configuration approach. A code generator that produces Promela, which is the input format for the SPIN model checker, allows us to simulate as well as model check properties of transaction configurations. Currently we work on extending the prototype to accept different configuration models and we look at coupling other analysis tools to it.

References

1. A. Beugnard, J.-M. Jézéquel, N. Plouzeau, and D. Watkins. Making components contract aware. *Computer*, 32(7):38–45, July 1999.
2. P. K. Chrysanthis and K. Ramamritham. *ACTA: The SAGA Continues*, chapter 10, pages 349–397. Morgan Kaufmann Publishers, 1992.
3. P. K. Chrysanthis and K. Ramamritham. Synthesis of extended transaction models using ACTA. *ACM Trans. Database Syst.*, 19(3):450–491, 1994.
4. T. Clark, A. Evans, S. Kent, and P. Sammut. The MMF Approach to Engineering Object-Oriented Design Languages. In Proceedings of the Workshop on Language Descriptions, Tools and Applications, LDTA2001. April 2001.
5. L. G. DeMichiel, L. Ümit Yalcinalp, and S. Krishnan, editors. *Enterprise JavaBeans Specification, Version 2.0*. Sun Microsystems, 2001.
6. A. Gokhale, D. Schmidt, B. Natarajan, J. Gray, and N. Wang. *Model-Driven Middleware. In Middleware for Communications*, chapter 7. John Wiley and Sons, 2004.
7. A. Kleppe and J. Warmer. Unification of Static and Dynamic Semantics of UML: A Study in redefining the Semantics of the UML using the pUML OO Meta Modelling Approach. http://www.klasse.nl/english/uml/uml-semantics.html, 2003.
8. A. Kleppe, J. Warmer, and W. Bast. *MDA explained: the practice and promise of the Model Driven Architecture*. Addison-Wesley Professional, 2003.
9. S. Loecher. Model-Based Transaction Service Configuration for Component-Based Development. In *7th Workshop on Component-Based Software Engineering (CBSE7), Edinburgh, Scottland, Workshop Proceedings, Volume 3054 of LNCS. Springer.*, March 2004.
10. S. Loecher. Modellbasierte Konfiguration von Transaktionsdiensten. In *Modellierung 2004, Gemeinsame Konferenz von zwoelf Fachgruppen der GI, Marburg, Germany, Proceedings zur Tagung, LNI Volume P-45*. Gesellschaft für Informatik, March 2004.
11. S. Loecher and H. Hussmann. Metamodelling of Transaction Configurations - Position Paper. In *Metamodelling for MDA, First International Workshop, York, UK*. University of York, November 2003.
12. J. Miller and J. Mukerji, editors. *MDA Guide Version 1.0*. www.omg.org, May 2003.
13. J. E. B. Moss. *Nested Transactions: An Approach to Reliable Distributed Computing*. PhD thesis, Massachusetts Institute of Technology, 1981.
14. Object Management Group (OMG). Transaction service specification, version 1.2, May 2001.
15. Object Management Group (OMG). Unified Modeling Language Specification, version 1.5. Document number formal/03-03-01, Object Management Group, March 2003.
16. M. Prochazka. *Advanced Transactions in Component-Based Software Architectures*. PhD thesis, Charles University, Faculty of Mathematics and Physics, Department of Software Engineering, Prague, 2002.
17. R. Rouvoy and P. Merle. Abstraction of Transaction Demarcation in Component-Oriented Platforms. In *International Symposium on Distributed Objects and Applications (DOA'03), Rio de Janeiro, Brasil, 16-20 June 2003*, 2003.
18. J. P. Sousa and D. Garlan. Formal Modeling of the Enterprise JavaBeans Component Integration Framework. In *Proceedings of FM'99*, volume 1709 of *LNCS*, Toulouse, France, Sept. 1999. Springer Verlag.
19. C. A. Szyperski. *Component Software*. Addison Wesley, 1998.

Alice: Modularization of Middleware Using Aspect-Oriented Programming

Michael Eichberg and Mira Mezini

Department of Computer Science,
Software Technology Group,
Darmstadt University of Technology, Germany
{eichberg, mezini}@informatik.tu-darmstadt.de

Abstract. In this paper, we identify three problems with current component middleware. First, the implementation of services is usually not modularized, making it hard to adapt the platform to application specific needs, to exchange services to cope with changing requirements or to use it on different devices. Second, mapping components to objects results in a complex programming model and is making the component code dependent on the used component framework. Third, application level crosscutting concerns are not modularized.

To solve these problems, we propose an aspect-oriented programming approach, complemented by standard Java 1.5 annotations to provide meta information about the components, and a sophisticated query language for pointcut designation based on annotations.

1   Introduction

Current middleware for component-based software development (CBSD), based on the Enterprise JavaBeans (EJB) [1] or CORBA Component Model [2], provide good separation of concerns between the business logic (implemented by the components) and the technical infrastructure needed to run the business logic (implemented by the container). The container implements m iddleware services e.g., to authenticate users, to make an application remotely accessible, to provide transaction handling, etc., and transparently invokes those services at well-defined points during the execution of the business logic.

Without the dedicated support by the component middleware the implementation, respectively the invocation and orchestration of middleware services, would be scattered around and tangled with the business logic. Such services, respectively their invocation, would be crosscutting the business logic [3]. Component middleware modularize this crosscutting. However, we observe three problems with this modularization.

The first problem concerns the complexity of the programming model. To achieve the separation of the business logic from the middleware services, current approaches force the developer to map component concepts onto language constructs designed to express lower-level concepts such as objects (i.e. Java classes

T. Gschwind and C. Mascolo (Eds.): SEM 2004, LNCS 3437, pp. 47–63, 2005.
© Springer-Verlag Berlin Heidelberg 2005

and interfaces in EJBs), often involving coding conventions. This complicates the programming model and defeats the benefits of static type checking [4,5]. A more direct support for the concept of distributed components in the programming model in use would make the business logic more maintainable and would foster reusability.

Second, middleware services are themselves generally not well modularized from each other. A modularization of the services into well encapsulated and decoupled modules is important to support adaptable component environments that can be tailored to specific application's needs [4,5]. The ongoing discussion about the "correct" persistence service [6,7] supports the observation that adaptable containers / application servers are needed. The vision is a virtual container composed out of a set of services per application.

Finally, current environments modularize only a predefined set of services defined by the respective component models; they lack openness along with a uniform approach for modularizing arbitrary application level aspects such as e.g., application specific authorization policies or aspects of the business logic itself. It is desirable to have a uniform mechanism for modularizing middleware as well as application specific concerns.

Motivated by these observations, we propose a new approach to the design of component middleware frameworks, called Alice. Our approach combines a minimal container concept with aspect-oriented programming [8] and annotations [9]. In Alice, business logic is declared and implemented in plain Java interfaces and classes, while crosscutting services are implemented in aspects.

Alice uses standard Java 1.5 annotations [9] to decorate Java interfaces that declare a component type. The idea is that components have additional semantics, as compared to plain objects; e.g., session or entity semantics. In Alice, such component properties are expressed by annotations rather than by coding conventions; at deployment-time the properties are evaluated, i.e. it is ensured that a component implementation confirms to the properties declared in its annotations.

The annotations are also used by the services, which are implemented in aspects and select well-defined points in the execution of the component where the service injects semantic effect. We will argue that annotations allow to select relevant join points based on semantic properties.

In Alice, the container consists in a minimal core fulfilling two roles. It serves as an assembler that, given a set of components and services deployed in it, makes sure that components and services are instantiated and the dependencies between them are resolved. In addition, the container serves as an extended class-loader that injects the semantics declared by the annotations into the components and weaves the functionality defined in aspects.

This paper presents the overall architecture of Alice and shows how it address the problems of current middleware platforms. Furthermore, we discuss the relation between Alice and other aspect-oriented proposals. We argue that the combination of aspect-oriented and container concepts supplemented by annotations makes Alice unique among the other aspect-oriented approaches to design of middleware platforms for component-based software development. Further, we explain that such a combination is actually needed.

The paper is structured accordingly. In Sec. 2 we present Alice. Sec. 3 discusses how Alice address the problems of component middleware platforms discussed above. In Sec. 4, we discuss Alice in relation to other aspect-oriented approaches. Sec. 5 summarizes the paper and outlines areas of future work.

2   Alice

This section is structured in 4 subsections, one for each element in the overall architecture of Alice. First, we discuss how annotations are used to declare a component's type and properties. Second, we present the implementation of services. Next, the functionality to enable an interaction between a component and a service is shown. At last, we explain the functionality of the Alice environment that brings all pieces together.

2.1   The Component Model / Annotations

A central feature of Alice is the use of Java 1.5 annotations [9] to provide meta-information about components and services. For components such meta-information includes the type of the component as well as structural and behavioral properties of it. For instance, in the following listing the annotation **Session** is used to declare that **ShoppingCart** defines a session component's interface[1]:

```
1 @Session public interface ShoppingCart {
2    @Authorize(role="Customer") public void checkout() { ... }
3    ...
4 }
5 public class ShoppingCartImpl implements ShoppingCart{ ... }
```

Note that the annotation is attached to the interface and not to the implementing class(es). This is consistent with the general statement that the interface defines a component's contract and the type of the component is part of such a contract.

Not only components, but also their methods, can be decorated with annotations. For instance, the annotation **Authorize** can be used to decorate business methods for which authorization is required. In the example above, this annotation is used to define that the **checkout** method can be executed, if and only if the caller has the **Customer** role (the value **"Customer"** of the annotation member **role** (in line 2), determines the required role of the user).

Note that annotations are not merely syntactic labels attached to the component. They effect the semantics of the component in an important way. The annotation **Session** associated with the interface **ShoppingCart** determines properties of every component that implements this interface. The defined properties depend on the chosen component model. However, Alice is not restricted to a

---

[1] A stateful Session Bean in EJB [1] terminology.

particular component model. The semantics of an annotation can be freely defined, but have to remain stable as soon as the annotation is used for the first time.

For an EJB-like component model, an example of a structural property to be fulfilled by session bean classes is that all fields must be declared either **private** or **public static final**. Examples of behavioral properties in the same model are: "Sessions should never start threads and should not handle concurrent access on their own". To give a more concrete intuition of how annotations define part of the component's semantic in Alice, consider an excerpt of a possible definition of the **Session** annotation for an EJB-like component model in the following:

```
1  Annotation to define a type as being a session component, i.e.  ...
2  */ @Target({ElementType.TYPE}) @Documented // Java meta
3  annotations
4  @Validate({"Session.xirc"})
5  public @interface Session { /* empty */ }
```

To read this code, one has to keep in mind that Java 1.5 annotations are program elements that can themselves be annotated with other annotations, called meta-annotations. The **Target** and **Documented** annotations used in the definition of **Session** above (line 3) are standard Java meta-annotations: in the concrete case, they specify that the **Session** annotation (a) can only be used to decorate type declarations (**Target**), and (b) that its usage should be part of the documentation of the decorated elements (**Documented**).

The **Validate** meta-annotation is used to bind structural/behavioral properties that the annotation imposes on the implementation of the components decorated with it. In our example, checks for those properties are defined in the file **Session.xirc**. That is, **Session.xirc** contains the logic for checking that any class that implements an interface annotated as **Session** does not explicitly use synchronization primitives, does not create threads, and that all its fields are declared as private or final public. In Sec. 2.4 we will go into more details as how this logic is expressed and executed in the Alice environment. For now, it is sufficient to note that for every class annotated with **Session**, all checks defined in **Session.xirc** will be evaluated and violations will be reported. Variations on this session semantics can be encoded in another annotation, call it **Session-Special**. A well-defined related set of annotations defines the component model in use in Alice; such models can co-exist.

2.2   Implementation of Services

Recall, that service denotes every implementation of crosscutting functionality. In Alice a service is a Java class decorated with the **Service** annotation; it implements crosscutting functionality by means of Pointcut & Advice [10]. We use the terms pointcut, join point and advice as defined by AspectJ [11]. Join points are well-defined points in the execution of a program; pointcuts are queries for selecting sets of such points that participate in a crosscutting structure; advice defines behavioral effect at the selected join points.

In Alice an advice is a standard Java method with a special signature and an `Advice` annotation. The parameter of the method is a `Context` object encapsulating the available context at a selected join point. The return type has to be `Object` and represents the result of the advice evaluation; it is used instead of the result of the original functionality at the selected join point.

For illustration, we discuss the development of a service for role-based authorization. In a non-aspect-oriented implementation the code for role-based authorization would be scattered around several modules. This is why role-based authorization is used as a typical example of a crosscutting concern [12]. Sample code implementing a role-based authorization in Alice is shown in the following listing.

```
1   @Service public interface RoleBasedAuthorization {  /* empty */ }
2
3   public class RoleBasedAuthorizationImpl implements RoleBasedAuthorization {
4
5       private Authentication authentication;
6       public RoleBasedAuthorizationImpl(Authentication authentication){
7           this.authentication = authentication;
8       }
9
10      @Advice (pointcut="implementingMethods(
11              annotatedMembers(annotatedTypes('alice.ex.annotation.Session'),
12                              'alice.ex.annotation.Authorize',
13                              'role', 'Customer' ) )")
14      public Object onExecution(Context context){ return authorize(context,"Customer"); }
15
16      private Object authorize(Context context, String role) {
17          User user = authentication.getUser( context.getThis() );
18          if (VALIDATE USER) return context.proceed();
19          else GENERATE ERROR;
20      }
21  }
```

Such a service will select all method calls to be checked for authorization by their property of having the annotation `Authorize` and will check if the authenticated user has the correct role. Hence, the authorization service is dependent on an authentication service. To make this dependency explicit the constructor of the class `RoleBasedAuthorizationImpl` in the above listing declares a parameter with formal type `Authentication` (line 6). At creation time, a service implementing this interface will be injected by the environment. Here we use the techniques of constructor-based dependency injection [13]. That is, the constructor of a component defines the dependencies on the services that are required. So, whenever a new component is instantiated an instance of a service is passed to the component to resolve the dependency. If a dependency cannot be resolved an exception is thrown and the component will not be loaded.

The most important part of the service is the definition of the pointcut (line 10) as part of the `Advice` annotation. The pointcut first selects all interfaces annotated with the `Session` annotation (line 11). For each selected interface, `annotatedMembers` will determine all methods decorated with the `Authorize` annotation (line 12) and whose `role` element (line 13) is set to `''Customer''` (line 13). So far, we have selected the method declarations of our concern. Now, we have to determine the implementations of the selected method declarations (line 10); only there advice can join the business logic.

Each service will be instantiated once by the environment at start-up time, i.e. a service is a singleton [14] and started before any component is loaded. When terminated the environment will notify the services to enable a controlled shutdown. The differences between a component and a service are summarized in the following table:

	Service	Component
number of instances at runtime	1	0..*
can define pointcuts & advice	yes	no
can be injected	yes	no
lifecycle	controlled by the environment	freely definable
instantiated	at load time	at runtime

2.3   Interaction Between Components and Services

Interactions between services and components can be in either direction: from a component to a service and vice versa.

The interaction from a component to a service is enabled by constructor-based dependency injection. For illustration, imagine a shopping cart component that - as part of its business logic - generates an order confirmation on checkout, starting with "Dear Mr/Ms CustomerName" (line 2). Hence, the component must interact with the authentication service (line 3) to get the name of the current user (line 4).

```
1    public void checkout(){
2        String confirmation = "Dear Mr/Ms ";
3        User user = authenticationService.getUser(this);
4        confirmation += user.getName();
5        ...
6    }
```

For this purpose, the component defines a constructor that expects as a parameter a reference to an authentication service (line 3). Hence, whenever the component is instantiated the environment will pass a reference to the instance of a corresponding service. Note that AuthenticationService is the common interface of all authentication services and not a concrete implementation.

```
1  public ShoppingCartImpl implements ShoppingCart{
2      AuthenticationService authenticationService;
3      public ShoppingCartImpl(AuthenticationService authenticationService){
4          this.authenticationService = authenticationService;
5      }
6      ...
7  }
```

Let us now consider the interaction of a service with a component. An interaction is required in this direction for services that control the life cycle of components. If the component cannot appropriately react to such externally caused changes in its life cycle, it might not work correctly afterward. This requires that the component developer is aware of all possible state changes. They are defined by the annotation used for this component. As a result, services that would change the state of a component in an undefined way cannot be used.

For illustration, let us assume that the Session annotation defines that the possible states of a session component are "does not exist", "ready" and "passive" and that the semantics is basically the same as those of Enterprise Java Stateful Session Beans [1]. Further, the callback methods slcActivate, slcPassivate and slcRemove to signal state transitions to the component are defined by the SessionLifeCycleListener interface.

If the developer of a component now implements this interface she/he ensures that the component will be called back at each state transition. In the following code, an interaction with a legacy Enterprise Information System is closed or (re-)established depending on the life cycle event.

```
1  public class ShoppingCartImpl implements ShoppingCart, SessionLifeCycleListener {
2      // REFERENCE TO THE LEGACY ENTERPRISE INFORMATION SYSTEM
3      private transient Interaction interaction;
4      public void slcActivate() {
5          Connection connection = ...;
6          this.interaction = connection.createInteraction();
7      }
8      public void slcPassivate() { interaction.close(); }
9      public void slcRemove(){ slcPassivate(); }
10     ...
11 }
```

2.4   The Alice Environment

The Alice environment represents a minimal core with a twofold role:

◇ It provides management functionality to (a) handle the life cycle of services, (b) instantiate components, and (c) resolve the service to service and component to service dependencies.
◇ It provides an extended load-time weaver that (a) checks the properties defined by annotations, (b) enables to plug-in code transformers, and (c) weaves advice functionality.

The manager role was discussed as part of the previous sections (dependency injection); in the following, we will elaborate on the weaver role.

At load-time, Alice "decompiles" a Java class file to an equivalent XML representation using BAT2XML [15]. This XML representation is used in the intermediate stages performed by the loader. At the end of the extended loading process, the XML file is converted back to a standard Java class file and passed to the Java Virtual Machine.

The first step at load time is to validate that any decorated class, be it a component, service, or annotated helper class, satisfies all properties defined by its annotations, if any. Restrictions on structural and behavioral properties of components are defined as queries in the functional query language XQuery [16], especially designed for XML data sources. The queries defined by the annotations will be run against the XML representations of the annotated class (elements) and every selected item will be reported [17].

For illustration, the following query detects the violations of component properties defined along with the Session annotation (section 2.1). This query is defined in Session.xirc, the value of the meta-annotation Validate associated with the Session annotation. The first line selects all subtypes of an interface with the Session annotation; the "." in subtypes(.) represents the set of all elements decorated with the annotation for which Validate is a meta-annotation. Lines 3–5 are XPath [18] expressions that select violations of one of the defined properties. Line 3 selects methods with synchronization code, line 4 selects invocations of Thread.start() and line 4 selects declarations of non-private and non-public-final fields.

```
1  let $classes := subtypes(.)
2  return
3    $classes//method[@synchronized = "true"] | $classes//monitorenter |
4    $classes//invoke[@methodName="start" and @declaringClassName="java.lang.Thread"] |
5    $classes//field[not(@visibility ="private") and not(@visibility="public" and @final="true")]
```

The second step at load-time performs code generation and / or transformation required to implement some services. For example, to implement a passivation service[2] [19] it is necessary that all references to the component are fully controlled by the service. Otherwise, the service could be bypassed leading to faulty runtime behavior [20].

Controlling all references to a component can be achieved by generating a transparent proxy [14] object and passing it to other components instead of the direct reference[3]. Since the proxy is transparent for the entire program except for the passivation service the service has now the necessary control over the "direct references" to the component and can successfully passivate and activate the component. The component itself needs eventually to be transformed in order to replace some references to this by references to the wrapping proxy.

A class that is successfully validated will be transformed, if necessary, by passing it to all applicable transformers in the order specified in the configuration file of the environment. A transform er is itself provided as a service that implements the Transformer interface. The latter defines a single method, which will be called by the environment to pass a representation of the byte code of a class to be transformed; the method returns the transformed class and / or other generated classes.

Before actually transforming a class a transformer checks its applicability by consulting the annotations of the class. E.g., it does not make sense to apply the proxy transformation to helper classes.

---

[2] A passivation service is used to achieve scalability. It removes a component from main memory that was not accessed for a certain amount of time (this process is called *passivation*) and writes it to secondary storage. Directly before the next access the component is restored (this is called *activation*) to handle the method call.

[3] In EJB the bean developer would pass the EJBObject to the other component.

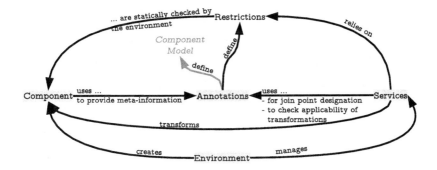

Fig. 1. An overview of Alice

The transformation step can be done by executing a set of XSL Transformations [21]. A service that relies on a specific code transformation / generation service can make this dependency explicit by using the standard dependency injection mechanism, even though, it does not need to explicitly interact with the transformation service.

The last step is the weaving of aspects. The pieces of advice to weave are determined by the services. Hence, all services that define advice need to be loaded at startup before the classes to be advised. In Alice, XQuery is also used as the pointcut language, as proposed in [22]. The weaving step evaluates the pointcut queries defined in the services to select elements in the code that might yield a join point at runtime. These are the XML elements where to weave advice.

Fig. 1 summarizes the discussion of this section as well as the previous sections. It depicts the relationship between annotations and the defined restrictions, components, services and the environment.

3   Alice and Current Component Models

This section evaluates Alice w.r.t. the problems of current component models identified in the introduction. In addition, it briefly discusses the relation between Alice and JBoss [23] one particularly advanced and modular implementation of the EJB component model. Last but not least, we shortly discuss Alice in relation to the upcoming EJB 3.0 specification [24].

Evaluation of Alice. Alice does not suffer from the problems of current component middleware discussed in the introduction.

First, by means of checked semantic annotations, Alice provides a mechanism for introducing component concepts in a principled way without restricting itself to a particular component model. Annotations play in Alice almost the role of new language constructs for expressing component semantics. They define checked properties of elements decorated by them, just as language constructs would define new semantics that is incorporated for by the language compiler. Hence, there is no need for unchecked coding conventions and other workarounds which introduce accidental complexity [25]. In contrast to language constructs that have a fixed semantics, Alice is capable of accommodating several component models.

Second, by encapsulating various crosscutting concerns into separate aspects, and by its ability to load and incorporate only services that are required by the business components, Alice enables a modular lightweight architecture of the middleware functionality; the middleware functionality is composed out of individual services based on application requirements.

Third, as already mentioned, services in Alice can be used to encapsulate any crosscutting concern, be it middleware or application level. This enables a uniform programming model and an open platform.

JBoss(Standard). The standard JBoss application server [23] implements the concept of a micro kernel architecture based on JMX [26]. This kernel provides a basic infrastructure on which all components and services rely. Hence, it serves as a least common denominator for the components as well as the services to plug in. Due to this architecture it is possible to exchange a service (e.g., to exchange a service for transactions using optimistic locking against one using a pessimistic locking strategy). However, the implementation is still bound to this very specific application server and the usage of a service or a component always requires the core JBoss application server and thus forces a specific architecture and / or design.

EJB 3.0. The programming model of the next version of the Enterprise Java Beans (3.0) [24] will rely on the use of annotations to make the development of components easier. Annotations will be used to automatically generate the necessary (Local-, Remote-, ...) interfaces and to make an explicit interaction with the container possible. However, modularization of the infrastructural services as well as separation of (business) concerns are not addressed. Also, the component model is fixed and using other types of components not defined in the model will be difficult.

4   Alice and Other AO Models

In this section we compare Alice with other aspect-oriented approaches. In particular we make a deeper comparison of Alice and AspectJ [11] since AspectJ represents the most mature aspect-oriented language available and the conceptual model of AspectJ is incorporated by multiple other approaches [27, 28, 29].

AspectJ [11] can also be used to modularize individual middleware services. It does not constrain the development of components and aspects (services) in any particular way and is already successfully used in many projects [30, 31, 32, 33] and especially for the implementation of infrastructural services [34, 35, 36, 37]. Alice is similar to AspectJ, as far as the underlying AO model is concerned. It complements the AO model, however, with a minimal container concept to better serve the specific needs of distributed component-based software development.

In the following, we briefly emphasize, that such a complement is needed mainly for three reasons.

First, as indicated in Sec. 2.4, some services require sophisticated code generation and / or transformation, e.g., the generation of proxies for the passivation service. However, as discussed in [20] generating proxy objects is not supported by AspectJ's inter-type declarations; using a different generation mechanism instead (e.g. Java's dynamic proxies) is also problematic [20].

Second, even though AspectJ can be used to enforce design properties [38, 12], it was not designed to enforce structural properties; in [39], we argue that AspectJ's declare warning / error constructs provide only limited support for checking properties of the program structure. In our context this implies that AspectJ's support for checking the applicability of a service to a specific class is limited; e.g., it is not possible to detect synchronized blocks within a class - a service aspect for handling concurrent access would conflict with such a class.

Third, AspectJ lacks a mechanism to enable components to require the presence of an aspect in a deployment environment without committing to a particular implementation. However, such a mechanism is needed, a component that needs to get an authenticated user requires an authentication aspect, otherwise it cannot be used[4].

These three tasks are performed by the container in Alice - besides weaving aspects. In addition to complementing the AO concepts with a container, another difference between Alice and AspectJ concerns the pointcut language. In [40] the authors discuss the problem of arranged patterns: Often pointcut definitions are based on naming conventions which leads to a coupling between an aspect and the components. Such a coupling is not acceptable for systems with hundreds of components; a clear separation between the component developers and the developers of the infrastructural services is needed[5]. A better separation is achieved in Alice by using annotations to select join points in pointcuts. Now, one might argue that adding annotations in the component code is also a form of crosscutting. We will discuss this issue in a dedicated place in Sec. 5.

HyperJ [41, 42] supports a flexible and multi-dimensional separation of concerns. In contrast to AspectJ (and similar approaches), HyperJ does not require that all aspects (concerns) are coded relative to the same model, instead each concern can be modeled according to its most appropriate domain model. However, HyperJ supports a more coarse-grained join point model than AspectJ. E.g., it is not possible to add functionality before, after or around a field access, which is often required for the implementation of services such as persistence. Further, the integration of different hyperslices relies on the matching of method / class names making it hard to develop off-the-shelf reusable services. Detailed

---

[4] Using aspectOf would bind the component to a particular implementation of the service.

[5] In case of the success stories mentioned at the beginning of this section the implementation of the infrastructural services using AspectJ were done by the same people who developed the base application.

knowledge about a hyperslice (implementing a concern) is required before a hypermodule (specifies the interaction of multiple hyperslices) can correctly be specified.

The approach described by Duclos et al. in [43] combines the ideas of AspectJ, containers and Meta-Object Protocols (MOPs), resulting in a programming model where aspects can be developed independent of the component application. An aspect user language controls the weaving and code generation step to create necessary classes (like proxies for instance) for the components as well as the interaction between an aspect and the component virtual environment (CVM). The CVM builds the least common denominator on which the components and aspects rely. However, in contrast to our approach they have a very limited pointcut language restricted to aspectualizing the CVM. Using aspects to model cross-cutting business functionality is not intended. Neither support to check the applicability of an aspect for a set of components nor the interaction between a component and a service are addressed.

In [37] and [44] Zhang and Jacobsen analyze three different CORBA [2] ORBs, by mining for aspects inherent in these middleware implementations and applying AspectJ to modularize these concerns. Besides the common aspects such as logging and monitoring, they identify various domain-specific aspects related to the creation and handling of objects in CORBA. In [45] they describe the successful modularization of several of those aspects in the CORBA ORB ORBacus and provide encouraging results with respect to the achievable level of modularization using AOP. In [46] they build on top of these results and develop the method of horizontal decomposition, a set of principles for guiding the aspect-oriented decomposition of a middleware system. The basic idea is to identify a minimal core and then to use aspects to extend the functionality of the core to provide additional services. A similar idea was also presented by Hunleth et. al. [47] but a detailed discussion of their architecture is not available. However, in contrast to Alice the minimal core identified by Zhang and Jacobsen already provides substantial middleware service (e.g. distribution). Further, every aspect is developed in relation to a particular core making an aspect dependent on it and susceptible to changes if the core evolves. But, they also note that the refactorization of the ORB is not complete and that they have not yet achieved a fully aspect oriented middleware platform. Further, in contrast to our work, their work builds upon an existing component model and implementations of it and is geared toward identifying and refactoring as many concerns as possible in that particular context, using an existing AOP approach.

JBoss AOP [28] is a small framework for aspect-oriented programming which comes with some pre-defined aspects (for transactions, etc.). The set of supported join points and and the pointcut languag are basically a subset of those supported by AspectJ but with the additional support for annotations (metadata). However, JBoss AOP is based on intercepting the original control flow and invoking so-called interceptors which execute the advice functionality. JBoss AOP has no support for introductions or other forms of code generation / transformation. Further, it proposes no standard way for the interaction between a component and a service (e.g. security) and checking of structural properties is also not possible. The Spring (AOP) Framework [48] and Jac [29] are similar to JBoss AOP. They are also interceptor based approaches with practically the same features and limitations.

AspectJ2EE [5] is geared toward a modularized implementation of the infrastructural services offered by an EJB container as an aspect library. The architecture enables to add or modify services. As in our approach the components are aspectualized at deploy time. However, in contrast to Alice AspectJ2EE is limited in several ways: (1) all components must be developed according to the EJB component model. This severely restricts the usability of AspectJ2EE as a general platform for component based software development and makes the components dependent on the EJB component framework. (2) adding additional aspects or modifying existing ones is possible but no mechanism exists to check that an aspect can actually be used for a component. (3) Aspects can only be defined for Enterprise JavaBeans and not for all classes of a project.

5   Annotations and Crosscutting

In this section, we briefly consider the question whether or not annotations introduce crosscutting. Our discussion focuses only on the particular use of annotations in Alice; a general discussion of the issue is out of the scope for this paper.

We argue that in their particular use in Alice, annotations do not add crosscutting. The reason is that annotations are not used in Alice as "syntactic anchors" to bind non-functional aspects to a component. Such a use would indeed re-introduce non-modularized crosscutting. The primary function of annotations in Alice is to declare that the annotated element has a certain guaranteed behavior; they make implicit information explicit, e.g., that a method is a business method, or that session handling is required. These are inherent properties of a component and are independent of the application of which it is a part of.

In our opinion, annotations that describe a property of a component should be defined along with it. They are in our view a substitute for the lack of component language constructs. As such, they have benefits not related to modularizing crosscutting concerns such as, better documentation and enforcement of properties. Furthermore, the component developers know exactly the properties of their component. So, they should specify them along with the component.

For annotations that are application specific (e.g., annotations declaring the transaction properties of a method), a step at the very beginning of the weaving process could be added that processes `declare annotations` statements as envisioned for the next version of AspectJ [11]. A `declare annotations` statement would allow a modularization of the decision which methods have a certain property (e.g., are transactional).

6   Future Work

The main goal of our work was to present a concise programming model that represents a significant improvement when compared with the current state-of-the-art in CBSD. Thus far, we did not target compilation and execution speed and due to the heavy usage of XML improvements of our prototype needs to be made before it can be used for larger middleware projects. Further, the mechanisms used to control the transformation process and to ensure that a component is appropriately transformed are sufficient for projects with few different types of transformations but if more different transformations are to be carried out more sophisticated mechanisms are required to ensure the integrity of the system, i.e. to check that two transformations do not influence each other in an unpredictable or unwanted manner. These topics as well as a throughout evaluation are going to be addressed in future work.

7   Summary

We have presented a programming model that allows the separation of infrastructural services in off-the-shelf reusable aspects. This is made possible by a set (of standardized) annotations which are used by the component developer to provide additional information about the component and the join points for aspects. The aspect developer uses the annotations to bind the functionality to a component without requiring any knowledge about a component's concrete implementation. We have further presented a model how to handle interactions between a component and a service and how to deal with the interaction of components with legacy systems. The entire functionality is provided by a small fully generic environment that does not imply a specific component model. To the best of the authors knowledge this is the first approach that fully separates all concerns of a middleware platform in different aspects. By doing so, a level of adapatibility and genericity of a middleware platform for CBSD is achieved that was not available before.

References

1. DeMichiel, L.G.: Enterprise JavaBeans Specification, Version 2.1. SUN Microsystems (2003)
2. Group, O.M.: Corba components 3.0. Specification formal/02-06-65, OMG (2002)
3. Masuhara, H., Kiczales, G.: Modeling crosscutting in aspect-oriented mechanisms. In: Proceedings of the 17th European Conference on Object-Oriented Programming, Springer (2003) 2–28
4. Pichler, R., Ostermann, K., Mezini, M.: On aspectualizing component models. Software Practice and Experience **33** (2003) 957–974
5. Cohen, T., Gil, J.Y.: AspectJ2EE = AOP + J2EE - towards an aspect based, programmable and extensible middleware framework. In: Proceedings of the 18th European Conference on Object-Oriented Programming, Springer (2004)

6. Jordan, D., Russell, C.: JDO or CMP? http://www.onjava.com/lpt/a/3763 (2003)
7. Tate, B.: For JDO, the time is now. http://www.devx.com/Java/Article/20422/1954?pf=true (2004)
8. Kiczales, G., Lamping, J., Menhdhekar, A., Maeda, C., Lopes, C., Loingtier, J.M., Irwin, J.: Aspect-oriented programming. In: Proceedings of the 11th European Conference on Object-Oriented Programming, Springer (1997) 220–242
9. Bloch, J.: A metadata facility for the java programming language. Java Specification Request 175 (2002)
10. Masuhara, H., Kiczales, G.: Modeling crosscutting in aspect-oriented mechanisms. In: Proceedings of the 17th European Conference on Object-Oriented Programming, Springer (2003)
11. Kiczales, G., Hilsdale, E., Hugunin, J., Kersten, M., Palm, J., Griswold, W.G.: An overview of aspectj. In: Proceedings of the 15th European Conference on Object-Oriented Programming, Springer (2001) 327–355
12. Laddad, R.: AspectJ in Action. Manning (2003)
13. Fowler, M.: Inversion of control containers and the dependency injection pattern. http://martinfowler.com/articles/injection.html (2004)
14. Gamma, E., Helm, R., Johnson, R., Vlissides, J.: Design Patterns. Addison-Wesley (1995)
15. Eichberg, M.: BAT2XML. http://www.st.informatik.tu-darmstadt.de/BAT (2004)
16. Boag, S., Chamberlin, D., Fernndez, M.F., Florescu, D., Robie, J., Simon, J.: XQuery 1.0: An XML query language. Working draft 12 november 2003, (W3C)
17. Eichberg, M., Mezini, M., Ostermann, K., Schfer, T.: Xirc: a kernel for cross-artifact information engineering in software development environments. In: Proceedings of the 11th IEEE Working Conference on Reverse Engineering, IEEE Computer Society (2004) to appear.
18. Berglund, A., Boag, S., Chamberlin, D., Fernández, M.F., Kay, M., Robie, J., Siméon, J.: Xml path language (xpath) 2.0. Working draft 12 november 2003, (W3C)
19. Völter, M., Schmid, A., Wolff, E.: Server Component Patterns: Component Infrastructures Illustrated with EJB. John Wiley & Sons (2002)
20. Eichberg, M.: The proxy inter-type declaration. In: Proceedings of the third AOSD Workshop on Aspects, Components, and Patterns for Infrastructure Software. (2004)
21. Kay, M.: Xsl transformations (xslt) version 2.0. Working draft 12 november 2003, (W3C)
22. Eichberg, M., Mezini, M., Ostermann, K.: First-class pointcuts as queries. In: Proceedings of the Second ASIAN Symposium on Programming Languages and Systems, Springer (2004) to appear.
23. JBoss Inc.: JBoss 3.2. http://www.jboss.org (2003)
24. DeMichiel, L.G.: Enterprise JavaBeans Specification, Version 3.0. Java Specification Request 220 (2004)
25. Brooks, F.P.: The Mythical Man-Month. Addison Wesley (1995)
26. Sun Microsystems: Java management extensions (JMX). White paper (1999)
27. Mezini, M., Ostermann, K.: Conquering aspects with caesar. In: Proceedings of the 2nd International Conference on Aspect-Oriented Software Development (AOSD), ACM Press (2003) 90–99

28. JBoss Inc.: JBoss aop beta3. http://www.jboss.org (2004)
29. Pawlak, R., Seinturier, L., Duchien, L., Florin, G.: Jac: A flexible solution for aspect-oriented programming in java. In: Proceedings of the third International Conference on Metalevel Architectures and Separation of Crosscutting Concerns, Springer (2001) 1–24
30. Walker, R.J., Baniassad, E.L.A., Murphy, G.C.: An initial assessment of aspect-oriented programming. In: Proceedings of the 21st International Conference on Software Engineering, (IEEE Computer Society) 120–130
31. Lippert, M., Lopes, C.V.: A study on exception detecton and handling using aspect-oriented programming. In: Proceedings of the 22nd International Conference on Software Engineering, ACM Press (2000) 418–427
32. Bodkin, R., Colyer, A., Hugunin, J.: Applying aop for middlerware platform independence. In: 2nd International Conference on Aspect-Oriented Software Development. (2003) Practitioner Reports.
33. Colyer, A., Clement, A.: Large-scale aosd for middleware. In: Proceedings of the 3rd International Conference on Aspect-Oriented Software Development, ACM Press (2004) 56–65
34. Rashid, A., Chitchyan, R.: Persistence as an aspect. In: Proceedings of the 2nd International Conference on Aspect-Oriented Software Development, ACM Press (2003) 120–129
35. Soares, S., Laureano, E., Borba, P.: Implementing distribution and persistence aspects with aspectj. In: Proceedings of the 17th Conference on Object-Oriented Programming, Systems, Languages, and Applications, ACM Press (2002) 174–190
36. Gudmundson, S.: An Aspect-Oriented Distribution Service (1999)
37. Zhang, C., Jacobsen, H.A.: Refactoring middleware with aspects. IEEE Transactions on Parallel and Distributed Systems **14** (2003) 1058–1073
38. Shomrat, M., Yehudai, A.: Obvious or not? regulating architectural decisions using aspect-oriented programming. In: Proceedings of 1st International Conference on Aspect-Oriented Software Development, ACM Press (2002) 3–9
39. Eichberg, M., Mezini, M., Schäfer, T., Beringer, C., Hamel, K.M.: Enforcing system-wide properties. In: Proceedings of the 15th Australian Software Engineering Conference, IEEE Computer Society (2004)
40. Gybels, K., Brichau, J.: Arranging language features for more robust pattern-based crosscuts. In: Proceedings of the 2nd International Conference on Aspect-Oriented Software Development, ACM Press (2003) 60–69
41. Ossher, H., Tarr, P.: Using multidimensional separation of concerns to (re)shape evolving software. Communications of the ACM **44** (2001) 43–50
42. Tarr, P., Ossher, H., Harrison, W., Stanley M. Sutton, J.: N negrees of separation: multi-dimensional separation of concerns. In: Proceedings of the 21st International Conference on Software Engineering, IEEE Computer Society (1999) 107–119
43. Duclos, F., Estublier, J., Morat, P.: Describing and using non functional aspects in component based applications. In: Proceedings of the 1st International Conference on Apect-Oriented Software Development, ACM Press (2002) 65–75
44. Zhang, C., Jacobsen, H.A.: Quantifying aspects in middleware platforms. In: Proceedings of 2nd International Conference on Aspect-Oriented Software Development, ACM Press (2003) 130–139
45. Zhang, C., Jacobsen, H.A.: Re-factoring middleware systems: a case study. In: On The Move to Meaningful Internet Systems 2003: CoopIS, DOA, and ODBASE, Springer (2003) 1243–1262

46. Zhang, C., Jacobsen, H.A.: Resolving implementation convolution in middleware systems. In: Proceedings of the 19th Conference on Object-Oriented Programming, Systems, Languages, and Applications, ACM Press (2004) to appear.
47. Hunleth, F., Cytron, R., Gill, C.: Building customizable middleware using aspect oriented programming. citeseer.ist.psu.edu/hunleth01building.html (2001)
48. Johnson, R.: Introducing the spring framework. http://www.theserverside.com/articles/article.tss?l= SpringFramework (2003)

Service Discovery Protocol Interoperability in the Mobile Environment

Yérom-David Bromberg and Valérie Issarny

INRIA-Rocquencourt,
Domaine de Voluceau, 78153 Le Chesnay, France
{David.Bromberg, Valerie.Issarny}@inria.fr

Abstract. The emergence of portable computers and wireless technologies has introduced new challenges for middleware. Mobility brings new requirements and is becoming a key characteristic. Mobile devices may move around different areas and have to interact with different types of networks, services and may be exposed to new communication paradigms. Thus, mobile distributed systems need to dynamically detect and adapt their interaction protocols to interoperate with services available in the environment. As a result, middleware for mobile devices must overcome two heterogeneity issues to provide interoperability in the mobile environment, i.e, heterogeneity of discovery protocols and of interaction protocols between services. Whereas adaptation techniques from reflective middleware are suitable for the latter, it is more problematic for the former if both issues are addressed concurrently. Specifically, reflective mechanisms consume too many resources like bandwidth, memory and CPU, which are limited on the mobile devices. This paper first highlights why current solutions to interoperability fail to realize service discovery protocol interoperability with both high performance and low resource consumption. Second, this paper addresses this open issue by using software architecture concepts enhanced with event-based parsing techniques to provide efficient, lightweight and flexible mechanisms to bring full service discovery interoperability to any existing mobile platform.

1 Introduction

In the mobile computing domain, middleware holds a predominant role. Communication relationships amongst application components involve the use of protocols, making applications tightly coupled to middleware. Additionally, to overcome wireless networks constraints, like limited bandwidth, poor network quality of service and either voluntary or forced frequent disconnection, several communication models have arisen. Thus, as it exists many styles of communication and consequently many styles of middleware, we have to deal with middleware heterogeneity [1]. Significantly, an application implemented upon a specific middleware cannot interoperate with services developed upon another. Similarly, we cannot predict at design time the requirements needed at run-time since the execution environment is not known. However, no matter which underlying communication protocols are present, mobile nodes must both discover

T. Gschwind and C. Mascolo (Eds.): SEM 2004, LNCS 3437, pp. 64–77, 2005.

and interact with the services available in their vicinity. More precisely, service discovery protocols enable mobile nodes to find and use networked services without any previous knowledge of their specific location. Several Service Discovery Protocols (SDP), like Jini [2], SLP [3], UPnP [4] and Salutation [5], are now available. And, with the advent of both mobility and wireless networking, SDPs are taking on a major role, and are the source of a major heterogeneity issue across middleware. Furthermore, once services are discovered, applications need to use the same interaction protocol to allow unanticipated connections and interactions with them. Consequently, a second heterogeneity issue appears among middleware. Summarizing, middleware for mobile devices must overcome two heterogeneity issues to provide interoperability in the mobile environment, i.e.:

1. Heterogeneity of service discovery protocols, and
2. Heterogeneity of interaction protocols between services.

In addition, both SDPs and interaction protocols are not protected from evolution across time. Indeed, an application may neither interact correctly nor be compatible with services if they use different versions of the same protocol [6]. Interoperability is also difficult between devices made by different manufacturers as they can implement differently a standardized protocol. Protocol evolution increases communication failure probability between two mobile devices.

As outlined above, interoperability among entities of a spontaneous ad hoc network, which is formed by the random arrival of mobile devices for short periods of time, is becoming a real issue to overcome. A portable computer must be aware of its dynamic environment that evolves over time, and further adapt its communication paradigms according to the environment. Thus, mobile distributed systems must provide efficient mechanisms to detect and interpret protocols currently used, which are not known in advance. Furthermore, detection and interpretation must be achieved without increasing consumption of resources that are limited on the mobile devices. This paper introduces base mechanisms for achieving interoperability among heterogeneous SDPs, which consider the above mobility requirements. We reuse concepts from software architecture enriched with event-based parsing techniques to drastically improve SDP interoperability, enabling mobile applications to be efficiently aware of their environment. The originality of our approach comes from the trade offs achieved among efficiency, interoperability and flexibility. Our solution may further be applied to any existing middleware platform.

In the following, we first examine how reflective middleware manages interoperability among heterogeneous SDPs, highlighting the current drawbacks that need to be addressed to provide efficient SDP interoperability (§2). This leads us to investigate a solution grounded in the software architecture domain to overcome the limitation of reflective middleware (§3). Then, we present the design of our proposal to bring both efficient and flexible SDP interoperability (§4). Finally, we conclude by a summary of our contribution (§5).

2   Reflective Middleware to Cope with Middleware Heterogeneity

New techniques must be used to both offer lightweight mobile systems and support their adaptation according to the dynamics of the mobile environment. Classic middleware are not the most suitable for the mobile domain. Their design is based on fixed network and resources abundance. Moreover, network topologies and bandwidth are fixed over time. Hence, quality of service is predictable. Furthermore, with fixed network in mind, the common communication paradigm is synchronous and connections are permanent. However, many new middleware solutions, designed to cope with mobility aspects, have been introduced, as surveyed in [7]. From this pool of existing middleware, more or less adapted to the constraints of the mobile environment, reflective middleware seem to be flexible enough to fulfill mobility requirements, including providing interoperability among networked services.

A reflective system enables applications to reason and perform changes on their own behavior. Specifically, reflection provides both inspection and adaptation of systems at runtime. The former enables browsing the internal structure of the system, whereas the latter provides means to dynamically alter the system by changing the current state or by adding new features. Thus, the middleware embeds a minimal set of functionalities and is more adaptive to its environment by adding new behaviors when needed. This concept, applied to both service discovery and interaction protocols, allows accommodating mobility constraints. This is illustrated by the ReMMoC middleware [1], which is, at this time, the only one to overcome simultaneously SDPs and interaction protocols heterogeneity. The ReMMoC platform is composed of two component frameworks [1, 8]: (i) the binding framework that is dedicated to the management of different interaction paradigms, and (ii) the service discovery framework that is specialized in the discovery of the SDPs currently used in the local environment. The binding framework integrates as many components as interaction protocols supported by the platform. The binding framework can dynamically plug on demand, one at time or simultaneously, different components corresponding to the different interaction paradigms (e.g., publish/subscribe, RPC...). Correspondingly, the service discovery framework is composed of as many components as of SDPs recognized. For example, SLP and UPnP can be either plugged together or separately, depending of the context. Obviously, such plug in of components applies only to components that are specifically developed for the ReMMoC platform. It is further important to note that the client application is specific to the ReMMoC API but is independent from any protocol, the interested reader being referred to [9] for further details on the mapping of an API call to the current binding framework.

Although ReMMoC enables mobile devices to use simultaneously different SDPs and interaction protocols, this still requires the environment to be monitored to allow ReMMoC to detect over time the SDPs and interaction protocols that need be supported/integrated, due to the very dynamic nature of the mobile environment. Such a knowledge about the environment may be made available from a higher level, which would provide the environment proxie updated by context-based mechanisms that are passed down to the system [1, 10]. But, this increases the weight and the complexity of the overall mobile system. Alternatively, the system can either periodically check or continuously monitor the environment. However, a successful lookup depends on the pluggable discovery components that are embedded. The more there are components, better is the detection. But, the size of the middleware and the resources needed grow with the amount of embedded components. That is particularly not recommended for mobile devices. Furthermore, as long as the current SDP has not been found, the middleware has to reconfigure itself repeatedly with the available embedded components to perform a new environmental lookup until it finds the appropriate protocol. As a consequence, this leads both to an intensive use of the bandwidth already limited due to the wireless context, and to a higher computational load. To save these scarce resources, a plug-in component, called discoverdiscovery, dedicated to SDP detection operations, has been added to the ReMMoC service discovery framework. In an initialization step, m ini-test-plug-ins, implemented for each available SDP, are connected to discoverdiscovery to perform a test by both sending out a request and listening for responses. Once the detection is achieved, a configuration step begins by load-ing the corresponding complete SDP plug-ins.

The above M ini-test-plug-ins are lightweight and so consume fewer resources. Nevertheless, they increase the number of embedded plug-ins, do not decrease the use of the bandwidth and finally have to be specifically implemented. Last but not least, rather than embedding as many components as possible to provide the most interoperable middleware, it seems to be more efficient to design an optimized lightweight middleware, which enables loading from the ambient network new components on demand to supplement the already embedded ones [1, 11]. But, still, it is necessary to discover, at least once, the appropriate protocols to interact with a service providing such a capability. This is rather unlikely to happen since we do not know the execution context (i.e., all potential available resources and services at a given time).

Summarizing, solutions to interoperability based on reflective techniques do not bring simultaneously interoperability and high performance. The SDP interoperability issue needs to be revisited to improve efficiency of SDP detection, interpretation and evolution. Furthermore, the ReMMoC reflective middleware does not provide a clean separation between components and protocols. In fact, pluggable components are tied to their respective protocols. For example, to maintain interoperability between several versions of the same SDP, a pluggable component is needed for each version. We need a fine grained control over protocols. Our approach is thus to decouple components from protocols with the use of concepts inherited from software architecture enhanced with event-based parsing techniques.

3   Software Architecture to Decouple Components from Protocols

Software architecture concepts, like components and connectors to decouple applications from underlying protocols, offer an elegant means for modeling and reasoning about mobile systems [12]. Components abstract computational elements and bind with connectors that abstract interaction protocols, through interfaces, called ports, which correspond to communication gateways [13]. Similarly, connectors bind with components through connector interfaces named roles (see Figure 1). Regarding the issue of achieving protocol interoperability,

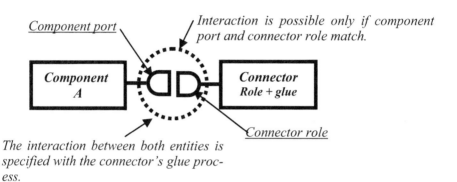

Component port

Interaction is possible only if component port and connector role match.

Component A   **Connector Role + glue**

Connector role

The interaction between both entities is specified with the connector's glue process.

Fig. 1. Components decoupled from protocols

this may be addressed through reasoning about the compatibility of port and role. This may be realized using, e.g., the Wright Architecture description language [14]. Wright defines CSP-like processes to model port and role behaviors. Then, compatibility between bound port and role is checked against, according to the CSP refinement relationship. However, the Wright approach does not bring enough flexibility with respect to dealing with the adaptation of port and role behavior so as to make them match when they share an identical aim, as, e.g., in the case of service discovery. To overcome the aforementioned limitation, [6] reuses the architectural concepts of component, connector, port and role. However, port and role behaviors are modeled by handlers of unordered event streams rather than by abstract roles processes. The challenge is then to transform protocol messages into events, and interpret them according to a protocol specification. To achieve this, an event-based parsing system, composed of generator, composer, unit, parser and proxy, is used (see Figure 2). A protocol specification feeds a generator that generates a dedicated parser and composer. The former takes, as input, protocol messages that are decomposed as tokens and outputs the corresponding events. The latter does the invert process; it takes series of events and transforms them into protocol messages. Parser and composer form a unit, which is specific to one protocol. Generators are able to generate on the fly new units, as needed, for different specifications. As a result, whatever

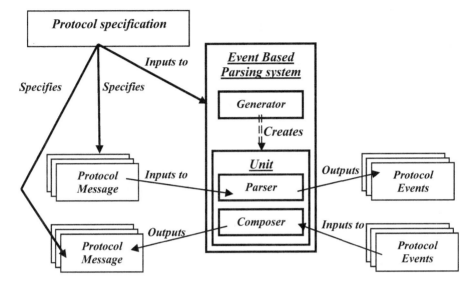

Fig. 2. Event based parsing system for achieving protocol interoperability

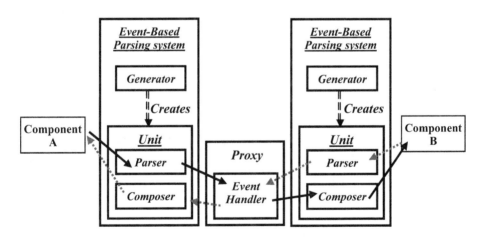

Fig. 3. Interaction between two components

is the underlying protocol, messages from a component are always transformed
into events through the adequate parser and conversely, events sent towards a
component are always transformed into protocol messages understood by this
component through its adequate composer. Furthermore, events are sent from
one component to another through a proxy whose role is to forward handled
events to the composer of the remote component (see Figure 3). The latter can
either discard some events if they are unknown or force the generator to produce
a new unit more suitable to parsed events. Thus, any connector gets represented

as a universal event communication bus, which is able to transport any event, independently of any protocol, as the protocol reconstruction process is let to each extremity. Thereby, event streams are hidden from components and so protocol interoperability is maintained.

Summarizing, event-based parsing is interesting in theory for its flexibility, and opens new perspectives to overcome protocols heterogeneity. However, it is still confined to theory: it has been applied only to protocol evolution issue, as it is simpler to test protocol interoperability between two similar protocols that differ with only small changes. Therefore, [6] addresses heterogeneity issues neither for SDPs nor for interaction protocols but brings interesting concepts. In the next section, we show how event-based parsing applied to software architecture enables efficient SDP detection and interoperability in the mobile environment.

4   Event-Based Parsing for Discovery Protocol Interoperability

With the emergence of mobility and wireless technologies, SDP heterogeneity becomes a major issue. ReMMoC is currently the only middleware to provide a first approach to resolve this issue through the use of the pluggable component philosophy. However, as stated earlier, this solution incurs high resource consumption (i.e., bandwidth, memory and CPU). Our objective is to provide a much more powerful solution, dedicated to the ad hoc network context, which both induces low resource consumption and introduces a lightweight mechanism that may be adapted easily to any platform. To achieve this challenge, we reuse the component and connector abstractions, and event-based parsing techniques from software architecture. Moreover, as our aim is to provide interoperability to the greatest number of portable devices, we base our technology on IP. The following first briefly introduces conceptual similarities among SDPs (§4.1), and then details our solution, addressing SDP detection (§4.2) and interoperability (§4.3).

4.1   Conceptual Similarities Among SDPs

The majority of SDPs support the concepts of client, service and repository. In order to find needed services, clients may perform two types of request: unicast or multicast. The former implies the use of a repository, equivalent to a centralized lookup service, which aggregates services information from services advertisements. The latter is used when either the repository's location is not known or there does not exist any repository in the environment. Similarly, services may announce themselves with either unicast or multicast advertisement depending on whether a repository is present or not. From the aforementioned approaches, two SDP models are identified, irrespectively of the repository's existence:

1. The passive discovery model, and
2. The active discovery model.

When a repository exists in an environment, the main challenge for clients and services is to discover the location of the repository, which acts as a mandatory intermediary between clients and services [3]. In this context, using the passive discovery model, clients and services are passively listening on a multicast group address specific to the SDP used and are waiting for a repository multicast advertisements. On the contrary, with an active discovery model, clients and services send multicast requests to discover a repository that sends back a unicast response to the requester to indicate its presence. In a "repository-less" context, a passive discovery model means that the client is listening on a multicast group address that is specific to the SDP used to discover services. Obviously, the latter periodically send out multicast announcement of their existence to the same multicast group address. In contrast, with a repository-less active discovery model, the roles are exchanged. Thereby, clients perform periodically multicast requests to discover needed services and the latter are listening to these requests. Furthermore, services reply unicast responses directly to the requester only if they match the requested service. To summarize, most SDPs support both passive and active discovery with either optional or mandatory centralization points.

Note that although service repositories reduce both bandwidth consumption and time for service location, they are not adequate to the dynamic nature of the mobile domain. All the entities from an ad hoc network form spontaneously a purely peer-to-peer architecture, which does not rely on any centralization point. Thus, SDPs, like Jini [2], exclusively based on a lookup server, break the peer-to-peer model and hence, conceptually, it is not advised to use it. However, we introduce a solution to SDP interoperability that supports almost all types of SDPs. The only exception is for the Jini SDP that is tied to the Java language and hence makes it harder to achieve interoperability because it requires that all mobile devices embed a Java virtual machine. In addition, properties of other SDPs must be Java byte-code encoded to allow interoperability with Jini clients. Addressing such an issue is part of our future work so as to fully support SDPs interoperability.

The two next sections detail our solution to SDPs interoperability, which is compatible with both the passive and active discovery models. However, when the SDP provides both models, the passive discovery model should be preferred over the active discovery model. Indeed, with the latter, the requester's neighbors do not improve their environment knowledge from the requester's lookup because services, that the requester wishes to locate, send only unicast replies directly to the requester. So, the services' existence is not shared by all the entities of the peer-to-peer network. Thus, it is unfortunate to not take benefit from the bandwidth consumption caused by the clients' multicast lookups. In this context, services' multicast announcements provide a more considerable added value for the multicast group members. Secondly, in a highly dynamic network, mobile devices are expected to be part of the network for short periods of time. Thus,

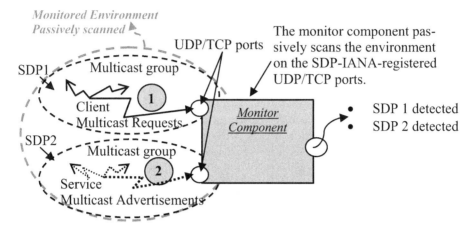

Fig. 4. Detection of active and passive SDPs through the monitor component

services' repetitive multicast announcements provide a more accurate view of their availability. Therefore, the passive discovery model saves more the scarce bandwidth resources than the active discovery model.

4.2 SDP Detection

Basically, all SDPs use a multicast group address and a UDP/TCP port that must and have been assigned by the Internet Assigned Numbers Authority (IANA). Thus, assigned ports and multicast group addresses are reserved, without any ambiguity, to only one type of use. Typically, SDPs are detected through the use of their respective address and port. These two properties form unique pairs. The latter may be interpreted as a permanent SDP identification tag. Furthermore, it is important to notice that an entity may subscribe to several multicast groups and so may be simultaneously a member of different types of multicast groups. These only two characteristics are sufficient to provide simple but efficient environmental SDP detection. Due to the very dynamic nature of the ad hoc network, the environment is continuously monitored to detect changes as fast as possible. Moreover, we do not need to generate additional traffic. We discover passively the environment by listening to the well-known SDP multicast groups. In fact, we learn the SDPs that are currently used from both services' multicast announcements and clients' multicast service requests. As a result, the specific protocol of either the passive or active service discovery may be determined. To achieve this feature, a component, called monitor component, embeds two major behaviors (see Figure 4) :

1. The ability to subscribe to several SDP multicast groups, irrespectively of their technologies; and
2. The ability to listen to all their respective ports.

Figure 4 depicts the mechanism used to detect active and passive SDPs in a repository-less context. The monitor component, located at either the client side or service side, joins both the SDP1 and SDP2 multicast groups and listens to the corresponding registered UDP/TCP ports. SDP1 and SDP2 are identified by their respective identification tag. However, SDP1 is based on an active discovery model. Hence, clients perform multicast requests to the SDP1 multicast group to discover services in their vicinity. The monitor component, as a member of the SDP1 multicast group, receives client requests and thus is able to detect the existence of SDP1 in the environment as data arrival on the SDP1-dedicated UDP/TCP port identifies the discovery protocol. Still, in Figure 4, SDP2 is based on a passive discovery model. So, services advertise themselves to the SDP2 multicast group to announce their existence to their vicinity. Once again, similarly to SDP1, as soon as data arrives at the SDP2-dedicated UDP/TCP port, the monitor component detects the SDP2 protocol. The monitor component is able to determine the current SDP(s) that is(are) used in the environment upon the arrival of the data at the monitored ports without doing any computation, data interpretation nor data transformation. It does not matter what SDP model is used (i.e., active or passive) as the detection is not based on the data content but on the data existence at the specified UDP/TCP ports inside the corresponding groups.

This component is easy to implement, as both subscription and listening are solely IP features. Hence, all the mobile middleware based on IP support the monitor component. Obviously, the latter maintains a simple static correspondence table between the IANA-registered permanent ports and their associated SDP. Hence, the SDP detection only depends on which port raw data arrived. Therefore, the SDP detection cost is reduced to a minimum.

Our monitor component can be either integrated into the ReMMoC middleware or considered as one primary element from a larger software architecture that we describe in the next section. The current ReMMoC discoverdiscovery plug-in may in particular be replaced by our monitor component, which avoids both implementing mini-test-plug-in for each available SDP and their loading just to perform SDP detection. In this way, we save both scarce bandwidth consumption and computation resources. However, once the detection is achieved, further processing is left to the appropriate SDP plug-in. The ReMMoC SDP configuration step then stays unaltered.

4.3   SDP Interoperability

From a software architecture viewpoint, SDP detection is just a first step towards SDP interoperability and represents a primary component. The main issue is still unresolved: the incoming raw data flow, which comes to the monitor component, needs to be correctly interpreted to deliver the services descriptions to the application components. To support such functionality, we reuse event-based parsing concepts (see Figure 5). As a result, upon the arrival of raw data at monitored ports (step 1), the monitor component detects the SDP that is used, and sends a corresponding event to the generator (step 2), that instantiates the appropriate parser (step 3) to successfully transform the raw data flow into a series of events

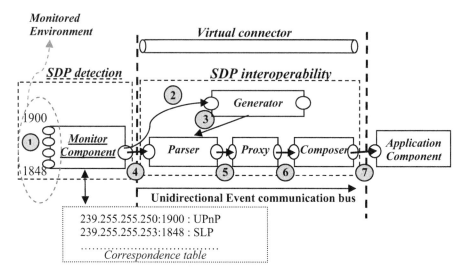

Fig. 5. SDP detection & interoperability mechanisms

(step 4). The parser extract semantic concepts as events from syntactic details of the SDP detected. Then, the generated events are delivered to a proxy (step 5). In its turn, the proxy forwards handled events to the local components' com-posers (step 6). Contrary to [6], parser and composer are not coupled by type. As events bring the necessary abstraction from the SDP syntactic details, events from a parser specific to one SDP are understood by a composer dedicated to another SDP.

The communication between the parser and the composer does not depend on any syntactic detail of any protocol. They communicate at a semantic level through the use of events. In fact, a fixed set of common events has been de-fined for all SDPs. The set of common events is itself an event subset of a larger event set dedicated to each SDP. For example, a subset of events generated by a UPnP parser is successfully understood by an SLP composer whereas specific UPnP events, due to UPnP functionalities that SLP does not provide, are sim-ply discarded from the SLP composer, as they are unknown. Event streams are totally hidden from components as they are reconstructed through composers (step7 in Figure 5). Monitor component and local application components are therefore virtually connected through a connector, which acts as a universal event communication bus. Consequently, interoperability is guaranteed to ex-isting applications tied to a specific SDP without being altered. Similarly, fu-ture applications do not need to be developed with a specific middleware API to get the SDP interoperability property. Furthermore, application components continue to use their own native service discovery protocol without using the virtual connector, which is unidirectional. Hence, there is no return path and the generator needs to instantiate neither a dedicated parser nor a dedicated composer to translate replies from the native SDP to the discovered SDP. This makes drastic computation resources economies. Moreover, it is important to note that our SDP interoperability may be applied to both service provider and client application. On the former side, requests, which are generated by clients using protocols other than the service provider's native SDP, are automatically detected thanks to the m onitor com ponent and transparently translated through the virtual connector into new semantically equivalent requests but understood by the service provider. Then, the latter replies, according to its native protocol, to the client. The virtual connector acts like a "SDP translator". However, this conversion process is without losses as it is based on the greatest common denominator of the different SDP functionalities. For example, SLP does not manage UPnP eventing mechanism [4] and consequently related messages are simply discarded but this is not a loss as SLP does not support it anyway. On the client side, the same mechanism occurs : received messages, generated by services using a different discovery protocol from the one used by the client are trans-lated to new messages semantically equivalent but syntaxically different according to the client's native SDP.

5   Conclusion

Service discovery protocol heterogeneity is a key challenge in the mobile computing domain. If services are advertised with SDPs different than those supported by mobile clients, mobile clients are unable to discover their environment and are consequently isolated. Due to the highly dynamic nature of the mobile network, available networked resources changed very often. Therefore, this requires a very efficient mechanism to monitor the mobile environment without generating additional resource consumption. In this context, inspection and adaptation functionalities offered by reflective middleware are not adequate to support service discovery protocol interoperability, as they induce too high resource consumption. This paper has addressed this challenge, providing an efficient solution to achieving interoperability among heterogeneous service discovery protocols. Our solution is specifically designed for highly dynamic ad hoc networks, which requires both minimizing resource consumption, and introducing lightweight mechanisms that may be adapted easily to any platform. An implementation will soon be released to validate both its design and efficiency.

Once services are discovered, applications further need to use the same interaction protocol to allow unanticipated connections and interactions with them. In this context, the ReMMoC reflective middleware introduces a quite efficient solution to interaction protocol interoperability. The plug-in architecture associated with reflection features allows mobile devices to adapt dynamically their interaction protocols (i.e., publish/subscribe, RPC etc.). Furthermore, [15] proposes to use ReMMoC together with WSDL [16] for providing an abstract definition of the remote component's functionalities. Client applications may then be developed against this abstract interface without worrying about service implementation's details. However, the solution discussed in [15] suffers from a major constraint: service and client must agree on a unique WSDL description.

But, once again, in a dynamic mobile network, the client does not know the execution context. Therefore, it is not guaranteed to find exactly the expected service. Client applications have to find the most appropriate service instance that matches the abstract requested service. In addition, this leads to the dynamic composition of services, which must account for mobility constraints and in particular related resource limitation. This issue is addressed by the WSAMI middleware [17], which introduces enhanced WSDL specification for mobile services and a dedicated middleware to allow a service instance to be automatically selected and composed upon a user request, according to the services that may be retrieved in the environment However, if WSAMI provides interoperability to Web services in the mobile environment, it is still a SOAP based middleware, and hence does not deal with interoperability among components using heterogeneous interaction protocols. We are currently investigating solutions to this issue so as to complement our solution to SDP interoperability and thus support middleware interoperability, as required by today's mobile environment.

Acknowledgements

This work has received the support at the European Commission through the IST program, as part of the UBISEC project (http://www.ubisec.org). The authors would like to thank Paul Grace for providing us with detail about ReMMoc. They are further grateful to anonymous reviewers for useful comments.

References

1. Grace, P., Blair, G., Samuel, S.: Middleware awarness in mobile computing. In: Proceedings of the 1st international ICDCS Workshop on Mobile Computing Middleware. (2003)
2. Sun: Jini architectural overview (1999) Technical White Paper.
3. Bettstetter, C., Renner, C.: A comparison of service discovery protocols and implementation of the service location protocol. In: Proceedings of the 6th EUNICE Open European Summer School: Innovative Internet Applications. (2000)
4. Universal Plug and Play Forum: Universal plug and play device architecture (2000)
5. Salutation Consortium: Salutation architecture (1998) White paper.
6. Ryan, N., Wolf, A.: Using event-based parsing to support dynamic protocol evolution. In: Proceedings of the 26th International Conference on Software Engineering (ICSE'04). (2004)
7. Mascolo, C., Capra, L., Emmerich, W.: Middleware for mobile computing (a survey) (2002)
8. Szyperski, C.: Component Software: Beyond Object-Oriented Programming. Addison Wesley (1998)
9. Coulson, G., Blair, G., Clarke, M., Parlavantzas, N.: The design of a configurable and reconfigurable middleware platform. Distributed Computing (2002)
10. Capra, L., Blair, G., Mascolo, C., Emmerich, W., Grace, P.: Exploiting reflection in mobile computing middleware. ACM Mobile Computing and Communications Review (2002)

11. Fu, X., Shi, W., Akkerman, A., Karamceti, V.: Cans: composable, adaptive network services infrastructure. In: Proceedings of the USENIX Symposium on Internet Tecnologies and Systems (USITS). (2001)
12. Issarny, V., Tartanoglu, F., Liu, J., Sailhan, F.: Software architecture for mobile distributed computing. In: Proceedings of the 4th Working IEEE/IFIP Conference on Software Architec-ture (WICSA). (2004) Oslo.
13. Garlan, D.: Formal modeling and analysis of software architecture: Components, connectors, and events. In: Third International School on Formal Methods for the Design of Computer, Communication and Software Systems. (2003)
14. Allen, R., Garlan, D.: A formal basis for architectural connection. ACM Transactions on Software Engeneering and Methodology (1997)
15. Grace, P., Blair, G., Samuel, S.: A marriage of web services and reflective middleware to solve the problem of mobile client interoperability. In: Proceedings of Workshop on Middleware Interoperability of Enterprise Applications. (2003)
16. Christensen, E., Curbera, F., Meredith, G., Weerawarana, S.: Web Services Description Language (WSDL) 1.1. W3C. 1.1 edn. (2001)
17. Issarny, V., Sacchetti, D., Tartanoglu, F., Sailhan, F., Chibout, R., Levy, N., Taloma, A.: Developing ambient intelligence systems: A solution based on web services. Journal of Automated Software Engineering (2004) To appear.

Formally Designing an Event-Based Application for Mobile Collaboration: A Case Study*

Pascal Fenkam and Mehdi Jazayeri

Technical University of Vienna, Distributed Systems Group,
A-1040 Vienna, Argentinierstrasse 8/184-1
{p.fenkam, m.jazayeri}@infosys.tuwien.ac.at

Abstract. The event-based style is recognized as a powerful paradigm for the construction of large-scale and complex distributed systems. The development of applications based on this concept is, however, currently ad hoc and informal. To remedy this situation, we have developed the LECAP methodology. This paper presents a case study of the application of the methodology to the analysis of a platform for mobile team collaboration. This case study shows that LECAP is indeed applicable to real-life examples. Further, we claim that a component developed for one architectural style is not necessarily deployable in the context of another style. Finally, we show where tool support is needed to enhance the methodology's usability.

1 Introduction

Despite the acceptance of the event-based (EB) architectural style as an integration mechanism for CBSE [1] and a communication mechanism for loosely coupled environments [3, 4, 5] the development of applications based on this paradigm remains an ad hoc and informal process. Consequently, as EB systems proliferate, including in safety-critical domains, it remains difficult to reason about the correctness and reliability of such systems. We have attempted to apply well established software construction principles to the design of an EB peer-to-peer platform for mobile collaboration called MOTION (MObile Teamwork Infrastructure for Organizations Networking). The main components of this platform were formally specified, the specification validated against the informal requirements, and the implementation of the components tested against the specification [6]. These components proved to be robust in a client-server based prototype. Surprisingly, however, their integration into an EB peer-to-peer environment revealed some severe unexpected and undesired behavior. This experience motivated us to develop LECAP (Logic of Event Consumption and Publication) [7, 8], a framework for constructing correct EB applications. This

---

* This work is supported by the Austrian Research Foundation Fond (FWF) through the RAY project (Number P16970-No4).

T. Gschwind and C. Mascolo (Eds.): SEM 2004, LNCS 3437, pp. 78–90, 2005.

paper presents the first case study in formal stepwise development of EB applications. We show the redesign of the MOTION's user management component to fit the requirements of the EB and the peer-to-peer architectural styles.

In general, while theories show how to carry a task, case studies are the measure of their practicability. This is one of the contributions of the paper. In addition, the paper justifies our claim that a component developed for deployment in the context of one architectural style (in our case client/server) does not necessarily behave well in the context of another architectural style (event-based and peer-to-peer). Finally, the paper identifies where tool support is needed to enhance the methodology's usability.

The remainder of the paper is organized as follows. The next section gives an overview of the LECAP framework. Section 3 presents an overview of the MOTION platform while Section 4 proposes a formal specification of the MOTION's user management system. Section 5 shows how to discharge local properties of components based on their specifications that are composed in Section 6. Global properties of applications are discharged in Section 7. Section 8 discusses our experience and Section 9 concludes the paper.

2   An Overview of LECAP

LECAP is a framework for the construction of correct EB applications which includes a core programming language (a while-parallel language extended with an event announcement construct), techniques for the specification of EB applications, rules for the top-down development of components, and rules for the composition of specifications. Due to the lack of space, readers interested in a comparison of LECAP with other approaches are directed to [7, 8, 2].

LECAP distinguishes the following steps in the development process:

1. Designing the architecture of the desired application,
2. Developing the formal specifications of the components,
3. Verifying local properties of these components,
4. Composing the specification of the whole application starting with the specifications of the components,
5. Discharging the composition proof obligations,
6. Verifying the global properties of the application,
7. Refining the component specifications to implementations,
8. Integrating the components by means of an integration framework.

Applied to our case-study, the first step concerns the MOTION architecture which is overviewed in Section 3. The second step is tackled in Section 4 while the steps 3 to 6 are discussed in Sections 5 to 7.

3   Overview of MOTION

MOTION is a platform we designed and prototyped in the MOTION project [12] where the needs of two well known organizations were addressed. The platform has a service architecture supporting mobile teamworking by taking into account different connectivity modes of users, providing access support for various devices, supporting distributed search of users and artifacts, offering effective user management facilities.

The MOTION platform was constructed by assembling different components including a user management and access control component, an XQL engine, a repository, an artifact manager, etc. These components are integrated into the platform by means of the EB architectural style implemented by PeerWare [10] (see Figure 1).

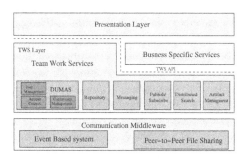

Fig. 1. The MOTION Architecture

The MOTION platform is based on a peer-to-peer (p2p) architecture, by which we mean that each device may host and manage a service independently of the behavior of other devices. The justification of this architecture can be found in [12]. This paper focuses on user management in a p2p environment.

4   Component Specification

The user management functionality has gained increasing attention and importance in distributed environments and is provided in the MOTION platform by DUMAS (Dynamic User Management and Access control System).

The MOTION platform supports various kinds of devices (see Figure 2) that have different capabilities and that cannot, therefore, be equally used for storing data such as user profiles and access control data. To support this heterogeneity of devices we give the end-users the possibility to specify which profiles they would like to store on their devices. For instance, an end-user, say Jane, may configure her system such that only profiles of her nearest colleagues are stored on her PDA. In terms of services, we may say that each device hosts a user management service. Although the implementation of this service may be the same for all peers, the content of the repository is not the same; Jane's profile may be stored on peer A but not on B. One of the main challenges in such an architecture is to keep the profiles of all users consistent. Any change to Jane's profile on one peer needs to be taken into consideration on (perhaps propagated to) other peers.

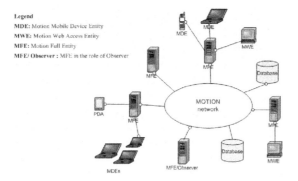

Fig. 2. The Conceptual View of MOTION

Although this may resemble the traditional data-consistency requirement in distributed systems we suspect that there are more difficulties in this case. First, a peer may suddenly decide not to be interested in Jane's profile anymore (depending on the interest of the owner of the peer). Next, the user management service on one peer has no knowledge about peers interested in events it announces. Third, each peer stores only profiles it is subscribed to. Finally, a peer interested in Jane's profile may be offline when some changes are made to this profile.

We use a notation that resembles the VDM-SL [11] notation for specifying the user management facility of MOTION. We lack place to present this notation.

4.1 Data Modeling

We present the datatypes defined in our specification and useful for understanding this paper. Access control models are based on three notions: principals, subjects, and access rights. A principal is anything capable of possessing access rights. In our model, we identify two types of principals: users and groups. Each user/group has an identifier of a not further defined type (declared with **token**).

$$
\begin{aligned}
ID &= token; \\
UserID &= ID; \\
GroupID &= \langle default \rangle \mid ID; \\
RightID &= ID; \\
PrincipalID &= UserID \mid GroupID;
\end{aligned}
$$

A subject is anything (other than an access right or a principal) on which an access right may be owned (e.g. files). The only requirement on these elements is to have an identifier. Subjects are not registered in the repository (defined below); we have no control over when they are created and destroyed.

$$
\begin{aligned}
SubjectID &= token; \\
Profile &= token;
\end{aligned}
$$

A profile is a set of user-specific information such as her expertise, her languages, her time-zone, etc. Such profiles may have complex structures that we do not want to specify at this level of abstraction.

A user is modeled with a set of data related to it: its parents, its access rights, its identifier, and its profile.

$$
\begin{aligned}
User :: \quad & \\
parents \quad & : GroupID\text{-set} \\
mainparent \quad & : GroupID \\
permissions \quad & : (RightID \times SubjectID)\text{-set} \\
name \quad & : UserID \\
profile \quad & : Profile \\
\text{inv } us \; \triangle & \\
& us.mainparent \in us.parents;
\end{aligned}
$$

A principal is either a group or a user. The definition of the datatype Group is not given in this paper.

$$Principal = Group \mid User;$$

We introduce the enumeration type Prog for referring to operations defined in this specification and that are elements of the event-based system's set of methods. We assume a system with a finite number of peers; each operation $operation_i$ corresponds to the operation operation running on peer i.

$$Prog = \langle impl\text{-}ebsimpleMu_1 \rangle \mid \cdots \mid \langle impl\text{-}ebsimpleMu_n \rangle \mid \langle mskip \rangle;$$

Next, we introduce a type EventName for classifying events. The only event name needed in the extract presented in this paper is $\langle UserProfileUpdate \rangle$.

$$EventName = \langle UserProfileUpdate \rangle;$$

An event is a composite type including the identifier of the announcing peer, a tag for identifying the performed state changes, and a payload. On the other hand, a subscription represents the set of events a peer is interested in.

$$
\begin{aligned}
Event :: \quad & \qquad\qquad\qquad Subscription = Event\text{-set}; \\
peerid \quad & : \mathbb{N} \\
action \quad & : EventName \\
payload \quad & : Subject;
\end{aligned}
$$

A binding associates each program (element of type Prog) to a subscription, i.e. the set of events the program is subscribed to.

$$Binding = Prog \xrightarrow{m} Subscription;$$

A repository is a map of subjects to their identifiers. The first invariant requires any element to be indeed mapped to its identifier. The second and third invariants require that the invariants of any user/group be satisfied. Five other invariants are omitted.

$$DB = SubjectID \xleftrightarrow{m} Subject$$

inv db $\triangle$
    let
        $inv0 = \forall x \in$ dom $db \cdot x = db(x).name,$
        $inv1 = \forall x \in$ rng $db \cdot$ is-$User(x) \quad \Rightarrow$ inv-$User(x),$
        $inv2 = \forall x \in$ rng $db \cdot$ is-$Group(x) \Rightarrow$ inv-$Group(x)$ in
    $inv0 \wedge inv1 \wedge inv2$

As devices may cache only parts of the whole set of information available in the system, each peer hosts a local repository. The state of the MOTION platform is, thus, composed of the sequence of peer repositories.

    state $System$ of
      $db : DB^*,$
      $\mathcal{B} : Binding$

      inv mk-$System(db, binding)$ $\triangle$
        $\forall i \in [1, \text{len } db] \cdot$ inv-$DB(db[i])$

      init sys $\triangle$
        $\forall i \in [1, \text{ len } db] \cdot db_i = \{\mapsto\}$
    end

The invariant of each peer is required to hold. The binding is currently empty as we do not know yet which program must be subscribed to which events.

4.2   Specification of Components

A number of operations are specified in our model. As an example, we discuss the operation for updating user profiles: the profile of the given user is replaced with the provided profile. Each operation is indexed with the identifier of the peer on which it is running. We, therefore, have a number of **len**db such operations in the system. Each of them only accesses the repository with the same index.

        ebsimpleMu$_i$(e : Event) $\triangle$
            await true **do** $simpleMu_i(e.body.name, \; e.body.profile)$ **od**

The specification is that of an operation that receives an event, extracts the identifier and the profile of the user that it wraps and submits them to an operation satisfying $simpleMu_i$ (Mu is used in analogy to the VDM operation μ for updating composite types) which is to be executed atomically.

On the other hand, $simpleMu_i$ is the specification of an operation, say $impl$-$simpleMu_i$ that is the basis for updating user profiles. The post-condition ensures that after execution, the local repository maps the given user identifier to a user with the given profile while any other information in the repository is unchanged. In addition, this method prepares the event to be announced through the announce construct of $muProfile_i$.

simpleMu$_i$(id : UserID, pr : Profile) $\triangleq$
> wr db
> pre $id \in \mathsf{dom}\ db_i$
> post $db_i(id) = \mu\,(db_i\,(id),\ profile \mapsto pr) \wedge db_i \lhd \{id\} = \overleftarrow{db_i} \lhd \{id\} \wedge$
> $\quad v.peerid = i \wedge v.action = \langle UserProfileUpdate \rangle \wedge v.payload = db_i(id)\ \wedge$
> $\quad \forall t \in [1, \mathsf{len}\ db] \cdot t \ne i\ \Rightarrow\ db_t = \overleftarrow{db_t}.$

While operations satisfying ebsimpleMu$_i$ are intended to be invoked by the EB infrastructure (it takes an event as input and announces no event), we provide the following operation to be used by end-users.

> **muProfile$_i$(id : UserID, prof : Profile)** $\triangleq$
> **await** true **do** $simpleMu_i(id,\ prof)$ **od; announce**(v_1)

Finally, the end-users are given the operation impl-userSubscribe satisfying userSubscribe for defining the kind of information they would like to store on their peers.

userSubscription$_i$(s : Subscription) $\triangleq$
> pre $\forall e \in s \cdot e.peerid \ne i\ \wedge\ e.action = \langle UserProfileUpdate \rangle$
> post $\mathcal{B} = \overleftarrow{\mathcal{B}} \dagger \{impl\text{-}ebsimpleMu_i \mapsto s \cup \overleftarrow{\mathcal{B}}\,(impl\text{-}ebsimpleMu_i)\}$

An operation impl-userUnsubscribe satisfying userUnsubscribe is also provided for unsubscribing. To avoid inconsistencies between the current peer and the remainder of the system, entries of the repository that match this subscription are also deleted.

userUnsubscribe(e : Event) $\triangleq$
> wr db_i
> post let
> $\qquad m = \langle impl\text{-}ebsimpleMu_i \rangle$
> $\qquad X = \{u \in \mathsf{rng}\ db_i\ |\ \exists\ e \in s \cdot e.payload = u\}$
> in $db_i \lhd \{e.body.name\} = \overleftarrow{db_i} \lhd \{e.body.name\} \wedge$
> $\qquad \mathcal{B} = \overleftarrow{\mathcal{B}} \dagger \{m \mapsto \overleftarrow{\mathcal{B}}\,(m) \setminus \{s\}\} \wedge \mathsf{rng}\ db_i \cap X = \emptyset$

5   Local Property Verification

The local property of interest is that any operation that satisfies one of the above specifications conserves the invariants of the repository. Considering that the binding is empty and that interference freedom is achived through the await construct, we deduce the following behavioral specification:

behavioral-muProfile$_i$(id : UserID, prof : Profile) $\triangleq simpleMu_i(id,\ prof)$

The proof obligation (PO) is subsequently formulated as:

Proof Obligation 1 $\forall\, u : UserID,\; p : Profile \cdot post\text{-}simpleMu_i(u, p) \;\Rightarrow\; inv\text{-}DB$

This PO is discharged by natural deduction along the following steps:

- Strengthening the pre-condition of $simpleMu_i$ with the assumption that the initial state satisfies the invariant of the repository,
- Applying the pre-rule to add this information into the post-condition,
- Observing that:
  - for any entry x in the domain of db_i, the invariant of $db_i(x)$ is satisfied and
  - for any x in the domain of db_i, $db_i(x).name = x$.

The second PO is that $impl\text{-}ebsimpleMu_i$ also conserves the invariant of the local repository and is discharged in the similar way.

6   Application Composition

The composition of specifications is done by subscribing specification of components to events in a way that reflects the architecture of the desired application.

6.1   Subscription of Components

The verification of the properties of this application is performed under some assumptions such as that of requiring subscriptions submitted by end-users to exclude events announced by the current peer (in this case the peer i).

If the owner of the peer i is interested in caching profiles satisfying the subscription s and the pre-condition $pre\text{-}userSubscription_i$, she uses the operation $userSubscribe$ to transform the binding into:

$$\mathcal{B} = \overleftarrow{\mathcal{B}} \dagger \{impl\text{-}ebsimpleMu_i \mapsto s \cup \overleftarrow{\mathcal{B}}\,(impl\text{-}ebsimpleMu_i)\}$$

Clearly, this binding requires the EB infrastructure to invoke the operation $impl\text{-}ebsimpleMu_i$ when an event matches the subscription s.

6.2   Identification of Affected Components

The next step in the composition of an EB application is the identification of components whose behaviors may be affected by a subscription. Since the operations $impl\text{-}ebsimpleMu_i$ announce no event, subscribing them to an event e only impacts their predecessors; by which we mean operations such that $impl\text{-}ebsimpleMu_i$ is invoked in some of their computations.

Starting with the empty binding, we subscribe $impl\text{-}ebsimpleMu_i$ to an event e where $e.name = \langle UserProfileUpdate \rangle$ and $e.peerid \neq i$ (as required by the precondition of $userSubscription_i$). The identifier $e.peerid$ of the subscribing peer may take any value different from i. The set of announcers of the event e is, therefore:

$$announcers(e) = \{impl\text{-}muProfile_j \cdot j \neq i\}$$

resulting in:

$$predecessors(impl\text{-}ebsimpleMu_i) = \{impl\text{-}muProfile_j \cdot j \neq i\}.$$

In general, predecessor(z) defines the set of programs such that the program z is triggered in some of their computations. It, therefore, depends upon the binding.

6.3   Derivation of Behavioral Specifications

We proceed to deriving the behavioral specifications of affected components. This process which is accompanied by the derivation and the discharge of composition proof obligations results in specifications that are used for the verification of global properties of the application.

The requirement is to derive the behavioral specification of each z in predecessors(impl-ebsimpleM u_i). Since, however, each operation z in predecessors(impl-ebsimpleM u_i) satisfies a specification of the form muProfile$_j$ (where $j \neq i$), it is enough to take an arbitrary impl-muProfile$_j$ and derive its behavioral specification.

Applying the announce rule and assuming that the binding is that obtained above, we derive:

$$\forall e \in events(impl\text{-}muProfile_j) \cdot subscribers(e) = \{impl\text{-}ebsimpleMu_i, mskip\}$$

and the behavioral specification of impl-muProfile$_j$ is therefore:

muProfile$_i$(id : UserID, prof : Profile) $\triangle$
    await true **do** $simpleMu_j(id, \; prof)$ **od**; $impl\text{-}ebsimpleMu_i(v)$

The PO for the correct behavior of this operation is given by the sequential rule:

Proof Obligation 2 **post**-$simpleMu_j(id, pr)$ $\Rightarrow$ **pre**-$ebsimpleMu_i(v)$

This PO is discharged straightforwardly after strengthening the pre-condition of impl-muProfile$_j$ with **pre-simpleM** u_i.

7   Global System Behavior

Based on the behavioral specifications computed in the previous section, we proceed to checking the behavior of the whole application.

7.1   Property I: Consistency

Scalability can be a serious problem in a p2p application. Among others, one of the obstacles to achieving this scalability in the MOTION platform is the requirement of replica consistency. We analyze our application with respect to this property. For any user identifier id and any two peers p and q such that $x \in$ dom $db_p \cap$ dom db_q it must be true that $db_p(x).$pro□le $= db_j(x).$pro□le. Formally, the requirement is formulated as:

Proof Obligation 3

$\forall\, p, q \in [1,\ \textit{len}\ db],\ x \in \textit{dom}\ db_p\ \cap\ \textit{dom}\ db_q \cdot db_p(x).profile = db_j(x).profile.$

PO3 is an invariant that must also be ensured before execution of operations, which means that the pre-conditions of methods must be strengthened with this assertion resulting in:

muProfile$_j$(id : UserID, pr : Profile) $\triangleq$

    pre **pre**-$simpleMu_i \wedge$ **pre**-$simpleMu_j \wedge C_1$

    post **post**-$simpleMu_i\ |\ $**post**-$simpleMu_j$

Despite this refinement, any attempt to discharge C_1 fails. To see why, let us assume that the peers 124 and 125 have each an entry corresponding to the user identifier id in their respective local repositories. We also assume that the peer 124 is subscribed to updates concerning the user id while the peer 125 is not. If a peer 123 now updates the profile of the user id (and subsequently announces an event), the peer 124 will receive the event while the peer 125 will not, leading to an inconsistency between the peers 124 and 125. To avoid such situations, we need to add an invariant to the repositories. We require that if there is an entry with identifier id in the local repository db_i of peer i, then, this peer must be subscribed to updates related to this identifier. The invariant is formulated as:

$inv4 \stackrel{def}{=} \forall\, i \in [1, \textsf{len}\ db],\ id : UserID,\ e : Event\ \cdot$
$\qquad\qquad (id \in \textsf{dom}\ db_i\ \wedge\ id = e.payload.name)\ \Rightarrow\ e \in \mathcal{B}_1(\langle ebsimpleMu_i \rangle)$

We further strengthen the pre-condition of the above specification resulting in the following specification that is used for discharging PO3 by natural deduction.

        muProfile$_j$(id : UserID, pr : Profile) $\triangleq$

        wr db

        pre **pre**-$simpleMu_i \wedge$ **pre**-$simpleMu_j \wedge C_1 \wedge$ inv-$System$

        post **post**-$simpleMu_i\ |\ $**post**-$simpleMu_j \wedge \overleftarrow{\textbf{pre}\text{-}muProfile_j}$

The property has been shown for the case where impl-ebsimpleMu u_i is the only operation interested in events named $\langle$UserProUleUpdate$\rangle$. In this case, there is no concurrency. Let us now assume that another operation impl-ebsimpleMu u_k is subscribed to these events, resulting into concurrency. The binding is now defined as:

$\mathcal{B}_2 = \{\ impl\text{-}ebsimpleMu_i \mapsto \{x : Event \cdot\ x.action = \langle UserProfile\ Update\rangle \wedge x.peerid \neq i\}\},$
$\qquad impl\text{-}ebsimpleMu_j \mapsto \{\},$
$\qquad impl\text{-}ebsimpleMu_k \mapsto \{x : Event \cdot\ x.action = \langle UserProfile\ Update\rangle \wedge x.peerid \neq k\},$
$\qquad \textbf{mskip} \mapsto \{x : Event\}\}$

which results into the following definition of subscribers:

$\forall e : Event\cdot$
$e.action = \langle UserProfileUpdate \rangle \wedge e.peerid = i \Rightarrow$
$\qquad subscribers(e) = \{impl\text{-}ebsimpleMu_k, mskip\}$
$e.action = \langle UserProfileUpdate \rangle \wedge e.peerid = k \Rightarrow$
$\qquad subscribers(e) = \{impl\text{-}ebsimpleMu_i, mskip\}$
$e.action = \langle UserProfileUpdate \rangle \wedge e.peerid \notin [i, k] \Rightarrow$
$\qquad subscribers(e) = \{impl\text{-}ebsimpleMu_k, impl\text{-}ebsimpleMu_i, mskip\}$

Since, however, any event announced by muProfile$_j$ is such that e.peerid = j $\notin$ [i, k], the following specification is derived by application of the announce rule followed by the skip rule.

behavioral-muProfile$_j$(id : UserID, prof : Profile) $\triangleq$
  await true do $simpleMu_j(id, prof)$ **od**; $\{ebsimpleMu_i(v) \| ebsimpleMu_k(v)\}$

The proof by natural deduction is constructed by finding A_i and A_k such that the following holds.

- $A_i \mid post\text{-}ebsimpleMu_k(v) \Rightarrow A_i$,
- $A_k \mid post\text{-}ebsimpleMu_i(v) \Rightarrow A_k$,
- $post\text{-}ebsimpleMu_i(v) \Rightarrow A_i$,
- $post\text{-}ebsimpleMu_k(v) \Rightarrow A_k$,
- $post\text{-}ebsimpleMu_j(v) \mid (A_i \wedge A_k) \Rightarrow C_1$.

7.2   Property II: Non-volatility of User Data

Although end-users are allowed to specify the kind of data they would like to store on their devices, an organization may choose to configure one fixed peer say i, to store all user data. In such a configuration, we must show that the peer i always has the current version of any user profile in the system. This PO is formulated as:

Proof Obligation 4 [C2]
$\forall t \in [1, len\ db],\ x : UserID \cdot db_i(x).profile = db_t(x).profile$

This is a global invariant of the platform that must hold after the execution of each impl-muProxle$_j$. The proof is by distinguishing two cases:

- x $\neq$ id; in this case, the entry db$_t$(x) is kept unchanged for any t and from the validity of C$_2$ in the initial state, one derives that db$_i$(x) = db$_t$(x) holds.
- x = id; the validity of C$_1$ after the execution of impl-muProxle$_j$ is applied to infer that db$_i$(x).proxle = db$_t$(x).proxle for any peer t such that x $\in$ dom db$_t$.

8   Discussion

The properties C$_1$ and C$_2$ about the MOTION platform presented in this paper are examples of those requirements that could not be checked in the original formal design that were oriented towards client/server applications. And, in fact, they were not required. Discharging the related proof obligations was possible only after some changes to the specification of our components. For instance, the mutual exclusion construct was inserted in the specification of $implmuProple_j$ that was not part of our original specification. As another example, discharging C_1 required the formulation of the invariant inv_4.

The analysis of the MOTION platform in the LECAP framework is, thus, a successful exercise in that it allows discovering and correcting design flaws of the original proposal. In addition, this shows that the LECAP is indeed applicable to non-trivial case studies. In fact, we claim that the MOTION case study is a complex case study in that components can be subscribed and unsubscribed dynamically. We have intentionally chosen such a case study to exercise our approach.

Tool support is important for the acceptance of a formal technique. Ideally, such tools must be oriented towards automating the software engineering process. We have experienced this necessity in the MOTION case study and believe that many steps of LECAP can be efficiently supported by CASE tools. Such tools may be built by combining PO generators with automatic analyzers (e.g. Alloy[9]) or model checker.

On the other hand, this analysis was only possible with the use of an abstract mutual exclusion construct that helps in controlling interference. A construct with the required semantics does not yet exist in practice. We are working on a prototype implementation for the Siena middleware.

9   Conclusions

Formally designing the user manager of the MOTION platform in the context of the EB style was an intriguing exercise. The specification presented in this paper is part of a larger effort in establishing a methodology for the construction of reliable event-based applications.

In general, we found that the LECAP methodology is indeed applicable to non-trivial real-life cases. The redesigning the MOTION system revealed a significant number of design shortcomings that could not be detected before. An example of such shortcomings is that the invariant $inv4$ presented in Section 7 was not specified before (see [6]), and hence, the consistency PO could not be proven.

The component that we specified in this case study was already specified, validated, and verified in another context were its robustness could be achieved. Its misbehavior in the context of the event-based paradigm suggests that the assumed architectural style must be part of the description of a component. A component designed, validated, and verified in the context of the client/server style, for instance, does not necessarily behave well in the peer-to-peer or event-based styles.

The LECAP methodology is still experimental. As such, many areas of improvement are possible, both in the methodology and in its applicability. In the first place, the VDM notation used in this paper is still experimental. A more usable notation must be investigated.

In this paper we have reported the results of a case study in applying the LECAP methodology in the redesign of a component of the MOTION platform.

We have shown how reasoning and validation about properties of the system can be carried out both about local properties and global properties. Although our experience is promising, the case study also identified some deficiencies that point the way to needed future work.

References

1. D. J. Barret, L. A. Clarke, P. L. Tarr, and A. E. Wise. A framework for event based software integration. *ACM Transactions on Software Engineering and Methodology*, 5(4):378–421, 1996.
2. Jeremy S. Bradbury and Juergen Dingel. Evaluating and improving the automatic analysis of implicit invocation systems. In *Proceedings of the 9th European software engineering conference held jointly with 10th ACM SIGSOFT international symposium on Foundations of software engineering*, pages 78–87. ACM Press, 2003.
3. Mauro Caporuscio, Antonio Carzaniga, and Alexander L. Wolf. Design and evaluation of a support service for mobile, wireless publish/subscribe applications. *IEEE Transactions on Software Engineering*, 29(12):1059–1071, December 2003.
4. Antonio Carzaniga, Elisabetta Di Nitto, David S. Rosenblum, and Alexander L. Wolf. Issues in supporting event-based architectural styles. In *Proceedings of 3rd International Software Architecture Workshop, Orlando FL, USA*, pages 17–20, November 1998.
5. Gianpaolo Cugola, Elisabetta Di Nitto, and Alfonso Fuggetta. Exploiting an event-based infrastructure to develop complex distributed systems. In *Proceedings of the 20th International Conference on Software Engineering (ICSE 98)*, pages 261–270, 1998.
6. Pascal Fenkam, Harald Gall, and Mehdi Jazayeri. Constructing CORBA Supported Oracles: A Case Study in Automated Software Testing. In *Proceedings of the 17th IEEE Automated Software Engineering Conference, Edinburgh, Scotland*, pages 129–138, September 2002.
7. Pascal Fenkam, Harald Gall, and Mehdi Jazayeri. A Systematic Approach to the Development of Event-Based Applications. In *Proceedings of the 22nd IEEE Symposium on Reliable Distributed Systems (SRDS 2003), Florence, Italy*. IEEE Computer Press, October 2003.
8. Pascal Fenkam, Harald Gall, and Mehdi Jazayeri. Constructing Deadlock Free Event-Based Applications: A Rely/Guarantee Approach. In *Proceedings of FM 2003: the 12th International FME Symposium, Pisa, Italy*, LNCS, pages 632–657. Springer Verlag, September 2003.
9. Daniel Jackson. Alloy: A lightweight object modelling notation. *ACM Transactions on Software Engineering Methododlogy*, 11(2):256–290, April 2002.
10. Gian Pietro Picco and Gianpaolo Cugola. PeerWare: Core Middleware Support for Peer-To-Peer and Mobile Systems. Technical report, Dipartimento di Electronica e Informazione, Politecnico di Milano, 2001.
11. Nico Plat and Peter Gorm Larsen. An Overview of the ISO/VDM-SL Standard. In *ACM SIGPLAN Notices*, pages 76–82. ACM SIGPLAN, September 1992.
12. Gerald Reif, Engin Kirda, Harald Gall, Gian Pietro Picco, Gianpaola Cugola, and Pascal Fenkam. A web-based peer-to-peer architecture for collaborative nomadic working. In *10th IEEE Workshops on Enabling Technologies: Infrastructures for Collaborative Enterprises (WETICE), Boston, MA, USA*, pages 334–339. IEEE Computer Society Press, June 2001.

Supporting Generalized Context Interactions

Gregory Hackmann[1], Christine Julien[2], Jamie Payton[1], and
Gruia-Catalin Roman[1]

[1] Department of Computer Science and Engineering,
Washington University in St. Louis
{ghackmann, payton, roman}@wustl.edu
[2] Department of Electrical and Computer Engineering,
The University of Texas at Austin
c.julien@mail.utexas.edu

Abstract. In context-aware computing, applications' behavior is driven
by a continually-changing environment. Mobile computing poses unique
challenges to context-sensitive applications and middleware, including
the ability to run on resource-poor devices like PDAs and the necessity
to limit assumptions about the network. Though middlewares exist to
provide context-awareness to applications, they do not address the limitations inherent in dynamic mobile environments. This paper discusses a
lightweight approach to context-sensitivity that takes into account these
considerations. We explore the use of modularization to tailor service discovery policies for applications, as well as leveraging existing language
constructs to simplify creation and aggregation of different context types.
We also discuss an implementation of these concepts, along with three
sample applications that can automatically propagate changes in context
to clients running on devices from mobile phones to desktop computers.

1 Introduction

Traditionally, context-aware computing refers to an application's ability to adapt
to its environment. Calendar or reminder programs [1] use time to display per-
tinent notifications to users. Tour guide applications [2, 3] display information
based on the user's current physical location. Still other programs implicitly attach context information to data, e.g., to research notes taken in the field [4].
Each of these applications independently gathers context information from the
required sensors and tailors the provision of context.

With the increasing popularity of communicating mobile devices, context-
aware computing has moved from a target environment of an autonomous device
to a sophisticated network of connected devices, all providing context information to each other. This enables powerful applications that allow complex interactions across a dynamic network of heterogeneous devices. Presenting context
to software engineers, however, has received little attention. Building context-
aware applications like those above has required each developer to independently
construct mechanisms to monitor and collect context information.

T. Gschwind and C. Mascolo (Eds.): SEM 2004, LNCS 3437, pp. 91–106, 2005.
© Springer-Verlag Berlin Heidelberg 2005

In this paper, we introduce CONSUL, a middleware solution that simplifies access to context information. By providing abstractions for complex network transactions, we allow novice programmers to build applications that utilize context information collected from a heterogeneous environment. We significantly simplify the development task by removing the need to handle the intricate network programming necessary to collect the information and instead present an accessible yet expressive and extensible interface for using context information.

In the next section, we outline the requirements of a context monitoring middleware for dynamic mobile environments. Section 3 examines existing solutions. Section 4 details the architecture and implementation of CONSUL, and Section 5 discusses three sample applications developed with the middleware. In Section 6, we address relevant issues, including discovery mechanisms, the separation of discovery and sensing, and higher level concerns associated with context-gathering. Conclusions appear in Section 7.

2   Problem Definition

Context items are pieces of data sensed about the environment, e.g., location, temperature, link latency, etc. The environment is open, meaning hosts contributing context information can join or leave the network at any time. We assume a heterogeneous and dynamic environment containing resource-constrained devices such as environmental sensors, cellphones, PDAs, and laptops.

Programming the collection and monitoring of dynamic contexts can be burdensome. A programmer must identify the desired source, contact the provider, collect the context items, and interpret them. Typically, the developer must use network programming mechanisms that require knowing the identity and location of the provider. In open and dynamic environments, it is often infeasible to rely on such a priori knowledge. Mobility compounds the problem since the movement of context providers requires management of network disconnections. In addition, given the wide array of devices available and the multitude of applications that run on them, the collected pieces of context are likely to be in diverse formats that require unification. Finally, the set of available context items is not static; applications continuously inject context items into the environment.

We aim to simplify application development by reducing the complexity of handling context collection and monitoring in dynamic environments. We achieve this goal through a middleware that hides the details of these tasks. The following are requirements of such a middleware infrastructure.

- **Decoupled communication.** We must assume no advance knowledge of communication partners.
- **Transparent monitoring of context.** Issues associated with distribution, mobility, and unpredictable connectivity should be hidden. Moreover, the process of determining how context changes are presented should be relegated to the infrastructure.
- **Generalized treatment of context.** Context should be generalized so applications interact with different types of information in a similar manner.

- **Extensibility.** Given the openness of the environment, the infrastructure should adapt to the inclusion of new context users and providers with little or no intervention from a system administrator.
- **Scalability.** To scale to large networks, a decentralized solution is necessary.
- **Accommodate small devices.** The middleware primitives must have a lightweight implementation to account for resource-constrained participants.

In the remainder of the paper, we examine how current solutions fall short of meeting these requirements and propose a new middleware infrastructure designed to facilitate rapid development of context-aware applications.

3   Related Work

In this section, we review examples of systems which support context-aware application development. We focus on three well-known systems: Stick-e Notes, CALAIS, and the Context Toolkit. For brevity, other context-aware systems such as CoolTown [5], Gaia [6], and Confab [7] are not discussed.

3.1   Stick-e Notes

Stick-e Notes [8, 9] favors ease-of-use and serves as a precursor for many context-sensitive middlewares. In Stick-e Notes, virtual notes are attached to physical phenomena like times, places, and events. The decision of when a note is in context is included within the note itself; the SGML structure of each note includes a section to semantically describe when it is to be triggered. Exactly what it means to trigger a note is left to the discretion of the client application.

This model is unique in that end-users need only basic SGML knowledge to create notes. However, significant trade-offs are made for the sake of ease-of-use. First, context is determined by the note and not the client, which limits flexibility. For example, a note may be triggered when the user enters a range of locations, but it is not possible for a user traveling in a car to trigger notes within a greater range of distances than a user on foot. In addition, the model provides no way to disseminate notes; the client either have them or be able to obtain them using some external mechanism. This limits the applicability of this model to dynamic environments.

3.2   CALAIS

CALAIS [10] offers an alternative for providing location-based context by allowing applications to register with sensors to receive notifications of state changes. Location is stored in a central database, which tracks physical objects (like Active Badges [11]) and uses spatial algorithms to determine which room contains these objects. This location information is automatically delivered to registrants. A simple language allows contexts to be aggregated into more-complex contexts. The use of callbacks and context aggregation addresses the most serious shortcomings of Stick-e Notes by allowing clients to determine context from a number of sources, which automatically notify the client of any state change.

CALAIS relies extensively on CORBA, which is too heavyweight for practical use on many mobile devices. Additionally, it is geared for a specific type of contextual information. Finally, the design of the location service necessitates a central server capable of processing complex spatial relationships, which raises additional performance and scalability issues.

3.3   Context Toolkit

The Context Toolkit [12] provides hooks for automatically discovering context-providing "widgets", which can be aggregated within the middleware to form more complex contexts. Unlike CALAIS, Context Toolkit does not depend on any specific back-end for communication between devices; by default it uses XML over HTTP for communication, but this can be swapped out to accommodate other communication mechanisms.

This model is not without its own shortcomings. First, the Context Toolkit is large and complex, which limits its use on resource constrained devices. This complexity also hinders the task of creating new widgets [13]. Finally, the movement of context aggregation functionality away from the client and into the middleware unnecessarily limits the types of aggregations that can be performed.

3.4   Observations

Despite their shortcomings, these systems identify several desirable characteristics of context-sensitive middleware. These characteristics, further refined in [14], form a list of challenges to meet when writing such a middleware. First, the context providing infrastructure must be independent of platform and programming language. Second, the system should adapt to changing context resources. Moreover, the system should adapt to changing context information and propagate these changes to applications. Third, the infrastructure must require minimal administration to be able to scale to large numbers of devices. Fourth, context should be treated universally to promote code reuse. Finally, to allow incorporation of resource-constrained devices, the middleware must remain lightweight.

4   A Middleware for Environmental Monitoring

Existing solutions fall short of meeting application needs, specifically on resource-constrained devices in highly dynamic networks. To address these concerns, we developed CONSUL (CONtext Sensing User Library), which provides application developers access to context information through a simplified interface. This eases programming and places the ability to build context-aware applications in the hands of novice programmers. Figure 1 shows CONSUL's architecture. In the figure, the solid gray components define CONSUL. The white components we assume to exist, and the cross-hatched component is what an application developer provides. In this section, we discuss the implementation of these components and show how developers use CONSUL to build context-aware applications.

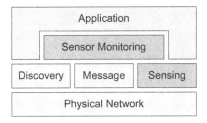

Fig. 1. The architecture of an application using CONSUL

4.1   Foundational Components

In building CONSUL, we assumed the existence of several components. First, CONSUL builds on a physical network which includes the physical hosts and the connections (wired or wireless) that allow the hosts to communicate. On top of this, our middleware also relies on an existing message passing mechanism. The final component that we assume to exist is a network discovery mechanism. For the remainder of this paper, unless otherwise explicitly specified, we rely on the simplest discovery mechanism: one that informs a host of all one-hop neighbors, i.e., other hosts in direct communication. We intentionally separate discovery from sensing to allow each application to select its own discovery mechanism. We further examine this choice and its separation from context sensing in Section 6.1.

4.2   CONSUL

As shown in Figure 1, two components contribute to providing the environmental monitoring functionality: the sensing component and the sensor monitoring component. Figure 2 shows the internal class diagrams for these two components and how they interact with each other and the application.

Sensing. The sensing component allows software to interface with sensing devices connected to a host. Each device has a corresponding piece of software (a monitor). In CONSUL, each monitor extends an **AbstractMonitor** base class and contains its current value in a variable (e.g., the value of a location monitor might be represented by a variable of type **Location**). An application can react to changes in monitor values by implementing the **MonitorListener** interface and registering itself with the monitor. To ensure that any listeners registered receive changes, the monitor should perform these changes through the **setValue()** method in the base class. Applications can also call the **getMonitorValue()** method provided by the base class to obtain these values on demand.

Figure 3 demonstrates an example class that extends **AbstractMonitor** to collect GPS information. From CONSUL's perspective, the important pieces are how the extending class interacts with the base class. The details of communicating with a particular GPS device are omitted; their complexity depends directly on the particular device and its programming interface.

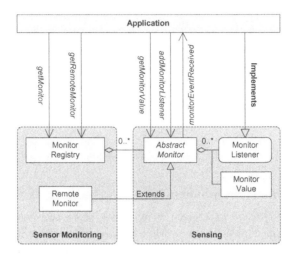

Fig. 2. The internal class diagrams for the components of CONSUL

```
public class GPSMonitor extends AbstractMonitor{
  public GPSMonitor(...){
    //call the AbstractMonitor constructor
    super("GPSLocation");
    //set up serial connection to GPS receiver
    ...
  }
  public void serialEvent(SerialPortEvent event){
    //handle periodic events from GPS receiver
    ...
    //turn GPS event into a GPSLocation object
    ...
    //set local value variable, notify listeners
    setValue(gpsLocation);
  }
}
```

Fig. 3. The GPSMonitor Class

To assist application developers, CONSUL includes several `MonitorValues` for programmers to use when building monitors or constructing more complex `MonitorValues`. These values reside in a library to which application developers can add new types. For example, the library contains an `IntValue` that can be used for sensors whose state can be represented as a single integer value. There are also aggregate values, e.g., `DateValue`, that build on the simple value types. In addition to being available for developers to use, they also serve as examples for defining new values. Figure 4 shows a class that extends `ArrayValue` to aggregate GPS coordinates (represented by `DoubleValues`).

```
public class GPSLocation extends ArrayValue {
  public GPSLocation(double latitude, double longitude) {
    super(new IMonitorValue [] {
      new DoubleValue(latitude), new DoubleValue(longitude)
    });
  });
  public double getLatitude() {
    return ((DoubleValue)getValues()[0]).getValue();
  }
  public double getLongitude() {
    return ((DoubleValue)getValues()[1]).getValue();
  }
}
```

Fig. 4. The GPSLocation Class

Sensor Monitoring. The sensor monitoring component maintains a registry of monitors available on the local hosts (local monitors) and on hosts found by the discovery package (remote monitors). As described above, local monitors make the services available on a host accessible to applications. To gain access to local monitors, the application requests them by name (e.g., "Location") from the registry, which returns a handle to the local monitor.

To monitor context information on remote hosts, the monitor registry creates RemoteMonitors that connect to concrete monitors on remote hosts. These RemoteMonitors serve as proxies to the actual monitors; when the values change on the monitor on the remote host, the RemoteMonitor's value is also updated. To access remote monitors, the application provides the ID of the host (which can be retrieved from the discovery package) and the name of the monitor to the registry's getRemoteMonitor() method. This method creates a proxy, connects it to the remote monitor, and returns a handle. The application can then interact with this handle as if it were a local monitor.

5   Example Applications

In this section, we present three applications, and for each show how using CONSUL extensively simplified the programming task.

5.1   Stock Viewer

In the first application, stock quotes are delivered to handheld devices. Behind the scenes, servers advertise stock information by acting as monitors. Clients running on J2ME-enabled devices automatically discover advertised stocks and display them to users who can select a stock and view its current value. Implementing the stock ticker using CONSUL is straightforward and requires minimal "from scratch" coding.

Since we do not have access to a J2ME-enabled mobile phone, the screenshots below are taken from a laptop running the MIDP Emulator from Sun's J2ME

Fig. 5. Left: the client stock ticker on a mobile phone emulator, displaying a list of discovered stock monitors. Right: the client displaying the value of a selected stock

```
DiscoveryServer discovery = DiscoveryServer.getServer();
discovery.setProxy(true);
discovery.start();
MonitorRegistry registry = new MonitorRegistry(p);

registry.addMonitor(new StockMonitor("MSFT"));
registry.addMonitor(new StockMonitor("YHOO"));
registry.addMonitor(new StockMonitor("T"));
```

Fig. 6. A Stock Ticker Server

Wireless Toolkit. The emulator uses an 802.11b wireless connection to communicate with a stock server on a desktop computer. To simulate a low-bandwidth connection, the emulator caps the network throughput at 9600 bits/second.

A stock's value consists of its ticker symbol; current, low, and high dollar values; trading volume; and company name. Creating a custom StockValue class simply requires aggregating the predefined StringValue, IntValue, and DoubleValue classes in an ArrayValue.

The stock monitor inherits its ability to automatically notify clients of changes from the AbstractMonitor base class. The implementation of StockMonitor requires only a call to AbstractMonitor's setValue() method to update its value and propagate the update to clients. As shown in Figure 6, the server benefits from similar substantial code re-use. The simple code snippet shown assembles a fully-functioning context server from the CONSUL components and the two classes mentioned above. The first three lines start a device-discovery server. Then, a registry is created on a particular port (p) to allow remote hosts to query local monitors on port p. The final lines create local monitors for the MSFT, YHOO, and T stock tickers.

The client gains most of its functionality from CONSUL's discovery server and monitor registry components. Once the user interface code has been written, adding the stock querying functionality is almost trivial: four lines of code to begin finding stock servers, six lines to listen to monitors on discovered servers, and two lines to receive updated stock values. Such extensive code re-use allows rapid development of context-aware applications, shifting effort away from the back-end and toward the user interface.

In this application, the use of CONSUL decouples servers from specific clients, allowing for custom clients that can present stock information in various ways, e.g., a client that pops up a notification when a stock reaches a certain price.

Since CONSUL is very lightweight, the client can easily be run on resource-poor devices like mobile phones. The stock viewer application plus all required libraries consumes only 48 kilobytes. This small size also means that it is feasible to send the application to devices on-demand over-the-air.

The use of context-aware middleware places one restriction on the devices used as clients: they need full IP networking support. In this sample application, the server obtains stock information from a Web service. Web services have one distinct advantage over full-scale context-aware middleware: the clients only need basic HTTP networking support. This drawback does not necessarily reflect a general shortcoming of our middleware, but rather raises the issue of how useful context-sensitivity is in this scenario; stock information is widely available from well-known sources on the Internet. Despite our middleware's small footprint, from a practical point-of-view it may be overkill for retrieving stock quotes. The need for context-sensitive middleware is more pressing when the context sources are not public or must be discovered at runtime.

5.2   RFID-Activated Smart Room

In our second sample application, a server uses an attached RFID scanner to provide information about current occupants of a room. Information about a user's presence is collected by using wearable RFID tags and an RFID scanner on the door. A separate client stores predefined playlists for each person who might enter the room. This computer uses the continuously-updated list of people in the room to play music in the Winamp media player; it selects music from a "master" playlist made by intersecting the playlists of everyone in the room.

The client in turn serves as a monitor that provides information about the song currently playing, which can be displayed on a handheld. Another computer combines the MP3 player's context with the RFID context information to serve a Web page with a list of current occupants and the music.

The screenshots below show the application running on a Compaq iPaq and a desktop, which communicate using 802.11b and wired Ethernet (respectively). Additional desktops (not shown) run the RFID and playlist server applications.

Unlike the previous example, these contexts are not publicly available on the Internet nor from well-known sources, so device discovery is essential. We also expect the playlist to be updated in real time as the room's occupants change, i.e., the client requires "push" service, which CONSUL provides; Web services inherently provide "pull" information.

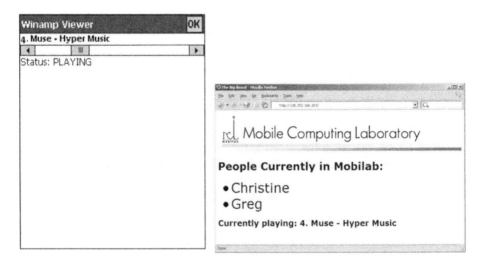

Fig. 7. Left: a client running on a PocketPC showing the current song being played. Right: a Web page showing the current song being played and the people in the room

The code to add context-sensitivity to this application is very similar to the previous application. Interestingly, the computer running the MP3 player acts both as a recipient of context information (a list of occupants) and as a provider (the current song). Once the RFID client was written, extending it to serve the MP3 player's contextual information required only a single line of code to instantiate a `WinampMonitor` and add it to the `MonitorRegistry` already in use to receive context from the RFID server.

Since these context monitors are re-usable components, extending this application is straightforward and transparent to the application. For example, a computer connected to an X10 controller could use the RFID context to automatically turn the lights off when the room is empty.

This application demonstrates that the monitors and values constructed using CONSUL are re-usable components just as CONSUL itself is. Multiple clients use the context provided by the RFID monitor and MP3 player monitor for different purposes, and the Web server drew context from multiple services. The `MonitorRegistry` class handles this transparently, so the programmer simply assembles applications from re-usable components.

Currently, the device discovery mechanism does not allow programmers to search for specific types of devices. Instead, clients retrieve a list of all the devices in the room. They must then collect a list of monitors running on the devices and select one or more monitors based on their names. This requires us to assume that a monitor's name reflects its function. For example, the clients interested in RFID information search for monitors named "RFID". This problem can be avoided by replacing the existing device discovery mechanism with a more-sophisticated discovery method as discussed in Section 6.1.

5.3   Ad Hoc Mobile Communication Protocol

The Network Abstractions protocol [15] provides context-sensitive routing in ad hoc networks by allowing an application to limit its operating context to a neighborhood within the ad hoc network. The protocol requires monitoring the values of sensors on the local host and on directly connected hosts in an ad hoc wireless network. To allow the size and scope of the neighborhood to be application-specific, each application can specify an abstract metric over arbitrary properties of hosts and links in the network. This metric calculates a logical distance from the application's local host to any other host, and includes a bound on allowable distances that restricts the hosts belonging to the neighborhood. As a simple example, an application might want to communicate with all hosts within three miles.

An implementation of this protocol can benefit from the use of CONSUL to access the host and link properties that define metrics. CONSUL relieves the protocol implementer and user from concerns associated with maintaining a consistent view of the values of the relevant sensors on local and remote hosts. For example, when the protocol builds a new context that it maintains over time, it can use the code in Figure 8 to register itself as a listener for the appropriate monitors. When changes in the monitor values occur, the protocol is automatically notified and can change the structure of the routing paths as needed.

```
ContextMonitorListener cml = new ContextMonitorListener(...);
AbstractMonitor m = registry.getMonitor("GPSLocation");
m.addMonitorListener(cml);

for(int i=0; i<neighbors.length; i++){
   AbstractMonitor m2
           = registry.getRemoteMonitor("GPSLocation", neighbors[i]);
   m2.addMonitorListener(cml);
}
```

Fig. 8. A Portion of the Network Abstractions Protocol using CONSUL

The code in the figure explains how, on behalf of a single application, the protocol uses CONSUL to build a network abstraction based on relative physical locations. The first line creates an instance of a monitor listener (the ContextMonitorListener). The protocol then retrieves the local instance of the GPSMonitor and adds the created listener to the monitor. This allows the protocol to be notified when the local host's location changes. Because this example metric is based on the physical distance between hosts in the network, the protocol must also register as a listener for changes in all the one-hop neighbors' locations. In the second portion of code, for each neighbor (in a list retrieved from the neighbor discovery component), the application adds its listener to the remote location monitor on the neighbor. Not shown is the fact that, when new neighbors are discovered, a listener must be added to their location monitors, and when neighbors move away, the listeners must be removed. Additional code within the listener also handles the reception of monitor events to adjust the metric values when the locations of the involved hosts change.

5.4   Comparisons and Lessons Learned

These sample applications demonstrate CONSUL's flexibility. They include components running on desktops, PocketPCs, an emulated mobile phone, and a variety of other mobile devices. This flexibility comes from CONSUL's small footprint and the fact that it does not rely on any language-dependent features. In comparison, CALAIS and Context Toolkit have large footprints and would very likely not run on smaller devices like PocketPCs or mobile phones.

The applications presented in this section required little programming effort to transform a stand-alone utility or viewer into a context-aware application because CONSUL encapsulates the functionality needed to find and propagate context information across a network. To implement the same applications in Stick-e Notes would require additional code to propagate context to clients.

The applications demonstrate that CONSUL promotes separation of concerns, modularity, and code reuse. In the smart room application, custom-made monitors and values were separated into re-usable components. A fairly complex smart room was built using simple components. This application also shows that CONSUL promotes the development of extensible context-aware systems.

6   Discussion

In this section, we examine issues that arise in the use of CONSUL. The first concern deals with the underlying mechanism of network discovery. We then discuss the importance of the separation of concerns, focusing on the separation of the two components within CONSUL and on the separation of CONSUL from network discovery. Another concern mobile computing developers express is the need to secure their information and devices. We discuss this in the context of sensor information that components make available. Finally, the CONSUL package provides a basis for building more sophisticated data interaction mechanisms, and we examine possibilities for these higher-level concepts.

6.1   Network Discovery

Well-known ad hoc mobile routing protocols generally use the simple network discovery mechanism assumed in Section 4. In these cases, all members of the network listen for any of their one-hop neighbors. However, this may cause problems in some target environments.

For example, conserving energy while discovering useful neighbor sets might be the driving design motivation. Birthday protocols [16] have been developed for static ad hoc networks where certain assumptions hold about the relationships between the devices. These networks are still quite dynamic, however, because nodes can be deployed and fail at various times, and require constant discovery.

Group communication mechanisms for mobile networks [17] can extend a node's neighborhood to include nodes to which it is not directly connected. Such protocols create a list of nodes with which a group member can reliably communicate. The integration of these group communication protocols with the CONSUL package allows applications to access sensor services available throughout the group instead of restricting remote sensing to one-hop neighbors.

Even in this brief overview, it becomes obvious that sophisticated discovery mechanisms can greatly enhance CONSUL. It is also apparent that the selection of the discovery mechanism depends heavily on a particular application's needs or operating environment. This factor plays heavily to our desire to separate the discovery mechanism from the CONSUL implementation.

6.2   Separation of Concerns

A key to software engineering is the identification and encapsulation of pieces of software related to a particular purpose. Software designed in accordance with the separation of concerns concept is highly modular and promotes code maintainability, reuse, and evolution. In CONSUL, we seek to provide a flexible and general middleware for context-aware application development in dynamic environments. As a result, CONSUL's architecture is highly modular.

Discovering the set of neighboring hosts that can contribute to an application's context is an important part of collecting context. In CONSUL, we separate the network discovery mechanism from the context interaction mechanisms (i.e., sensing and monitoring components). The discovery component constantly evaluates a host's set of neighbors. This neighbor set is used by other components in CONSUL to support context interaction. With this separation, we allow different methods of discovery to be used interchangeably without affecting how an application interacts with sensors.

In CONSUL, context interaction is further synthesized into components. The tasks associated with acquiring and reporting data are separated from those associated with acquiring sensors. The sensing component encapsulates sensing tasks (i.e., one-time and persistent query handling) within a monitor. The sensor monitoring component provides the application with a handle to monitors, local or remote, through the use of a monitor registry. With this separation, we place the responsibility on the sensor monitoring component for providing access to the desired monitors. Moreover, we eliminate the need for an application to use separate interfaces for interacting with local and remote monitors.

6.3   Security Concerns

CONSUL uses no encryption when sending monitor values between hosts. This avoids burdening resource-constrained devices with storing a large encryption library and decrypting values on-the-fly. However, monitors could be used to transmit sensitive data on insecure networks, justifying this burden. For these applications, an optional `EncryptedValue` class is included in CONSUL. This class wraps values with an encryption layer provided by the Bouncy Castle Crypto library [18]. Monitor programmers can use this class to encrypt values with a fixed symmetric key; access to monitor values can be controlled by distributing this key ahead-of-time to trustworthy clients. Clients without this key can still receive monitor values, but cannot decrypt them.

Since CONSUL's values are reusable components, the use of this generic wrapper adds only one line of code each to the monitor and client. Implementing more-sophisticated encryption schemes should be just as straightforward.

Unfortunately, this encryption layer does not address situations where untrustworthy clients should not know that certain monitors exist. This problem can be solved by incorporating access control into device discovery mechanisms.

6.4   Supporting Sophisticated Data Interaction

CONSUL is lightweight and provides simple data access. However, as discussed in this section, CONSUL can support high-level data handling and can be used to address data access issues important in context-aware application development.

Researchers are increasingly concerned with performing in-network data aggregation to reduce network communication. Approaches include directed diffusion [19], Tiny Aggregation (TAG) [20], and digest diffusion [21]. CONSUL can support data aggregation by employing a hierarchicy of monitors. An aggregation monitor is at the top of the hierarchy, and is constructed by registering persistent queries on neighboring monitors or aggregation monitors of the same name. An application receives query responses only from the top-level monitor.

Another data access issue of mounting concern is imprecise data. Recent work has allowed applications to detect and respond to imprecision. For instance, spatio-temporal relationships between sensor readings can be exploited in an online learning algorithm to predict current readings and detect abnormalities [22]. Other approaches quantify the tolerable level of uncertainty of a query and the level of uncertainty associated with a response [23]. A simple variation of these approaches could be employed using CONSUL, again through the use of a hierarchy of monitors. The top-level monitor registers a persistent query on other monitors of the same type and begins to calculate statistics about the monitor readings. If a reading is not within a specified threshold of the statistical expectation, the top-level monitor decides what to report to the application.

Researchers have also become interested in adaptively providing access to data and services given the quality of service required by the application and the state of the environment [24, 25]. CONSUL can be used to build such systems. CONSUL context monitors can be used to monitor properties associated with services that can affect an application's performance (e.g., a bandwidth monitor for a streaming video service). These monitors can be used by a quality of service evaluation component to adaptively provide optimal access to services.

7   Conclusions

In this paper, we presented CONSUL, a lightweight middleware designed to support context-aware application development. CONSUL simplifies context interactions by encapsulating sensing and monitoring tasks, and provides a simple API for accessing context. In CONSUL, context monitors perform sensing tasks, and handle one-time and persistent queries issued by applications. An application uses a monitor registry to obtain monitors. Thus, the responsibility for obtaining the desired monitor from a constantly changing set of monitors is placed on the middleware, and the application can interact with sensors using a unified API.

The applications presented highlight how CONSUL meets requirements for middleware designed for dynamic mobile environments; it is portable, scalable, adaptable, and applicable to small devices. The applications presented demonstrate CONSUL's use on a range of platforms. Since CONSUL's underlying communication mechanism is very simple, if the device discovery mechanism used for an application scales well, then CONSUL scales no worse than a standard client/server application. Adaptability is demonstrated in the smart room application by CONSUL's use of device discovery to find and replace sources of context. Finally, CONSUL has an extremely small footprint, and can be used in applications on a mobile phone, whose resources and features are limited.

References

1. Dey, A.K., Abowd, G.D.: Cybreminder: A context-aware system for supporting reminders. In: Proc. of the 2nd Int'l Symp. on Handheld and Ubiquitous Computing. (2000) 172–186
2. Abowd, G., Atkeson, C., Hong, J., Long, S., Kooper, R., Pinkerton, M.: Cyberguide: A mobile context-aware tour guide. ACM Wireless Networks **3** (1997) 421–433
3. Cheverst, K., Davies, N., Mitchell, K., Friday, A., Efstratiou, C.: Experiences of developing and deploying a context-aware tourist guide: The GUIDE project. In: Proc. of MobiCom. (2000) 20–31
4. Pascoe, J.: Adding generic contextual capabilities to wearable computers. In: Proc. of the 2^{nd}nd Int'l Symp. on Wearable Computers. (1998) 92–99
5. Kindberg, T., Barton, J.: A Web-based nomadic computing system. Computer Networks **35** (2001) 443–456
6. Romn, M., Hess, C., Cerqueira, R., Ranganathan, A., Campbell, R.H., Nahrstedt, K.: A middleware infrastructure for active spaces. IEEE Pervasive Computing **1** (2002) 74–83
7. Hong, J.I., Landay, J.A.: An architecture for privacy-sensitive ubiquitous computing. In: Proc. of MobiSys. (2004) 177–189
8. Brown, P.J.: The stick-e document: a framework for creating context-aware applications. In: Proc. of EP'96. (1996) 259–272
9. Brown, P.J., Bovey, J.D., Chen, X.: Context-aware applications: from the laboratory to the marketplace. IEEE Personal Communications **4** (1997) 58–64
10. Nelson, G.J.: Context-Aware and Location Systems. PhD thesis, University of Cambridge (1998)
11. Want, R., Hopper, A., Falco, V., Gibbons, J.: The Active Badge location system. ACM Transactions on Information Systems **10** (1992) 91–102
12. Dey, A.K.: Providing Architectural Support for Building Context-Aware Applications. PhD thesis, Georgia Institute of Technology (2000)

13. Yellin, D.M.: Stuck in the middle: Challenges and trends in optimizing middleware. SIGPLAN **36** (2001) 175–180
14. Hong, J., Landay, J.: An infrastructure approach to context-aware computing. Human-Computer Interaction **16** (2001)
15. Roman, G.C., Julien, C., Huang, Q.: Network abstractions for context-aware mobile computing. In: Proc. of the 24th Int'l. Conf. on Software Engineering. (2002) 363–373
16. McGlynn, M.J., Borbash, S.A.: Birthday protocols for low energy deployment and flexible neighbor discovery in ad hoc wireless networks. In: Proceedings of MobiHoc. (2001) 137–145
17. Huang, Q., Julien, C., Roman, G.C.: Relying on safe distance to achieve strong partitionable group membership in ad hoc networks. IEEE Transactions on Mobile Computing **3** (2004) 192–205
18. Legion of the Bouncy Castle, The: The legion of the bouncy castle. http://www.bouncycastle.org/ (2004)
19. Intanagonwiwat, C., Govindan, R., D.Estrin, Heidemann, J., Silva, F.: Directed diffusion for wireless sensor networking. ACM/IEEE Trans. on Networking **11** (2002) 2–16
20. Madden, S., Franklin, M., Hellerstein, J., Hong, W.: Tag: A tiny aggregation service for ad-hoc sensor networks. In: ACM Symp. on Operating System Design and Implementation. (2002)
21. Zhao, J., govindan, R., Estrin, D.: Computing aggregates for monitoring wireless sensor networks. In: 1st Int'l. Workshop on Sensor Network Protocols and Applications. (2003)
22. Elnahrawy, E., Nath, B.: Cleaning and querying noisy sensors. In: Proc. of the 2nd Int'l. Conf. on Wireless Sensor Networks and Applications. (2003) 78–87
23. Cheng, R., Prabhakar, S.: Managing uncertainty in sensor databases. SIGMOD Record, Special Section on Sensor Network Technology and Sensor Data Management **32** (2003)
24. Noble, B., Satyanarayanan, M.: Experience with adaptive mobile applications in odyssey. Mobile Networks and Applications **4** (1999)
25. Capra, L., Emmerich, W., Mascolo, C.: Carisma: Context-aware reflective middleware system for mobile applications. IEEE Trans. of Software Engineering Journal (TSE) (2003)

A Middleware Centric Approach to Building Self-adapting Systems

Svein Hallsteinsen, Jacqueline Floch, and Erlend Stav

SINTEF ICT, 7465 Trondheim, Norway
{svein.hallsteinsen, jacqueline.floch, erlend.stav}@sintef.no

Abstract. The use of handheld networked devices to access information systems by people moving around is spreading rapidly. Systems being used in this way typically face dynamic variation in their operating environment. This poses new challenges for system developers that need to build systems that adapt dynamically to the changing operating environment in order to maintain usability and usefulness for mobile users. In this paper we propose an approach to building such self-adapting systems where the adaptation is handled by generic middleware. Our approach builds on component frameworks and variability engineering to achieve adaptable systems, and property modelling, architectural reflection and context monitoring to support dynamic self-adaptation.

1 Introduction

Computers and networking technology are becoming an integral part of our living and working environment. The increasing mobility and pervasiveness of computing and communication enable new services and applications that can improve quality of work and life. When people are using handheld networked devices while moving around, significant variability is introduced in the operating environment for the provided services. For example, communication bandwidth changes dynamically in wireless communication networks, or user interface preferences change when on the move because light and noise conditions change. Under such circumstances, dynamic adaptation is required in order to retain usability, usefulness, and reliability of the application. This poses a significant challenge for application developers, and existing software development methodology and middleware technology give little support for such dynamic adaptivity. Solutions exist that support dynamic reconfiguration, but we lack means for describing dependencies between application and context, and for reasoning about the influence of context changes on application configuration.

In this paper we propose a middleware centric approach to building applications capable of adapting to dynamically varying requirements being developed in the FAMOUS[1] project. Our approach builds on the following main ideas:

---

[1] FAMOUS (Framework for Adaptive Mobile and Ubiquitous Services) is a strategic research programme at SINTEF funded by the Research Council of Norway.

T. Gschwind and C. Mascolo (Eds.): SEM 2004, LNCS 3437, pp. 107–122, 2005.

- Component frameworks as a means to build both applications and middleware that are capable of being adapted by reconfiguration.
- Annotation of components and compositions with property characteristics in order to discriminate between alternative configurations.
- implementation of adaptation management as generic middleware services exploiting architectural reflection.

Self-adaptation has so far typically been applied to mission critical systems, where software development cost has not been a limiting factor and considerable additional development effort to achieve the necessary flexibility has been acceptable. Our approach is instead targeted on everyday applications, where more cost effective ways to achieve self-adaptation must be found. For these systems self-adaptation does not need to be perfect, as long as it provides perceived benefit by better being able to maintain service quality and user satisfaction during dynamic variations in operating conditions and user requirements. We are thus talking about providing sufficient utility for everyday users, much in the same way as discussed by Shaw in [15].

The paper is organized as follows: First we briefly present some concepts central to our approach. Then we explain the approach and demonstrate it by walking through the design and test of a simple pilot application built on a prototype implementation of the middleware. Next we evaluate the approach based on the experience with the pilot application. Finally we discuss related research that has inspired our work before concluding and discussing plans for further research.

2   Foundations

In this section we briefly explain some central concepts of our approach.

M iddleware. We understand middleware as generally reusable software that enables the execution of sets of collaborating components in a heterogeneous and distributed execution environment. Typical examples are CORBA, MS COM+ and J2EE. In addition to the basic mechanisms facilitating configuration and deployment of component configurations and facilitating communication between components, such middleware typically also includes reusable components providing commonly needed services, for instance persistent data storage and user authentication. We believe that adaptation is a common concern for all sorts of applications intended for use in a modern distributed and partly mobile computing infrastructure and therefore should be supported by middleware.

C omponent Fram eworks. Szyperski [18] defines a component framework as "a dedicated and focused architecture, usually around a few key mechanisms, and a fixed set of policies for mechanisms at the component level". In our use of the concept we also include the components that can be plugged into the architecture to build working systems and rules constraining such building. A component framework may be fairly generic, supporting the building of almost any kind of component-based system, or more specific and meant to, support the implementation of a family of similar systems. A specific framework is usually a specialization of a more generic framework that constrains the architecture of system families. Our approach defines both a generic component framework: the FAMOUS adaptation middleware, and a specific component framework: the application framework.

Variability Engineering. In order to construct a useful component framework for a system family, one needs to understand the variation in requirements that it has to cover. Analyzing the need for variation and deciding on how to build this variability into a component framework is central in the design of product line or system family architectures [2] [20] and is often referred to as variability engineering.

Reflection. Maes [6] defines computational reflection as "the activity performed by a system when doing computation about (and by that possibly affecting) its own computation". Typically this means that the system has some sort of model of itself. By architectural reflection we understand making available a model of the system architecture at runtime and making use of it to affect the computation performed by the system. This principle is at the heart of our approach to adaptation.

3   Overall Architecture

An overview of our approach is given in Figure 1. Applications are built as component frameworks constructed to support the creation of application variants matching the different requirement sets that may occur during use. Application variants can differ in a number of ways, for example user interface style and modality, functional richness, quality properties provided to the user, how the components are deployed on a distributed computing infrastructure, and what resources and quality properties they need from the platform and network environment.

The adaptation middleware is responsible for creating and maintaining a suitable application variant based on the application framework.

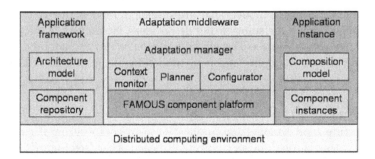

Fig. 1. Overall runtime architecture

The central components of the adaptation middleware are the adaptation manager, the context monitor, the planner and the configurator. The context monitor monitors the user context and the execution environment of the application and keeps the adaptation manager informed about changes. When changes occur that make the running variant of the application unsuitable in some manner, the adaptation manager will invoke the planner component, which consults the architecture model to generate plans for and evaluate other possible compositions of the application with respect to their suitability in the current context. If the best composition found is a sufficiently big improvement over the current composition, the adaptation manager instructs the configurator to dynamically reconfigure the application. The same mechanism is also used at application startup to find and set up the most appropriate initial application variant.

The architecture model of the application framework is a runtime representation of the application framework architecture, while the component repository stores the concrete components available for plugging into the framework.

In this paper we focus on the modelling of the application framework architecture and how this model is represented and used at runtime by the adaptation manager to make decisions about adaptation. There are also many challenges related to context monitoring and dynamic reconfiguration [16], but this is outside the scope of this paper.

4   Application Framework Architecture Model

The application framework consists of a model of the framework architecture and a set of components fitting into the architecture. Application variants suited for different situations may be created from the framework by populating the architecture with an appropriate set of concrete components. The architecture model defines the allowable compositions.

The adaptation middleware needs a model of the framework architecture that can be represented efficiently at runtime and serve the needs of both the planner and the configurator to understand the variability supported by the application framework and how to configure application variants with given properties. This model must cover the following aspects of the architecture: i) structure, ii) distribution, iii) variability and iv) property specifications. Furthermore it should be derivable from design time models that are similar to models the developers are already familiar with. Our solution builds on ideas introduced by architecture definition languages [8] such as Darwin [5] and Koala [19], and adopted by UML 2.0 [11], and on work on quality of service modelling in the context of UML [12].

4.1   Structure

The architecture model models an application as a composition of component roles collaborating through ports connected to each other (see Figure 2). A port either defines a service implemented by the role and offered to its collaborating components, or a service needed by the role from its collaborating components

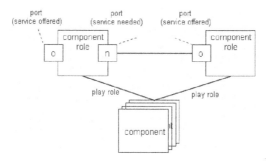

Fig. 2. Component roles and ports

in order to implement its offered services. Connections between ports are bidirectional, and the functional part of the service interaction is defined by required and provided interfaces at each end of the connection.

Hierarchical decomposition is supported through composite components. A composite component has an inner composition of roles and associated sets of candidate components, and may be seen as a sub-framework. At the root of this hierarchical decomposition is the role representing the application and its interaction with the user and the execution environment.

4.2   Distribution

The execution environment is modeled as a set of node roles connected by link roles. Distribution is modeled by associating component roles with abstract nodes of the computing infrastructure. This association means that the component playing the role in an application or component variant must be deployed on the associated abstract node. Mapping from abstract to actual nodes is performed at runtime. Component deployment can also be performed at runtime as part of preparations for reconfiguration, allowing small devices to save memory by avoiding keeping all components pre-deployed. The meta-information for a component can be deployed independently of the component, and the planner can utilize this information for all deployed and deployable components through the architecture model.

4.3   Variability

Variability is modelled by associating sets of alternative compositions to applications or composite components, or by associating sets of alternative components to component roles. The set of component can be extended by adding new alternative components that match a component role. Creating an application variant with given properties means selecting the appropriate alternative from each set. In this way one may vary the structure, the selected components and the distributions of the application.

Not all variability is naturally expressed in this way however. Therefore we also allow components that manage their own adaptation. Such components must define an adaptation port that is used by the adaptation manager to coordinate the adaptation of self-adapting components with its own activities.

4.4   Property Specifications

Basically adaptation management is about matching the properties of the application to the user needs and preferences and to the properties of the execution environment. For example, if the user is driving and prefers hands-free operation, the adaptation manager should find a configuration that offers this property. In order to do so the adaptation manager needs the following information:

- The user needs and preferences (as determined by the user context).
- The properties of the execution environment.
- The properties offered by application variants to the user and how they depend on the properties of the execution environment.
- The properties needed by the application from the execution environment.

To model this information we introduce property characteristics and property constraints. Property characteristics are quantifiable characteristics of the context or of an application or component variant. A property characteristic has a name and a value range. The value range may be specified as string, integer (optionally with range indicated), enumeration (with allowable values listed) or boolean. Some examples of property characteristics are given in Table 1.

A property constraint limits the allowed values of a property characteristic and typically expresses a need or an offer regarding a particular property characteristic. For example, using the property characteristics listed in Table 1, the constraint "haf = yes" associated with the user, indicates that the user needs hands-free operation, while the same constraint associated with a variant of an application, indicates that this variant offers hands-free operation.

Property characteristics and property constraints are similar to quality of service characteristics and quality of service constraints as defined by the proposed UML profile for modelling QoS and Fault tolerance submitted to OMG by I-Logix, Open-IT and THALES [12]. However, property characteristics are intended to be used more generally to describe also properties not naturally perceived as quality of service, like offer or need for various types of resources.

We associate property constraints with ports to describe the properties of the service associated with the port. In the case of a service offered, the property constraints associated with the port describe the offered properties. In the case

Table 1. Example property characteristics

Name	Value range	Explanation
avy	1:100	Availability of the service provided by an application
rsp	1:100	Response time of the service provided by an application
mem	1:100	Amount of memory of a computer
nbw	1:100	Bandwidth of a network connection
nsb	1:100	Stability of a network connection
haf	yes, no	Hands-free operation

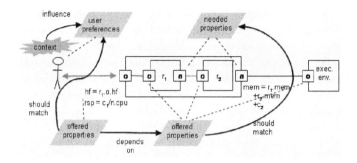

Fig. 3. Ports with property specifications

of a service needed the property constraints describe the needed properties. The properties of a composition or component are the aggregation of the properties of its ports.

Often the offered properties of a composition depend on the properties of the services it needs or by the properties of its constituent components. This is modeled by allowing a property constraint to be expressed as a function of other properties.

For example a property constraint describing a service offered by a component can be expressed as a function of one or more of the properties of the services offered to the component (and used in a given configuration), and/or of the properties of its constituent components.

The language for specifying such functions is not yet fully specified. So far we have used simple arithmetic expressions where properties used as operands are referred to by characteristic name, qualified by the port name, and for properties of roles in compositions, also the role name. Some examples of property annotations are given in Figure 3. More examples are given in the experimentation section below.

5 Adaptation Management

In this section we describe in more detail how the adaptation manager works. When a context change occurs, this is detected by the context monitor which notifies the adaptation manager. The adaptation manager then searches for the configuration that best fits the current context and resource situation of the application. The search is performed by using the planner component to iterate through plans for all possible application variants. A plan is generated by selecting a concrete component for each component role of the application. As some of the selected components can be composite components, the plan generation process continues recursively until all leaf nodes are selected. The best configuration is selected by computing a utility value for each plan with respect to the user preferences and properties of the execution environment. The utility value is computed by the utility function which is defined by the developer. The utility funciton is typically a weighted mean of the differences between the offered and needed properties. The weights in the utility function can represent changing user priorities, and can be adjusted at runtime. The variant with the highest utility is chosen. In order to avoid that the system is busy adapting all the time, the adaptation manager also has to evaluate whether the improvement is high enough to justify an adaptation. The evaluation is based on user-adjustable settings for a utility improvement threshold and adaptation delay.

During the configuration phase, the configurator component will go through the selected configuration plan attempting to perform only the minimum number of changes to the composition of the application. This is done by comparing the component roles in the new plan with those in the plan used in the current composition, and keeping all component instances where the same concrete component has been selected to play a role. Changes can involve creating, replacing and removing component instances, relocating component instances to other nodes, and adding and removing connections between components. To make sure these changes do not corrupt the current execution of the service, the component configurator pattern has been applied, and affected components are requested to suspend their activity before the reconfiguration occurs and to resume it when the changes are completed.

6   Experimentation

In order to demonstrate and experiment with the proposed approach we have built a middleware prototype and a simple application. In this section we walk through the design of the application framework and the behavior of the application in an example usage scenario.

The application domain is inspection and maintenance support for janitors where janitors use handheld PDAs during their work. Janitors in large organisations often need to do maintenance on a variety of technical installations, possibly spread over large geographic areas. Their work typically include several very different working situations, ranging from administrative work in a clean and quiet and connected office environment, through travelling between technical installations needing maintenance to doing repair work in rugged industrial environments with varying network coverage. We have chosen an application for organising the work, including support for tasks such as fault report registration, repair job definition, work assignment, and progress reporting.

The implementation environment is Java 2 Micro Edition, Personal Profile including RMI. In the prototype middleware the context monitor has been replaced by a context simulator to facilitate experimentation with the prototype.

6.1   Context Variations

We have identified a number of context parameters that vary during a typical working day of a janitor and that influence the needs and preferences of the janitor and the execution environment of the applications he is using:

- The network coverage varies from place to place and in some places there is no coverage at all.
- During some operations hands are busy and the janitor must use an audio based user interface.
- In some situations the janitor needs to use several applications concurrently and the device runs out of memory.

To be able to describe adaptation to these context variations we define a set of property characteristics that depend on context. The properties used in scenario are described in Table 1. For the sake of simplicity we have chosen a value range from 1 to 100 for all property characteristics except for the hands-free property characteristic. The value range is defined by the developer. The current prototype does not support varying user priorities. Fixed weights are associated to user preferences.

6.2   Application Design

In accordance with the proposed approach the application is designed as a component framework. An overview of the framework architecture in the form of an and/or-graph is given in Figure 4.

The root node has associated two alternative components. One is a medium client variant where the user interface and the application logic are deployed on the client device, while the shared database is deployed on the server. The internal architecture and the property annotations of this variant is shown at the left side of Figure 5. The other is a self-reliant client variant with also a local database replicating relevant data deployed on the client. The internal architecture and the property annotations of that variant is shown at the right side of Figure 5.

Two alternative components are associated to the UI role, which appears both in the thin and the self reliant client variants. One UI component implements a normal display-, pointer- and keyboard-based user interface, while the other implements a voice- and ear-based interface. The property characteristics of the UI are described in Figure 6. These properties directly influence the application properties.

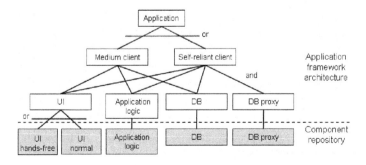

Fig. 4. Component framework overview

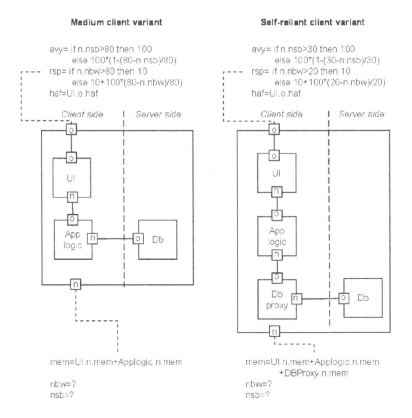

Fig. 5. Medium and self-reliant client variants

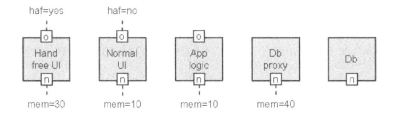

Fig. 6. Component repository with property annotations

The utility function is shown in Figure 7 together with the top level diagram for the application framework architecture showing the application and its context. The purpose of this diagram is to name the context objects of interest, here the user "usr" and the execution environment "exe", such that they can be referred to in the utility function.

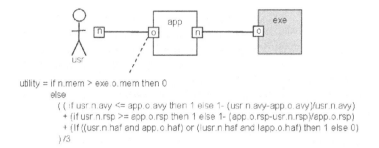

utility = if n.mem > exe.o.mem then 0
else
((if usr.n.avy <= app.o.avy then 1 else 1- (usr.n.avy-app.o.avy)/usr.n.avy)
+ (if usr.n.rsp >= app.o.rsp then 1 else 1- (app.o.rsp-usr.n.rsp)/app.o.rsp)
+ (If ((usr.n.haf and app.o.haf) or (!usr.n.haf and !app.o.haf) then 1 else 0)
) /3

Fig. 7. The utility function

6.3   Usage Scenario

We have simulated a possible usage scenario for the application described above, using a context simulator instead of a context monitor. An extract from a trace of the simulation is included in Table 2. In the following we walk through the simulation. Note that in the current middleware prototype, the variant with the highest utility is always chosen; the adaptation manager does not evaluate whether the improvement is high enough to justify an adaptation.

The janitor launches the application on his handheld computer to check his assignments for the day before he leaves home in the morning. He is also running a video player on the device showing morning news on a screen in the kitchen. The context description for this situation is given in Table 2. There is little memory and cpu because the video player uses a lot. The home wlan provides high capacity network connection. In this situation the medium client configuration is the best match and is chosen as the initial configuration. For the UI role the Normal UI is chosen since hands and eyes are available.

Table 2. Extract from trace of test run simulating usage scenario from the example

Context (changes in bold)						Utility (selected variant in bold)			
needed by user			offered by exec. env			s.r.cl.+	s.r.cl.+	m.cl.+	m.cl.+
haf	avy	rsp	mem	nbw	nsb	no.ui	hf.ui	no.ui	hf.ui
Initial situation									
no	80	30	30	70	90	0	0	**1**	0
Janitor shuts down video player									
no	80	30	**70**	70	90	1	0	**1**	0.66
Janitor drives away from house									
no	80	30	70	**30**	90	**1**	0	0.81	0.47
Janitor wants hands-free UI when driving									
yes	80	30	70	30	90	0.66	**1**	0.47	0.8
Janitor enters area with poor network coverage									
yes	80	30	70	30	**20**	0.61	**0.94**	0.24	0.58

The janitor notices that his first job is to fix the ventilation system in a large building which is causing problems. He checks if there are any special tools or spare parts that are recommended to bring, given the symptoms that has been reported. The janitor shuts down the video player, and walks out to his car to go to the building where the faulty installation is located. Now a lot of memory is freed, and this triggers the adaptation manager. In this situation (2nd line of Table 2) the self reliant client variant has the same utility as the one running, but since it is not better, no adaptation takes place.

As the janitor drives away from the house, he moves out of reach of the home WLAN and his handheld swithces to GPRS, causing a decrease in the network bandwidth (3rd line in Table 2). Now the self-reliant client is better and a reconfiguration takes place.

While he is driving the janitor wants to check a few details, but since his eyes and hands are busy with the driving, he prefers hands-free UI (4th line in Table 2). This causes the utility of the configurations with handsfree UI to increase and another reconfiguration occurs.

The building the janitor is heading for is part of an industrial plant located in a remote place with poor GSM coverage, and as he approaches the place the network stability decreases significantly (4th line in Table 2). Although this influences the utility values, the running configuration is still the best one and no adaptation occurs.

7   Evaluation

By building the prototype middleware and the pilot services as described above we have demonstrated that the proposed approach to adaptation is feasible. In this section we discuss the merits of the approach based on the experience from this exercise.

E■ectiveness of expressing variability. As illustrated by the example, we have been able to model interesting adaptive behaviour, and the possibility to include self-adapting components enables the resort to other ways than reconfiguration at the component level where this is not suitable. However, there are some limitations in our current approach that we should overcome.

Firstly the current adaptation manager requires that there is a manageable set of variants to be used in the algorithm that searches for the best configuration. This makes it difficult to deal with more continuous variation in properties as is achieved for example by varying buffer sizes, the resolution of images, or the precision of calculations. To cope with this we need a more sophisticated approach to evaluating properties in the planner.

Another limitation is that a property must be expressed as one value. The OMG draft standard allows a quality characteristic to be described in several "dimensions", and an extension in that direction would clearly improve the expressive power of the language for modeling properties.

Scaling to real life applications. The implementation of the pilot services is somewhat skeletal and has few components and variants. Thus we have little experience as to the scalability of the proposed approach. Issues that might threaten scalability are memory requirements of the runtime representation of the architecture model and memory and cpu requirements of the algorithm for selecting the best configuration. In particular the memory and cpu requirements of the algorithm for selecting the best configuration as it is currently implemented causes some concern: it is an exhaustive search of all possible configurations that generates a plan for the construction of each configuration in the form of an object structure.

The number of configurations depends exponentially on the number of variation points (or-nodes in the and-or graph). In a real application, the number of possible configurations may be quite high. On the other hand we believe there are many opportunities for employing various forms of heuristics to reduce the scope of the search.

Extra Burden on Developers. The additional tasks for the developers compared with traditional development are:

- Developing a framework rather than a single application.
- Providing the property annotations and the utility function.
- Providing the runtime representation of the framework architecture.
- Making components reconfigurable.

Developing the application as a framework with built-in variability is clearly an extra burden on the developers. However the alternative may be to develop several variants of the application for use in different contexts, and this may require more work than the work required to model variation and properties. After all it is now widely accepted that the component based system family approach is an efficient way to deal with varying requirements [2].

In the prototype the runtime representation for the application framework architecture model with the property annotations were hand-coded in Java. Once it had been designed, the implementation was fairly trivial. However, in a more complete implementation we foresee that this can be generated by tools from an annotated design time model in the same style as shown in the presentation of the pilot application design above.

Still, defining property characteristics and utility functions is not at all straight forward, and may require specially trained developers. We need more experience to say how difficult it will be to develop such models in typical cases. The definition of a standard vocabulary of properties and the development of adaptation patterns are approaches we foresee.

Size and complexity of the application framework architecture model A critical issue in all the considerations above is the size and complexity of this model. The key question is how accurate it must be to support useful adaptation to common context changes for everyday applications. At the moment our pilot application is too simple to draw conclusions about this.

8   Related Work

The QuA project [17] presents a component based platform able to dynamically plan and compose a service based on QoS specifications from a repository of available components. The approaches are similar in the sense that both are based on explicit modelling of the properties of components and compositions. However, while QuA so far has focused on initial configuration of services with media streaming as the application area, we have focused on dynamic adaptation to context with access to information systems from mobile clients as the application area.

The CASA framework [9] supports development of applications which need to dynamically adapt due to unreliable availability of resources in self-organized mobile networks. An XML-based contract specification language is used to describe application contracts, allowing resource requirements for different configurations to be computed. All application configurations must be specified explicitly, in contrast to our approach where configurations are created automatically by exploiting the variation capabilities of the framework architecture. CASA has focused on a peer-to-peer telecom architecture and defines a protocol for support service negotiations between distributed applications. We have not yet considered the coordination of the adaptation of multiple applications. This is an issue we plan to work with in the future.

The Aura project [10] addresses the dynamic composition of resource-aware services to support user tasks and proposes an efficient algorithm for searching the configuration space. Their approach is similar to ours in the sense that they also use properties to support reasoning on the suitability of service compositions to a particular situation. Although we reason and configure at the component level and take into account a wider set of properties (e.g. functional richness), we intend to investigate how this algorithm can be tailored to our approach.

Several approaches discuss the importance of adaptation in mobile computing middleware [7]. ReMMoC [4] or DynamicTAO and UIC [13] are representative approaches. These approaches focus on the adaptation of the underlying middleware rather than the adaptation of applications. For example, they enable different concurrency management, connection management or service discovery strategies to be selected. They exploit similar mechanisms as our approach, such as component frameworks and reflection. The key issues to be addressed are however slightly different. As the middleware offer basic services that multiple applications rely on, robustness, security and performance are central issues. On the other hand, differently from applications, underlying middleware is quite stable and remains the domain of expertise of few developers. The key issues for applications are acceptance by developers and usability.

An important issue during dynamic reconfiguration is the preservation of application consistency. In our approach, we apply the component configurator pattern [14], i.e. components affected by reconfiguration are requested to suspend and resume their activity before and after reconfiguration. We need to elaborate this approach with support for state preservation. Middleware oriented and software pattern based approaches have been proposed. In [1] a CORBA service is presented that allows dynamic reconfiguration with maximum transparency for the client and server side developers. In [3] software reconfiguration patterns based on statecharts are described.

9   Conclusion and Further Work

We have presented a middleware centric approach to supporting the building of applications capable of adapting to a dynamically varying context as is typical of mobile use. The proposed approach builds on the idea of achieving adaptability by building applications as component frameworks from which variants with different properties can be built dynamically.

In this paper we have focused on the modelling of the adaptation capabilities and the decision making related to adaptation, and we have demonstrated the feasibility of the approach by a walkthrough of an example application design and how it behaves in a typical usage scenario. We have also done prototype implementation of the proposed adaptation middleware and a simple pilot application for mobile use and we have done some simple tests.

The tests that we have done are promising although it is to early to draw firm conclusions about the performance of our approach in real life situations.

We are now doing a more elaborate implementation of the prototype middleware and will implement more complete pilot services. This will be used to do a more thorough evaluation of the proposed approach by analyzing the experiences from the development of pilot applications and by studying trial use of them and to evolve the ideas presented here.

References

1. Almeida, J.P.A., Wegdam, M., van Sinderen, M., and Nieuwenhuis, L., "Transparent Dynamic Reconfiguration for CORBA", in Proc. of the 3rd Int. Symposium on Distributed Objects and Applications, 2001, pp. 197-207.
2. Bosch, J., "Design & Use of Software Architectures - Adopting and Evolving a Product-Line Approach", Addison Wesley, 2000. ISBN 0-201-67494-7.
3. Gomaa, H. and Hussein, M., "Dynamic Software Reconfiguration in Software Product Families", in Poc. of the 5th Int. Workshop on Product Family Engineering (PFE), Lecture Notes in Computer Science, Springer-Verlag, 2003.
4. Grace, P. Blair, G.S., and Samuel, S. "ReMMoC: A Reflective Middleware to Support Mobile Client Interoperability", in Proc. of the International Symposium on Distributed Objects and Applications (DOA), 2003.
5. Magee, J., Dulay, N., Eisenbach, S., and Kramer, J., "Specifying Distributed Software Architectures", in Proc. of the Fifth European Software Engineering Conference, 1995.
6. Maes, P., "Concepts and experiments in computational reflection", in Proc. of OOPSLA'87.
7. Mascolo, C., Capra, L. and Emmerich, W., "Mobile Computing Middleware", Tutorial Summary, in Advanced Lectures on Networking, LN CS Vol. 2497. 2002. pp. 20-58.

8. Medvidovic, N., and Taylor, R.N., "A classification and Comparison Framework for Software Architecture Description Languages", IEEE Transactions on Software Engineer-ing, 2000, pp. 70-93.

9. Mukhija, A. and Glinz, M. "A Framework for Dynamically Adaptive Applications in a Self-organized Mobile Network Environment", in Proc. of the 24th International Conference on Distributed Computing Systems Workshops, 2004, pp 368-374.

10. Poladian, V., Sousa, J., P., Garlan, D., and Shaw, "M. Dynamic Configuration of Resource-Aware Services", in Proc. of the 26th Int. Conf. on Software Engineering, 2004.

11. OMG, "UML 2.0 Superstructure Specification", Final adopted specification. August 2003.

12. OMG, "UML Profile for Modelling Quality of Service and Fault Tolerance Characteristics and Mechanisms", OMG draft adopted specification November 2003.

13. Roman, M., and Kon, F., "Reflective Middleware: From Your Desk to Your Hand", in IEEE Distributed Systems Online Journal, Special Issue on Reflective Middleware, 2001.

14. Schmidt, D., Stal, M., Rohnert, H. and Buschmann, F., "Pattern-Oriented Software Architecture. Patterns for Concurrent and Networked Objects", John Wiley & Sons, Ltd, 2000. ISBN: 0-471-60695-2.

15. Shaw, M. "Everyday Dependability for Everyday Needs". Keynote speech at ISSRE 2002.

16. Stav, E., and Hallsteinsen, S., "Definition of adaptive architecture, FAMOUS deliverable D3.1-v1". SINTEF report STF90 A04046, 2004.

17. Staehli, R., Eliassen, F., Aagedal, J.Ø., and Blair, G., "Quality of Service Semantics for Component-Based Systems", in Proc. of the 2nd Int'l Workshop on Reflective and Adaptive Middleware Systems, 2003, pp. 153-157.

18. Szyperski, C., "Component Software: Beyond Object-Oriented Programming", Addison Wesley, 1997 (2nd ed. 2002, ISBN 0-201-74572-0).

19. van Ommering, R., van der Linden, F., Kramer, J., and Magee, J., "The Koala component model for consumer electronics software", IEEE Computer, Vol. 33, Nr. 3, March 2000, PP. 78-85.

20. van Ommering, R., and Bosh, J., "Widening the Scope of Software Product Lines - From Variation to Composition", in Proc. of the Second Software Product Line Conference (SPLC 2), 2002, pp. 328-347.

PlanetSim: A New Overlay Network Simulation Framework

Pedro García, Carles Pairot, Rubén Mondéjar, Jordi Pujol,
Helio Tejedor, and Robert Rallo

Department of Computer Science and Mathematics, Universitat Rovira i Virgili,
Avinguda dels Països Catalans 26, 43007 Tarragona, Spain
{pgarcia, cpairot, rrallo}@etse.urv.es

Abstract. Current research in peer to peer systems is lacking appropriate environments for simulation and experimentation of large scale overlay services. This has led to a plethora of custom made simulators that waste development resources and hinder fair comparisons between different approaches. In this paper we present a new simulation / experimentation framework for large scale overlay services with three main contributions: i) provide a unifying approach to simulation/ experimentation that eases the transition from simulation to network testbeds, ii) it clearly distinguish between the design of overlay algorithms (key based routing), and the applications and services built on top of them, iii) offer a layered and modular architecture with clear hotspots, and pervasive use of design patterns. We have used PlanetSim to implement and evaluate overlay networks such as Chord and Symphony, and overlay services such as Scribe application level multicast, and keyword query systems over distributed hash tables.

1   Introduction

In the last years, we have experienced an increasing interest in peer to peer systems from research settings but also from commercial vendors because of its mainstream use in the Internet. Furthermore, the growing bandwidth and computing power in the edges of the network foresee innovative massive applications of peer to peer technology.

We can classify peer to peer networks as structured or unstructured, depending on the way they are connected and how the data they contain is arranged. In a structured network the connections between nodes are of some regular structure, which allows deterministic and optimal lookup hops (typically O (log N)). In contrast to structured networks, nodes in unstructured networks do not share a regular structure and a unified identifier space. Lookups are thus normally achieved by flooding and using replication in the network.

Structured P2P networks are now a hot research topic and they represent an interesting platform for the construction of resilient, large-scale distributed systems. Moreover, structured networks can be used to construct services such

T. Gschwind and C. Mascolo (Eds.): SEM 2004, LNCS 3437, pp. 123–136, 2005.

as distributed hash tables (DHT), scalable group multicast/anycast (CAST) and decentralized object location and routing (DOLR). We focus our research in PlanetSim on structured overlays and the design and development of distributed services on top of them.

In general, both structured and unstructured networks are often called overlay networks because they are built on top of an existing network, usually on top of the Internet. At the moment, P2P networks usually do not map the underlying network or even do not take the layout of these networks into account. As we can see, these overlay networks are thus working at the application layer, and use transport protocols like TCP or UDP as communication channels between inter-connected peers.

P2P researchers are usually more interested in algorithm verification (number of hops, node stress, link stress) than in simulating the whole TCP/IP stack. As a direct consequence, researchers find existing network simulators too specific and low-level. Besides, those simulators exhibit a considerable lack of scalability for thousands of nodes. Another key problem is that the transition from simulated code to experimental code is still quite difficult to achieve.

This has led to the development of ad-hoc simulators (SimPastry, FreePastry, p2psim, DKS, Tapestry) from a high number of research groups, wasting expensive resources in infrastructure code and avoiding clean comparisons between different algorithms. With minor differences, all these ad-hoc simulators are poorly documented and do not show clear-cut software engineered designs. Due to these approaches it is quite difficult to reuse code and even harder to extend those simulators.

To address these limitations, we present PlanetSim, an object oriented simulation framework for overlay networks and services. The novel contributions of PlanetSim are the following:

1. PlanetSim presents a layered and modular architecture with well defined hotspots documented using classical design patterns. This can considerably reduce the learning curve and thus ease the development of new overlay services and algorithms.
2. PlanetSim clearly distinguishes between the creation and validation of overlay algorithms (Chord, Pastry) and the creation and testing of new services (DHT, CAST, DOLR) on top of existing overlays. Our layered approach cleanly decouples services built in the application layer using the standard Common API for structured overlays [2], and peer to peer algorithms built in the overlay layer.
3. PlanetSim also aims to enable a smooth transition from simulation code to experimentation code running in the Internet. Because of this, we provide wrapper code that takes care of network communication and permits us to run the same code in network testbeds such as PlanetLab. Furthermore, because we follow FreePastry's implementation of the Common API, our overlay services can easily run on top of Rice's FreePastry Java code. This enables complete transparency to services running either against the simulator or the network.

PlanetSim has been developed in the Java language to reduce complexity and smooth the learning curve in our framework. We however have profiled and optimised the code to enable scalable simulations in reasonable time. To validate the utility of our approach, we have implemented two overlays (Chord and Symphony) and a variety of services like CAST, DHT, and DOLR. We have proved that PlanetSim reproduces the measures of these environments and is also efficient in its network implementation.

This paper is organized as follows. Section 2 gives details of the PlanetSim framework architecture and services. We present the framework's validation using developed extensions in Section 3. Section 4 compares PlanetSim with related approaches, and finally we draw conclusions and present future work in Section 5.

2 PlanetSim Architecture

The overall model comprises a discrete event simulator (time-stepped) that uses a central step-clock to simulate timing. As we will explain in this section, most entities in an overlay simulator are related to the routing of messages between the nodes of the overlay. Nevertheless, overlay simulators must not forget the underlying network that sustains the overlay and thus include appropriate abstractions and mappings for both routing infrastructures.

We have decided to implement PlanetSim in Java in order to smooth the learning curve of the framework. We aim to create a framework that is easy to learn, easy to use, easy to extend, and easy to integrate with other frameworks. The main drawback of this decision is the performance penalty that Java imposes. We however have carefully profiled and optimised the code to enable massive simulations in reasonable time.

2.1 The Common API for Structured Overlays and FreePastry

To better understand the overall architecture we must first introduce the Common API for Structured Overlays and the FreePastry implementation. We propose a novel service to be supported by overlay simulators: a façade API to develop overlay services and applications on top of existing overlays. This API is based on the proposed Common API (CAPI) for structured Peer-to-Peer overlays published in [2]. The main motivation for this decision is the plethora of applications and services that can be built on top of structured overlays.

In [2] authors identify the Key based Routing (KBR) as the common denominator of services provided by any structured overlay. Every node in a structured overlay is thus responsible for a number of keys in the identifier space (key's root), and can route messages in O(log N) hops to the keys's root for any key.

On top of this Tier 0 KBR, structured overlays can be used to construct services like distributed hash tables, scalable group multicast/anycast and decentralized object location (see Figure 1). These services in turn promise to support novel kinds of distributed applications like notification systems, messaging,

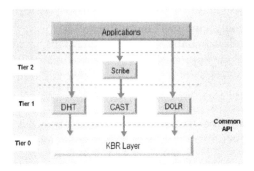

Fig. 1. Common API Diagram

content distribution networks and cooperative replication of archival storage. Furthermore, many traditional applications like Usenet or DNS have recently been re-architected on top of these decentralized architectures.

The common API offers two kinds of functions: the first ones for routing and processing messages in applications, and the second ones for accessing node's routing state information. The former include three kind of calls: *route*, *forward* and *deliver*. The *route* operation delivers a message to the key's root. Applications process messages by executing code in upcalls (*forward*, *deliver*) which are invoked by the underlying routing system. The *forward* upcall is invoked at each node that forwards a message and enables to override the default routing behaviour. The *deliver* upcall is invoked on the node that is root for a key upon the arrival of the message.

The second kind of functions for accessing node's routing state includes *local_lookup*, *neighbourSet*, *replicaSet*, *update*, and *range*. We will not explain each function due to lack of space, but all of them give information about routing state and identifier space information from running nodes.

Using these functions, the authors in [2] define the mapping to different overlay algorithms, and they also specify how to construct overlay services like DHTs, CAST or DOLR.

The common API (CAPI) promises a unifying layer to different DHT architectures, and thus enabling to run applications on top of different algorithms (Chord, Pastry, Tapestry). The API is however loosely defined and each research group is implementing its own version. This clearly hinders application interoperability and it only helps to improve understanding of applications in different DHTs through a common vocabulary.

After evaluating different overlay systems, we concluded that FreePastry is the cleanest and more advanced implementation of a structured overlay. They offer a clean object oriented implementation of the common API in the Java language. Besides, they have implemented several applications on top of this API like Scribe overlay multicast, replication systems like PAST and others. FreePastry is an active project and many research groups are using FreePastry code to create new innovative P2P services.

Nevertheless, FreePastry is also poorly documented and it is only extensible at the application level. It is not possible to implement and simulate other overlay algorithms apart from Pastry. Because of this, we have chosen to embrace FreePastry's common API implementation in our framework to leverage their existing code base and developers.

2.2   PlanetSim Layered Design

PlanetSim's architecture comprises three main extension layers constructed one atop another. As we can see in figure 2, overlay services are built in the application layer using the standard Common API façade. This façade is built on the routing services offered by the underlying overlay layer. Besides, the overlay layer obtains proximity information to other nodes asking information to the Network layer.

The Network layer dictates the overall life cycle of the framework by calling the appropriate methods in the overlay's Node and obtaining routing information to dispatch messages through the Network. As we explain later, the Network layer can be implemented either by the NetworkSimulator or NetworkWrapper. Developers can thus transition from simulation to experimentation environments in a transparent way.

We outline three main extension points (hotspots) in our framework:

- Application: Developers of overlay services like Scribe must extend the Application class to implement the required messaging protocol. Application methods are upcalls from the underlying layer and they notify of specific messages. The Application code can then send or route messages using the EndPoint (downcalls) as well as access underlying node routing state. Any application created at this level can then be run or tested against any structured overlay in the next layer.
- Node: Developers of overlay algorithms like Chord must extend the Node class to implement the required overlay protocol. The node provides incoming and outgoing message queues that permit to create the KBR infrastructure required in the upper layer. At this level nodes interchange messages using Ids and NodeHandles (IP Address + Id).
- Network: It is also possible to create customized Networks (RingNetwork, CircularNetwork, RandomNetwork) by selecting specific Id Factories and also to provide additional routing or proximity costs to the overall routing infrastructure.

As a direct consequence of this layered approach we can also identify two main user roles: ones interested in overlay services and others focused on overlay infrastructures. The former can thus develop and test different overlay services on top of different KBR schemes or even probe services without even care about the KBR layer. Other kind of users can be mainly interested in structured overlays and thus use the simulator to probe or compare a variety of KBR algorithms.

For example, in our research group, there are researchers working at the application layer developing new replicated DHT services, and also experimenting

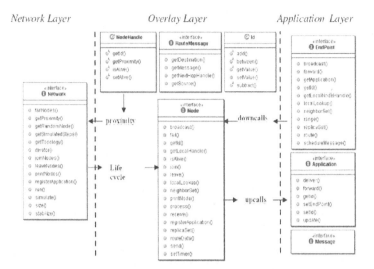

Fig. 2. PlanetSim class diagram

with query systems on top of different overlays. Another group is working at the overlay layer to compare security problems and solutions (BadNodes) over different overlays.

Application Layer

At this layer we have followed FreePastry's implementation of the Common API. In this line, the interfaces borrowed from FreePastry are Application, EndPoint, Message, RouteMessage, Id and NodeHandle. We can see that this API is a façade to the underlying routing system of the simulator. This layer can thus permit very easily to test applications like DHT or Scribe multicast over different implemented overlays like Chord or Symphony.

We outline the Application and EndPoint classes as the main implementers of the common API. The EndPoint is a façade to the underlying overlay Node and offers the *route* method and routing state methods like *replicaSet* or *range*. The Application is a hotspot containing the methods *deliver*, *forward* and *update* that will be invoked by the overlay layer accordingly on reception of messages. As we can observe, Application provides upcall messages invoked by the Node and EndPoint provides downcalls to access Node's routing state services.

In order to run an application (overlay service) in PlanetSim three configuration files are required: the simulator properties, the overlay properties, and the simulation properties.

To simulate an overlay we need to specify in those files a concrete Node (ChordNode) defining the overlay protocol, a concrete IdFactory (CircularId-Factory) and a specific Network (SimpleNetwork).

Each node includes a configuration file specifying different configuration parameters. For example, ChordNode file can define the number of bits in the identifier, stabilization period or other related parameters. Each Network can also be properly tuned defining its own parameters.

Finally, when a developer prepares an overlay simulation, he must define in a configuration file (overlay) several parameters like: Node Type (Chord, Symphony), Network Type, event file, log file, and others.

Configuration information is essential to accurately tune and probe new overlays or services, and to validate and compare existing results. The key concept here is that each hotspot includes its own configuration information file, and the final execution weaves the different components that create the running overlay testbed.

Overlay Layer

The main conceptual entity and obvious hotspot of this layer is the Node. A node contains incoming and outgoing message queues and methods for sending and receiving/processing messages. Each particular node must then include a complete behaviour or protocol that will dictate which messages to send in specific times and how to react to incoming messages. Furthermore, to create a new overlay, the embedded protocol must define its own messages with specific information to arrange the overlay. This also implies that developers should be able to define their own message types.

At the overlay layer, the communication is bidirectional with both the application and network layers. With the application layer, the Node notifies the Application of received messages (upcalls) and it is invoked by the EndPoint façade in order to route messages or obtain routing state information (downcalls).

Both the EndPoints and the Nodes exchange RouteMessage types. A RouteMessage contains source and target identifiers, as well as information regarding the next hop in the overlay. It is also possible to modify the next hop route at the application or overlay layers in order to alter the routing scheme.

With the network layer, the Node hotspot provides the template methods (*join, leave, fail* and *process*) that determine the life's cycle of every node. The method *process* contains the specific protocol each node maintains to create the overlay. Besides, every node has an incoming and an outgoing message queue; incoming messages are parsed every step in the *process* method, and the *send* method moves messages to the outgoing queue.

To identify nodes in the overlay, the simulator employs three main entities: Id, IdFactory and NodeHandle. Ids are custom number types of 32 to 160 bits that identify nodes in the overall key based routing scheme. The extensible IdFactory permits to define custom Id generation schemes in each overlay. Additionally, NodeHandles contain IP to Id value pairs for each node. Furthermore, a NodeHandle provides a *proximity* method that queries the Network to obtain network proximity information.

As we can see, we have many upcalls that define the Node's life cycle and registering of applications, and only one downcall to query the Network for proximity between Nodes.

Network Layer

This layer is the main actor who dictates the overall life's cycle. The simulator will run n simulation steps or until a specific goal (i.e. the network is stabilized) is achieved. In each step, the simulator moves outgoing messages to incoming queues for all nodes, and then calls the *process* method in each node to react to incoming messages.

Furthermore, the simulator must process events in different steps. Events are node joins, leaves, fails, or lookups. Events can be generated from an event file declaratively, or programmatically using simulator APIs.

The key hotspot is the Network: it represents the underlying network that the Simulator uses to route messages. The Network contains a mapping of Node-Handles to Nodes that permit to correctly dispatch messages from source to destination.

An overlay can run on top of different networks using different underlying protocols. Developers can define their own networks, with specific protocols. The network can also include latency or cost information, or even the topology and arrangement of real nodes in this network. We could then implement a GT-ITM (Georgia Tech Internetwork Topology Models) transit stub topology in a network that would add more real information about costs and latencies.

Furthermore, each node can try to calculate its network proximity to other node. This can be defined in a NodeHandle's *proximity* method, transparently invoking the Network's *proximity* method (following FreePastry's interface definition). Developers can then decide in the network which proximity metric to employ (ping, landmarks, etc).

Nevertheless, a simple overlay mostly focused on algorithm verification, probably will be more interested in a very simple Network –without proximity information worsening the simulator performance–. In the current version of PlanetSim, we only provide simple Networks like RingNetwork, or Circular-Network that do not include latency costs. It is however feasible to incorporate Peersim [8] or Brite [5] network information to define more realistic networks.

An ideal case at this point could be the integration of disparate frameworks: overlay frameworks with network simulation frameworks. The Network hotspot and Network factory extension point would theoretically permit to create such integration points. This is to say for example between J-sim and PlanetSim. Nevertheless, a more thorough study must be undertaken to study the feasibility of such integration. A C++ implementation of PlanetSim could also study the interoperability with NS [13] for example.

Another interesting feature of the simulator is to serialize to a file the full state of a simulation. This can be used for example, to stabilize a huge overlay network, serialize it, and later on begin the simulation from that point. This feature is extremely useful for large simulations and saves valuable computing time.

Finally, the Network can be replaced by a Network Wrapper. This wrapper then assumes the tasks of the Simulator, and it routes incoming and outgoing

Node's messages using appropriate TCP or UDP connections on top of a real IP network. It is also responsible for calculating the proximity metric between nodes and to optimize the communication channels, disconnection events and specific timeouts of the underlying IP network. The NetworkWrapper thus allows moving unchanged simulated code to a real Internet testbed like PlanetLab. However, note that Network Wrapper provides different methods than Network, it does replaces completely the simulator in the interaction with nodes. NetworkWrapper does not include *simulate* a method nor inherits or implements any Network class. Also note than we are still working in the NetworkWrapper and much work remains to be done at this point.

3   Validation

In order to validate the PlanetSim framework we have implemented two structured overlays (Chord and Symphony) and several overlay services and applications (Scribe and DHT applications). We believe that our results confirm the generality, accuracy, and performance of our infrastructure.

Chord [11] is a classical structured ring-based topology that assures O(log n) lookup hops with pointers (finger table) to log (n) nodes where n is the number of nodes in the system. Chord's lookup mechanism is robust in the face of node failures and re-joins but it requires a periodic and costly stabilization protocol.

Our implementation of the Chord protocol aims to be close to MIT's Chord specifications and our results coincide with MIT published statistics. We however use a 32-bit address space in this paper for performance reasons –although the simulator can be configured to use a maximum of 160 bits–.

We also implemented the Symphony [12] overlay protocol in order to compare a deterministic approach to routing (Chord) to a probabilistic one (Symphony). Symphony is inspired by Kleinberg's Small World model and constructs a ring topology where each node has few long distance links. Symphony demonstrates that with k = O(1) links per node, it is possible to route lookups with an average latency of $O(1/k \log^2 n)$.

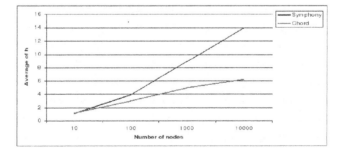

Fig. 3. Chord vs Symphony lookup hops

As we can see in figure 3, both algorithms scale gracefully with the increase in the number of nodes. Obviously, Chord performs better as a result of a bigger routing table and deterministic routing, but Symphony is less communication intensive with a very small maintenance algorithm. Like published results, Chord shows an average $1/2 \log_2(n)$ function and Symphony a $\log_{10}^2(n)$ function.

Furthermore, we have implemented and tested an efficient overlay broadcast algorithm [3]. We obtained the awaited results where all nodes are covered in the broadcast process and that no redundant messages are sent.

As example application, we present here the Scribe [1] application level multicast protocol. Scribe is a large-scale and decentralized event notification system built on top of an overlay layer. The overlay layer, originally a Pastry network [10], is used to maintain topics and subscriptions, and to build efficient multicast trees. Scribe's randomized placement of topics and multicast roots balances the load among participating nodes.

Simulation results indicate that Scribe scales well. It efficiently supports a large number of nodes, topics, and a wide range of subscribers per topic. Hence, Scribe can concurrently support applications with widely different characteristics. Results in our simulator also show that it balances the load among participating nodes, while achieving acceptable delay and link stress. Besides, implementing Scribe was straightforward by leveraging original FreePastry code based on the common API. Our layered approach also permits to test the Scribe algorithm in different overlays like Chord or Symphony. We do not show here graphical results due to lack of space.

3.1   Performance

One of the main goals of the PlanetSim framework is to achieve good performance for a high number of nodes. Due to the election of the Java language, we have been forced to spend a lot of resources in profiling and optimizing the simulator code. Besides, we have been faced with a constant compromise between clean designs and performing code.

Examples of such optimizations in our code are an efficient MessagePool that reuses messages, a custom Id class avoiding the Java's BigInteger, and static Singletons and Factories for loading Node, Message and Application types.

We run our experiments on 3 GHz (1 Gb RAM) Pentium 4 machines running Linux 2.4.24. We measured the time and steps required to stabilize Symphony

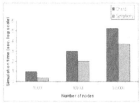

Nodes	Overlay	Steps	Time (sec)
1000	Chord	2515	8.5964
	Symphony	2149	2.164
10000	Chord	20504	1001.0365
	Symphony	20153	98.28
100000	Chord	203024	167962.848
	Symphony	200279	5037.671

Fig. 4. Chord vs Symphony stabilization time

and Chord networks of different sizes. As we can see in Figure 4, Symphony performs much better than Chord in simulation time.

Chord needs around 8 seconds to stabilize a 1000 nodes network, 16 minutes for 1000 nodes and 46 hours for 100000 nodes. Symphony requires 2 seconds for 1000 nodes, 98 seconds for 10000 nodes, and 1.3 hours for 100000 nodes. Note that the bars are shown in a base 10 logarithmic scale to improve visualization. These results clearly show that the overhead imposed by the Chord stabilization protocol is quite big compared to Symphony's maintenance algorithms.

We believe that these numbers demonstrate the feasibility of using Planet-Sim for large overlays. As future work, the distributed version of the simulator can even permit simulation of much higher number of nodes in an overlay network.

4   Related Work

First of all, we distinguish between network simulators and overlay simulators. The formers provide packet-level simulation of network protocols (TCP, UDP, IP, etc) over realistic Internet topologies. However, congestion-aware simulation including packet-loss and queuing delays is costly, leading to inappropriate scaling numbers for big overlays. Overlay simulators are usually more interested in evaluating overlay algorithms and its routing behaviour without even taking into account the underlying network layer. The excessive overhead and complexity of network simulators thus imposes an unnecessary burden to overlay evaluators and researchers.

For example, the NS [13] network simulator provides a standard framework for accurate simulation of network protocols. NS is appropriate to simulate networks in the link, switching and transport layer but it is not aimed for application level overlays. Besides, for smaller scale scenarios NS performs gracefully, but for overlays over a hundred nodes in size suffers considerable scaling problems. Another example is the J-Sim [14] network simulation framework that follows a component oriented approach. Similar to ns-2, J-Sim is a dual-language simulation environment in which classes are written in Java (for ns-2, in C++) and "glued" together using Tcl/Java. Being easier to use than Ns-2, J-Sim also lacks enough scalability and performance for big overlays.

Other network simulators like SFFNET and OMNET++ have also been successfully used for peer to peer applications. Particularly, OMNET++ provides a rich environment that enables both packet-level simulations and high-level overlay protocols. Nevertheless, all these network simulators are mainly aimed for packet-level protocols, and impose additional complexity to the user learning curve.

In the end, many research groups have created their own overlay simulators, sacrificing accuracy for scale. Examples of these include p-sim, FreePasty, Sim-Pastry, 3LS, PLP2P, and SimP^2. In the field of structured overlays, one of the pioneers is MIT's pspsim. This simulator currently supports many protocols, including Chord, Koorde, Kelips, Tapestry, and Kademlia. p2psim is protocol extensible, and it is pretty straightforward to develop new protocols by simply implementing the join() and lookup() low-level methods. Despite its protocol independence, p2psim provides no interface in order to simulate higher level applications. Besides, from the software engineering perspective, this simulator is poorly documented and difficult to extend for different purposes.

FreePastry [10], the Java open-source implementation of the Pastry structured P2P protocol includes as well, the possibility to simulate applications on top of this overlay network. As in PlanetSim, FreePastry provides a Common API [2] to the applications built on top of it, thus making it very easy for developers to create and simulate complex distributed applications. Protocol specific details remain hidden from the application-level point of view. However, FreePastry is highly tied to the Pastry protocol, and it does not permit simulation of its applications on top of other structured P2P protocols.

Another interesting approach is the one followed by MACEDON [9]. Macedon provides an infrastructure to ease development, evaluation, and iterative design of overlay algorithms. Applications are built using a C-like scripting language, and code is automatically generated for TCP/IP and ns [13]. Moreover, it follows a standard API which does not tie applications to any specific overlay network protocol. Large-scale emulation and evaluation tools are at the developer's disposal as well. Macedon is not limited to structured P2P networks, and it includes an impressive variety of protocols and applications such as AMMO, Bullet, Chord, NICE, Overcast, Pastry, Scribe, and SplitStream. Furthermore, MACEDON simplifies development of new overlays using a finite state machine (FSM) model for defining overlay protocols.

MACEDON is a very nice tool for overlay simulation but it follows a completely different approach than PlanetSim. MACEDON is mainly related to Domain-specific languages (DSLs) that generate functional code from domain specific representations. Besides, MACEDON currently supports only two types of overlays: distributed hash tables and application level multicast. We have created a layered and modular framework that is extensible at all levels, and that can even be integrated with other frameworks. DSLs like MACEDON are not designed to be extensible but instead to provide all possible functionalities and vocabularies in the domain language.

5   Conclusions and Future Work

We have presented the PlanetSim overlay simulation/experimentation framework that facilitates design and implementation of both overlay algorithms and overlay distributed services. PlanetSim has been carefully designed to provide clean hotspots that make the framework extensible at all levels. Extensibility and external integration is a main goal of our framework because we believe that it is quite difficult to offer all the services that overlay researchers require.

Furthermore, our adoption of FreePastry's object oriented implementation of the Common API for structured overlays is a key aspect to ease the transition from simulation code to network code and vice versa. Unlike other simulators, we clearly distinguish between overlay algorithms (key based routing), and the applications and services built on top of them. Another side benefit of this design decision is that we can easily leverage FreePastry application code like Scribe and others.

We believe that PlanetSim can be used in peer to peer research settings but also as an educational tool to better understand overlay algorithms and services. Besides, the Network Wrapper code permit users to easily test their designs over the Internet using existing infrastructures like PlanetLab.

Of course, and like many other frameworks, PlanetSim can fail to attract users and developers in the research and educational settings. There is now a big inertia in the research arena towards custom-made simulators that solve particular problems. This is sad because it avoids clear comparisons in a unified platform. Besides, the framework cannot acquire critical mass without external contributors delivering new algorithms and services.

We however plan to extend the framework to incorporate new services and algorithms in the short term. We outline an improved overlay visualization engine for overlay networks and services, and a distributed version of the simulator enabling simulation of huge number of nodes (0,5M to 1M). PlanetSim is an open source project that is being actively used in our University for research and educational purposes. We welcome future collaborations or extensions to the project. PlanetSim is available with full source code and GPL license in http://ants.etse.urv.es/planet.

Acknowledgements

This work has been partially funded by the Spanish Ministry of Science and Technology through project TIC-2003-09288-C02-00.

References

1. Castro, M., Druschel, P., et al, "Scalable Application-level Anycast for Highly Dynamic Groups", *Proc. of NGC'03,* September 2003.
2. Dabek, F., Zhao, B.Y., Druschel, P., Kubiatowicz, J., and Stoica I., "Towards a Common API for Structured Peer-to-Peer Overlays", 2nd *International Workshop on Peer-to-Peer Systems, IPTPS'03,* Berkeley, CA, February 2003.
3. El-Ansary, S.; Alima, L.O.; Brand, P.; et al. "Efficient Broadcast in Structured P2P Networks", 2nd *International Workshop on Peer-to-Peer Systems, IPTPS'03,* Berkeley, CA, February 2003.
4. Gummadi, K., Saroiu, S., et al., "King: Estimating latency between arbitrary Internet end hosts", *Proceedings of the 2002 SIGCOMM Internet Measurement Workshop.* Marseille, France, November 2002.
5. Medina, A., Lakhina, A., Matta, I., et al. "BRITE: An Approach to Universal Topology Generation", *Proceedings of the International Workshop on Modeling, Analysis and Simulation of Computer and Telecommunications Systems (MASCOTS 2001).* Cincinnati, Ohio, August 2001.

6. Pairot, C., García, P., Gómez Skarmeta, A.F., "DERMI: A Decentralized Peer-to-Peer Event-Based Object Middleware", *Proceedings of ICDCS'04*, Tokyo, Japan, pp. 236-243.
7. Pairot, C., García, P., Gómez Skarmeta, A.F., "Dermi: A New Distributed Hash Table-based Middleware Framework", *IEEE Internet Computing*, Vol. 8, No. 3, May/June 2004, pp. 74 – 84.
8. PeerSim Peer-to-Peer Simulator. http://peersim.sourceforge.net/
9. Rodriguez, A., Killian, C., Bhat, S., et al., "MACEDON: Methodology for Automatically Creating, Evaluating, and Designing Overlay Networks", *Proceedings of the USENIX/ACM Symposium on Networked Systems Design and Implementation (NSDI 2004)*, March 2004.
10. Rowstron, A., and Druschel, P., "Pastry: Scalable, decentralized object location and routing for large-scale peer-to-peer systems", *IFIP/ACM International Conference on Distributed Systems Platforms (Middleware)*, pp. 329-350, November 2001.
11. Stoica, I., Morris, D., Karger, D., et al. "Chord: A Scalable Peer-to-peer- Lookup Service for Internet Applications", *Proceedings of the ACM SIGCOMM 2001*, San Diego, CA, August 2001, pp. 149-160.
12. Singh, G.M., Bawa, M., Raghavan, P. "Symphony: Distributed Hashing in a Small World". *Proceedings of USITS'03*, Seattle, WA.
13. The Network Simulator – ns – 2. http://www.isi.edu/nsnam/ns/
14. J-Sim. http://www.j-sim.org/

Towards the Development of
Ubiquitous Middleware Product Lines

Sven Apel and Klemens Böhm

Department of Computer Science,
Otto-von-Guericke-University Magdeburg
{apel, kboehm}@iti.cs.uni-magdeburg.de

Abstract. Ubiquitous computing is a challenge for the design of middleware. The reasons are resource constraints, mobility, heterogeneity, etc., just to name a few. We argue that such middleware has to be tailored to the application scenario as well as to the target platform. Such tailor-made middleware has to be be built from minimal fine-grained components, and the system structure must be highly configurable, as we will explain. We propose to use the well-known mixin layer approach to build the flexible lightweight middleware envisioned. We show that the thoughtful use of mixin layers is promising in this specific domain and allows to deal with issues such as device heterogeneity and resource constraints. To do so, we present the design and implementation of a middleware and three configurations derived from it. Our evaluation criteria are the number of supported features and the memory footprint. The middleware configurations derived perform well in these respects.

1   Introduction

Ubiquitous computing [26] is becoming reality. Everyone is connected everywhere and at any time, to consume and provide information. Computers become more and more transparent [25]. Middleware plays a key role to let this vision become true. It supports the application programmer who builds distributed applications and services, e.g., for electronic health care or intelligent buildings (more examples in [26, 25]). Such middleware must deal with the various characteristics of ubiquitous computing scenarios, e.g., resource-constrained devices, heterogeneity, mobility, bandwidth fluctuations, connection interruptions. Conventional middleware is not sufficient in these respects. It targets at static distributed systems with fixed hosts where resources are not tightly constrained.

This article attempts to validate the following hypothesis: the combination of software engineering and distributed computing principles will support the development of advanced ubiquitous applications, middleware services etc. well. To do so, we focus on the resource constraints of partly mobile ubiquitous devices, e.g. cell phones, wearable microchips, smart cards, autonomous robots,

T. Gschwind and C. Mascolo (Eds.): SEM 2004, LNCS 3437, pp. 137–153, 2005.
© Springer-Verlag Berlin Heidelberg 2005

sensors, actuators, etc., and their heterogeneity in terms of hardware (e.g. processor, memory, communication media) and software (e.g. operating system, network protocol). We present a flexible middleware which one can easily port to different hardware and software. It provides a device-independent interface to applications. As the design and implementation method, we propose the mixin layer approach. Mixin layers are known as one method for the implementation of product-line architectures (PLA) [22, 1]. Middleware for ubiquitous computing should benefit from the PLA concept as well, in terms of configurability, reusability and extensibility. By deploying the mixin concept, we want to verify if this is indeed the case. More generally, we wonder if implementation of general middleware concepts in mixin layers is feasible. The answer is not obvious because some concepts are known as crosscutting concerns, or are formulated in an abstract, 'high-level' manner. Further, are mixin layers a good implementation method for middleware that one can easily port to other devices? To address these issues, we have designed and implemented a middleware PLA[1] presented here. We then describe three middleware configurations which are tailored[2] to fit three specific ubiquitous application scenarios. We do so to show that our approach can lead to flexible lightweight middleware for ubiquitous computing. The derivation of these configurations consists of only a few steps. This is not straightforward – only the thoughtful use of mixins and the careful deployment to the middleware domain results in such ease. If one designs the layers carefully such that there are only few fine-grained device-specific layers, portability is much easier. Further, we investigate the relationship between the memory footprints of the configurations and the number of features integrated: We observe that few features result in a small footprint. As a result, configurability of middleware does not necessarily collide with small footprint. This is an important finding because other approaches cannot provide such a degree of configurability in combination with small footprint, as Section 6 will explain. Finally, we say why these results can be generalized to other middleware.

This article is structured as follows: Section 2 introduces an ubiquitous computing application scenario and points to problems regarding middleware and applications. Section 3 reviews the software engineering methods deployed here. Section 4 presents our middleware, built according to the mixin layer approach. We then discuss implementation results and experiences concerning the configuration. Section 6 reviews related work. Finally, we conclude.

2   A Ubiquitous Computing Application Scenario

This section sketches an application scenario for ubiquitous computing. Based on this, we list challenges at the middleware and the application level. We point to the weaknesses of conventional middleware approaches.

---

[1] In the remaining article, 'middleware' and 'middleware PLA' are synonyms.

[2] We refer to tailoring as configuration process with special focus on memory footprint. To do so, unneeded functionality is removed consequently.

2.1   Application Scenario

With ubiquitous computing, computers become an even more integral part of everyday life. They act behind the scenes, transparently for humans. The scenario presented, in parts borrowed from [25], includes conventional aspects as well as more visionary ones. Starting point is a room with many common mobile and ubiquitous devices, e.g., PDA and Smartphones. They are general-purpose devices which include various communication media, e.g., WLAN, Bluetooth, IR, etc. If a person enters the room, the PDA can contact the embedded devices available. For instance, the PDA can communicate with the light switch to raise or dim the light. To facilitate this, the dimmer offers an appropriate service interface. A primitive dimmer only provides a basic service to dim or light up. A more complex dimmer can provide additional information about the minimum and maximum dim level or provide a timeout mechanism to adjust the light automatically. A 'more ubiquitous' scenario is that the light dimmer adjusts itself by communicating with the PDA behind the scenes. A person enters the room, and the light adjusts itself, using personal information from the PDA. Other devices in the room act more autonomously, e.g., a climate-control unit which adjusts the air condition to the current climate, to the current time of day and the current season as well as to the presence of a person. Further, think of a digital paper scrap which people use to take notes. Notes are then stored on a central notes server. A more common device is a home-entertainment system, including a music box, a dvd recorder and a TV set. It apparently provides a lot of controllable functionality and interacts with itself and the PDA extensively. For instance, it provides information on the TV program. This information can control the programming of the dvd recorder. In a more ubiquitous setting, the dvd recorder reacts to program changes or records telecasts which match a profile autonomously. The next step is that the dvd recorder in cooperation with the TV set learns the customs of persons and generates personal profiles itself.

2.2   Problems Occurring

In the scenario introduced, certain problems occur, which we describe next. Common middleware cannot deal with these problems, as we will explain.

Ubiquitous computing middleware must run on the various devices. Frequently, devices are embedded systems. They are developed for a special purpose, e.g., to control the light, and have a low resource consumption. Cost-effective thinking requires this, in particular if the number of these devices is huge. Next to these embedded special-purpose devices, general-purpose devices (PDA, Desktop PC, Server) are part of ubiquitous-computing scenarios. These devices are not resource-constrained and provide much more functionality. In our scenario, the PDA communicates with other devices, displays information (e.g., air-condition level) and processes it (e.g., television-program based programming of the dvd recorder). The spectrum of resources consumed is extremely broad, as well as the one of functionality provided.

Another challenge is to overcome the heterogeneity of devices. They use different hardware and software. The middleware must bridge them and must provide a well-defined device-independent interface to the application programmer. Hence, the middleware consists of device-specific and device-independent parts. Naturally, the device-independent part must be as large as possible (in relative terms) to maximize reusability.

Our middleware is supposed to hide these specifics, in order to support the development of ubiquitous applications. Conventional middleware approaches, e.g., CORBA, DCOM, Java-RMI, are not suitable for our scenario. They are too heavyweight and cannot be customized to application requirements. It would be quite impossible to port them to other devices or platforms and to get them to work in resource-constrained environments. The monolithic system structure prevents the reuse of logical device-independent functionality. However, research effort has tried to improve standard CORBA to fit ubiquitous computing. It has been shown that refactorization of CORBA implementations yields higher configurability [27]. However, our expectation in the long run is that customizability of carefully designed middleware product-lines is even higher. This is why we think that the issue merits attention. Finally, dynamic adaptation [20, 12] does not solve the problem in our specific context either, as Section 6 will explain.

All this motivates the design of a ubiquitous-computing middleware with the following features:

– minimal memory footprint and lightweight implementation, to save resources,
– run on heterogenous hardware and software,
– provide uniform device-independent application interface,
– customizability, reusability, and extensibility.

3   Relevant Software Engineering Issues

This section presents our solution to the problems discussed in Section 2. It uses the mixin layer approach. This is because this approach is known to facilitate configurable and reusable software, e.g., product-line architectures [22]. To ease understanding, we provide some background information on this software engineering method. The so-called collaboration-based design is a feasible design method to serve as a basis for mixin layer implementations. We briefly review it here as well. Finally, we outline the expected benefits of these approaches for ubiquitous computing, before looking at our realization in the next section.

3.1   Collaboration-Based Design

Parnas [19] introduced collaboration-based design first. The idea is to build software incrementally, using minimal building blocks and starting from a minimal base. Exchanging, adding and removing such building blocks, also called layers, yields reusability, extensibility, and customizability. Batory et al. have mapped this concept to the object-oriented world [1, 22]. They observe that a new software feature often extends or modifies numerous existing classes. Based on this observation, they perceive features as collaborations of class/object fragments, also referred to as roles. Figure 1 collaborations. Classes are arranged vertically $(c_1 - c_3)$. Collaborations are arranged horizontally and span several classes $(f_1 - f_3)$. Several features of a software system result in a stack of collaborations. In our context, examples of features are 'remote procedure calls' or 'remote object invocation'. Collabo-

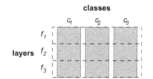

Fig. 1. Stack of collaborations

rations with the same interfaces are easily exchangeable. They are an instance of large-scale components [1]. A collaboration of objects implements a feature and is part of a layered stack.[3]

3.2 Mixin Layers

The mixin layer approach allows to implement collaboration-based designs. The mixin layer approach is based on the GenVoca component model [1] to support large-scale components, easy exchangeability, and syntactic consistency checking. These characteristics allow for the development of configurable and reusable software. Different languages can be used to implement mixin layers: C++ [23], AHEAD ToolSuite [2], Java Layers [7], Sather [17]. In the code snippets that follow we use the C++ notation.

Mixins are types whose super-types are specified parametrically [5]. Mixins facilitate the same sub-type specialization to be applied to different (super-)-types. In other words, they allow the specialization of multiple classes with a single reusable class. For example, think of the three unrelated classes `Buffer`, `Message`, `Printer`. Suppose that one wants to add a locking feature that restricts access to these objects. With conventional object oriented approaches, one must add a different sub-type to each class, e.g., `LockableBuffer`, `LockableMessage`, `LockablePrinter`. Each of these types adds the methods `lock()` and `unlock()`. With mixins in turn, a single mixin `Lockable` extends all of those super-classes (see Figure 2). Methods `lock()` and `unlock()` are defined only once. Instantiation of mixins generates new class hierarchies. For instance, the instantiation `Lockable<Buffer> lb;` generates the class hierarchy depicted in Figure 3.

```
1  template <class BaseType>
2  class Lockable : public BaseType {
3      bool m_locked;
4      void lock() {m_locked = true;}
5      void unlock() {m_locked = false;} }
```

Fig. 2. A simple mixin class for synchronization support.

Fig. 3. A lockable buffer

---

[3] We use the terms feature or layer as synonym for collaboration.

M ixin layers are mixins containing nested types which can be mixins them-selves [22]. Mixin layers are used to coordinate changes and extensions to classes that collaborate. The mixin layer approach allows to add a new feature/layer in form of a set of sub-classes to a software system using one implementa-tion unit. A single mixin layer is able to implement a feature that crosscuts multiple classes. Mixin layers are equivalent to collaborations, whereas nested mixins are equivalent to object roles. Consider the following example: A pro-gram library provides a buffer to store data elements and an iterator to tra-verse the data elements. A possible refinement is to store and manage arrays of data elements. Applying this new feature requires modifications of both buffer and iterator. Figure 4 depicts the two mixin-based feature implementations `BufferLayer` (Lines 1–4) and `ArrayBufferLayer` (Lines 5–8). The BufferLayer simply consists of a `Buffer` class and an `Iterator` class. `ArrayBufferLayer` is a mixin layer, which expects a template parameter (`BaseType`). Line 10 con-tains the instantiation of `ArrayBufferLayer` using `BufferLayer` as super-type. This instantiation connects both layers and their corresponding nested types (`Buffer`, `Iterator`) using inheritance (Lines 5–7). It refines the basic buffer abstraction with the array feature. This feature crosscuts the classes `Buffer` and `Iterator`. The 'Array' feature is encapsulated in a single implementa-tion unit. This eases the composition of mixin layers and therefore the con-figuration of the target software. To see this, think of ten further buffer fea-tures, e.g. locking, synchronization, complex data types. Composing the buffer implementation using these mixin layers requires only one instruction, e.g., `Lockable<Sync<...<ArrayBufferLayer<BufferLayer>>...>>buf;`. This exam-ple illustrates the ease of configuration of mixin layer-based implementations. (more examples in [1, 22, 2])

```
1   class BufferLayer {
2       class Buffer {};   // store simple data types
3       class Iterator {}; // traverses element-wise
4   };
5   template <class BaseType> class ArrayBufferLayer : public BaseType  {
6       class Buffer : BaseType::Buffer {/* stores arrays of elements */}
7       class Iterator : BaseType::Iterator {/* iterates array-wise */}
8   }
9   ...
10  ArrayBuffer<Buffer> abuf;
```

Fig. 4. A base and a mixin layer: the buffer abstraction and array management feature

3.3   Benefits for Ubiquitous Computing

Mixin layers offer several benefits for the development of middleware for ubiqui-tous computing. As mentioned before, this article focuses on resource constraints and heterogeneity.

Resource Constraints. Mixin layers offer modularity and flexibility and thus seem to be ideal candidates for the design and implementation of tailored software for ubiquitous computing. To accomplish this, the system components (the mixin layers) must be fine-grained. Middleware must be customized to the specific hardware and to the requirements of the application, e.g., performance.

Heterogeneity. Another issue is the heterogeneity of the devices involved. The objective of our middleware (as well as of other middleware) is to bridge this heterogeneity and to provide components which can work with different hardware, operating systems and network protocols. How can mixin layers help in this respect? An interesting feature of mixin layers in the middleware domain, for heterogeneous environments, is decomposition of middleware functionality into device-specific and device-independent components. The goal is to minimize the number of device-specific components. This leads to middleware which is easier to port to new platforms. Summing up, the thoughtful use of mixin layers seems to be promising to deal with heterogeneity in ubiquitous computing.

In summary, mixin layers might help to address the following issues in ubiquitous computing where common middleware solutions are not sufficient:

– resource constraints (step-wise refinements, minimal exchangeable layers)
– heterogeneity (composition of device-specific and device-independent layers)
– lack of customizability (mixin layer as large-scale components, separation of crosscutting concerns)

Admittedly, the mixin layer approach also has some disadvantages: It is not always practical to implement a feature as a single mixin layer. The implementation units of such features are often spread over several other feature implementations. Mixin layers only allow to refine related classes, namely those included in the stack of basic layers. Related approaches like aspect-oriented programming (AOP) [13] and multi-dimensional separation of concerns (MDSC) [18] can refine unrelated classes as well, using one implementation unit. AOP and MDSC support refinements on statement and expression level as well as a regular-expression based mechanism to specify code positions where refinements are applied (join points). On the other hand, they lack a component model, e.g., imported and exported interfaces or symmetric components. Hence, it is difficult to build configurable product-lines. The mixin approach in turn is sufficient for building the base functionality of our middleware, as we will explain in Section 4. In general the approaches mentioned are equivalent with regard to modularization of crosscutting concerns and customizability [2]. In the long run, we think that only a combination of these will lead to success, if more complex functionality is added, e.g., fault-tolerance or security. Each feature will be implemented using the appropriate method. However, these issues are beyond the scope of this paper. This paper in turn investigates the benefits and limits of mixin layers to build middleware product-lines.

4   Middleware Design

This section presents the design and implementation of a flexible lightweight middleware for ubiquitous computing, based on collaborations and mixin layers. To assess the benefits of these methods, the implementation of the following functionality should suffice: The middleware provides standard remote object invocation (ROI). Well-known subconcepts of ROI, e.g., marshaling, are part of the implementation, but are not discussed here. Moreover, we leave ubiquitous-computing specific features, e.g., server-initiated computation. Their implementation would not provide significant further insight (we argue). Our concern is the deployment of collaborations and mixin layers for ubiquitous middleware. Arguably, implementation of middleware functionality in mixin layers is not obvious. In addition, a solution must cope with devices that are resource-constrained and with heterogeneous environments. Our design described next, i.e., the specific arrangement of collaborations or the specific choice of the roles, is only one possible solution (but nevertheless appropriate, as we will show).

The result of collaboration-based design and of the mixin layer approach is a set of components. They can be composed to various middleware platforms. Subsequently, we refer to these platforms as configurations. When designing our middleware, we have found it natural to distinguish between components with client-side functionality and those with server-side functionality. The feature of managing and registering remote objects is server-side, but only the client sends requests to the server, to give some examples. Moreover, we identified some features used by client and server. This motivates the following terminology: general layers, client layers and server layers.

Several figures depict the collaboration/layer stack and the roles included. The rounded boxes represent roles (the dashed boxes mark derived roles) and the grey boxes in the background represent the collaborations. We organized the stack of layers in bottom-up order. We use UML-like arrows to represent relations between object roles (inheritance, composition, etc.). Explaining all roles in detail is beyond the scope of this article and is actually not necessary for understanding. We focus on the overall structure, and we say how to design collaborations and to implement mixin layers for ubiquitous middleware.

4.1   General Middleware Layers

The general layers provide basic functionality for both client side and server side. Figure 5 depicts the stack of general layers. The abstraction of basic messages form the bottom layer of the stack. These messages are transferred between client and server. A marshaling mechanism serializes messages; connections are based on sockets. Messages may have parameters that are typed. The parameters are used in higher layers as function arguments or to identify operations and instances on clients and servers. Our approach allows to decide at compile-time which data types are supported. Avoiding types that are not needed reduces the memory consumption. Other variation points, again well known, are the connection type (UDP or TCP), the direction of communication (unidirectional or bidi-

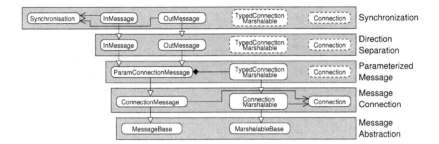

Fig. 5. The stack of general middleware layers

rectional) and the synchronization strategy (synchronous or asynchronous). The variation points as well as the different data types supported are implemented as different layer variants to enhance configurability. For instance, two different layers exist for the synchronization feature (synchronous and asynchronous). At configuration time, the programmer has to choose one.

4.2   Client-Side Layers

Based on the general layers, the client layers facilitate uni- and bidirectional messaging (see Figure 6). We use these messaging functions to implement remote function and class-function calls and remote object invocation. We use parameterized messages to deliver the identifications of functions, classes, objects and their arguments. Response messages deliver results. Next to function calls, we provide operations for creating and deleting objects.

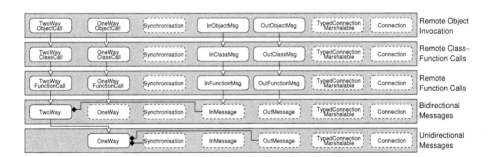

Fig. 6. The stack of client-side layers

4.3   Server-Side Layers

Figure 7 shows the server-side layers, but does not show all roles, due to space limitations. The server layers are shown as light grey boxes, the client layers as dark grey boxes. Client and server layers that correspond to each other are often required in combination, e.g., remote function calls and remote functions.

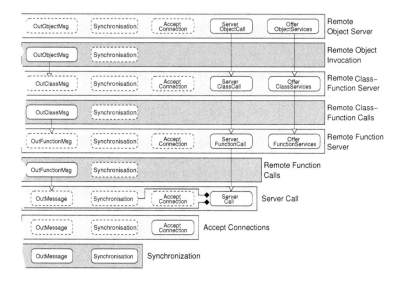

Fig. 7. The stack of server-side layers

This interleaving does not mean that a server implementation always requires the client layers and vice versa. If a configuration does not need certain client layers, one has to remove them during the configuration process (cf. Section 5). Consider the light dimmer from Section 2. It only needs to obtain incoming function calls, but does not need to issue remote function calls.

The basic server layers listen for client requests and accept connections. We have implemented a single-threaded and a multi-threaded variant. Our middleware deserializes incoming messages. Depending on the connection type chosen, the incoming messages are transferred using byte streams or datagrams. Based on these mechanisms, the server side provides a remote function server, a remote class-function server, and a remote object server. The programmer can use several functions for registering and managing remote functions, classes and objects. A client can specify the desired function or object as well as the desired operation (create, delete, invoke) using parameterized messages.

4.4   Implementation

In order to verify our hypotheses, we have implemented the middleware design presented so far in full (in C++). To do so, we have used the template mechanism, nested classes and parameter-based inheritance, as described in Section 3. To save implementation work, we use the gSoap communication library [10]. While designing and implementing the system, we have kept in mind that the communication library should be easily exchangeable, e.g., with a lightweight binary protocol. We have used the low-level functions only to (un-)marshal and to send or receive SOAP [4] messages. We have not used remote-function-call mechanisms or other high-level functions. gSoap is the only device-dependent part of our middleware. Because space is limited, we cannot discuss all issues at

```
1  template <class BaseLayer> class ROILayer : public BaseLayer {
2         class OutObjectMessage : BaseLayer::OutClassMessage {};
3         class InObjectMessage : BaseLayer::InClassMessage {};
4         class OneWayCall : BaseLayer::OneWayCall {};
5         class TwoWayCall : BaseLayer::TwoWayCall {}; };
```

Fig. 8. The Remote Object Invocation Mixin Layer

code level. Instead we refer to Figure 8. It depicts the interface of one mixin layer, the roi layer in C++. The layer has four nested classes (Lines 2–3) which represent the corresponding roles (cf. Figure 8). Each nested class inherits from the corresponding classes of the base layer, represented by `BaseLayer`. Beyond the short example the implementation examples from Section 3 and the discussion of design issues there should shed light on our implementation.

5   Results

This section discusses experiences from the implementation, together with three configurations: a sensor-actuator-system, a web service/client and a roi client/-service. They are useful for the scenario described in Section 2.

5.1   Configuration

Instantiation (combination) of the mixin layers configures new middleware platforms (see Section 3). A G enV oca grammar describes the possible configurations [1] (not shown here for lack of space). Using this grammar, we have calculated the number of configurations possible by adding the numbers of all combinations of layers of our middleware permitted: $192 * (2^n - 1)$ different server configurations, where n is the number of data types supported, and $96 * (2^n - 1)$ client configurations. As a result, the degree of configurability is high. This is required for tailoring the middleware to work in ubiquitous computing scenarios.

To convey the ease of the configuration procedure and the flexibility of the implementation, we now describe the three configurations we have derived.

Sensor-Actuator M iddleware. A sensor-actuator middleware is useful for ubiquitous devices like the our light dimmer, which only needs a small subset of the functionality. For communication between sensors and actuators, we chose asynchronous unidirectional remote procedure calls. In our scenario, a light sensor only needs the client features. We add the server-side features only to the actuators (a light dimmer), which receive messages. Figure 9(a) depicts the features chosen. In our example application, we have used the sensor to send a measurement to the actuator. Both devices display status information.

Remote-O bject-Invocation M iddleware. Our configuration of a remote-object-invocation (roi) middleware consists of nearly all layers implemented. It is used for ubiquitous devices which provide a rich set of functionality and provide many services. In our scenario, the home entertainment system runs a fully functional object server. Next to remote object invocations, remote function calls and remote class-function calls are also available. We have chosen synchronous communication. Figure 9(b) depicts the layers of the client and of the server. To complete the proof-of-concept implementation, we have implemented a simple service on top of the roi-middleware.

Web-Service Middleware. The web-service (ws) middleware supports the implementation of web services. This configuration is useful to access ubiquitous devices from the internet using SOAP [4]. Similarly, ubiquitous information systems like a digital newspaper can collect information from the Web and display it. The web-service middleware provides the following functionality: SOAP-conformant remote function calls as well as synchronous and asynchronous communication. When using gSoap, creating SOAP messages that conform to the standard is easy. Our web-service middleware is useful to implement all types of web-services and corresponding clients. Our example server can receive SOAP messages and can reply to every common SOAP client with the same interface. The analogous is true for our client as well. It can connect to any compatible web service. Figure 9(c) depicts the layers of the client and the server.

5.2 Discussion

Section 5.1 has shown that a broad range of configurations is possible. Moreover, Sections 3 and 5.1 have discussed the easy composition of layers to create a configuration. Some configurations may differ only in a few features. But the three examples show the broadness of the application scenarios supported. Let us now have a closer look at the resulting configurations. Figure 10 shows the memory footprint and the number of features supported, with a distinction between client-side and server-side. The memory footprint is the size of the binary code. We have obtained it using the linux `size` command. We have left aside the code of the underlying communication protocol library. The ws client is bigger than the roi client because it has to process and transfer additional web-service-specific information like namespaces, etc. The binary code size of clients ranges from 4423 to 6631 bytes and the one of the servers from 9310 to 32738 bytes. The server-side results show that the memory footprint of a minimal system configuration (the actuator) is only 28% of the one of the maximal system configuration (the roi server). At the client side, the minimal configuration is about 65%. The binary code size of the web service lies between them. This is because it has more features than the sensor-actuator middleware and much less features than the roi service. As a result, configuring middleware that does not waste resources is easy, using the mixin layer approach. As our implementation has shown, decomposition of middleware functionality into fine-grained components is possible (cf. Figure 9). With less features, the code size and the amount of data and consequently the binary code size decreases significantly (see Figure 10). So it is in the hand of the application programmer to tailor the middleware and fit it to the application requirements and target platform. Configurability and tailoring make it possible to build middleware for embedded ubiquitous devices.

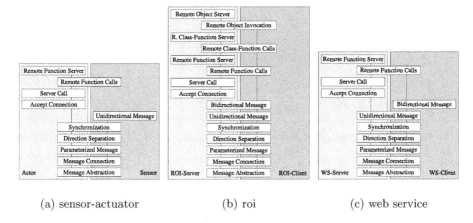

(a) sensor-actuator   (b) roi   (c) web service

Fig. 9. Three different middleware configurations

To deal with hardware and software heterogeneity, we differentiate between device-specific and device-independent layers. Only the layers which communicate directly with the hardware or the underlying software (operating system, protocol stack) are device-specific.

The reader should note that a performance analysis is not meaningful in the current context, for various reasons: (1) We have used a SOAP-based communication library. The overhead for parsing and generating the XML/SOAP messages would falsify performance numbers. (2) A direct comparesion to other middleware solutions, e.g. [11, 24, 16], is not meaningful, because the set of features implemented (communication protocol, marshaling strategy, data types supported, etc.) is different. – The design of mixin layers that results in configurations both with small footprint and good performance is an interesting issue, but is beyond the scope of this article (obviously, the problem is more difficult).

Finally, our results generalize to other middleware as well, not only in the ubiquitous computing domain. For example, one can build middleware for mobile computing using more large-scale components, to reduce the maintenance

configuration	size [byte]	features
sensor	4420	6
actor	9406	9
roi-client	6302	10
roi-server	32834	15
ws-client	6727	7
ws-server	11707	10

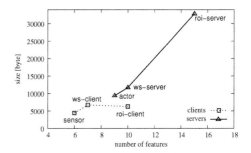

Fig. 10. Memory footprint and number of features of three configurations

overhead. Reflective architectures like [20] or [12] could be implemented using mixin layers and could work together with current base level components. However, reconciliation of the objectives performance, small memory footprint, as well as configurability, reusability and extensibility is an open issue.

6   Related Work

Conventional middleware technology (e.g. CORBA, SOAP, Java-RMI) hides the internal communication. It is designed primarily for fixed hosts with adequate resources and a static network structure. It does not run in non-conventional application scenarios, e.g., embedded systems and ubiquitous computing. Middleware technologies have emerged to meet the requirements of these scenarios, e.g., real-time constraints, reliability, as well as environment-specific issues, e.g., resource constraints, bandwidth fluctuation, connection interrupts, dynamic changes of network topology. However, some research has enhanced CORBA-based middleware to become flexible, customizable and lightweight: OpenCorba [15], OpenORB [3] and dynamicTAO [14] extend CORBA by a reflective architecture. These systems reify important characteristics of the behavior and of the structure of the middleware, such as scheduling strategy and resource management. The application can access and modify this information using a meta-interface. This allows to customize the middleware at runtime. A similar reflective CORBA-independent approach is CARISMA [6]. Its focus is on context-awareness and on policy conflict resolution. We for our part have focused on customizability at compile-time. By doing so, we do not need a reflective architecture which would consume a significant amount of resources (we argue). Furthermore, reflection is simply not needed in all ubiquitous devices and services. (Think of the primitive light dimmer.) On the other hand, mixin-based middleware may serve as a basis for a runtime-adaptable implementation, which combines the advantages of mixin layers and reflection.

UIC [20] and ReMMoC [12] are two examples of middleware with a focus on device heterogeneity. Both assume that different devices use different middleware technologies, e.g., SOAP, CORBA, Java RMI, and provide mechanisms to deal with this heterogeneity. UIC is based on dynamicTAO. It implements a reflective architecture and a minimal core of functionality. If the reflective architecture detects the presence of a remote device, it loads the adequate middleware component. ReMMoC uses a similar approach. While this is a significant contribution for conventional application scenarios, it seems to us that the runtime overhead of reflection may not always be acceptable in ubiquitous devices. Further on, reflection may not be required in some ubiquitous application scenarios.

TAO [21] is another prominent approach to achieve customizability, based on design patterns. We believe that modern component models have a stronger focus on modularization and configurability than design patterns. Moreover, the mixin layer approach supports the development of PLA well [2]. It is the high degree of configurability and tailoring that makes PLA a suitable candidate for the development of ubiquitous computing middleware.

Zhang and Jacobsen have shown how to improve customizability and flexibility of middleware by refactorization [27]. They utilized AOP to remodularize orthogonal, entangled middleware features, e.g., the dynamic programming model or portable interceptors. Colyer and Clement argue that AOP can help to cope with the rising complexity of middleware [8]. They have refactored several middleware crosscutting concerns successfully. They have argued that AOP can scale to size of commercial middleware projects. Our approach towards building a product-line does not focus on refactoring. Rather a carefully planned and designed middleware product-line makes refactoring unnecessary.

[24, 11, 16, 9] focus on middleware for embedded and real-time systems. Their work addresses performance and resource consumption issues. Tailoring and customization of middleware using modern software engineering methods are not discussed. But such methods are key to overcome device heterogeneity, resource constraints and lack of customization functionality.

7   Conclusion and Further Research

Software engineering methods advance the design and implementation of middleware for ubiquitous computing. We have proposed the use of collaboration-based design and mixin layers to build lightweight flexible middleware for this domain, to provide a device-independent interface to applications. We have implemented a set of fine-grained basic components. We have generated three middleware configurations, tailored to specific application requirements. The configuration phase consists of a few steps only. A GenVoca grammar describes the combinations permitted. As a result, tailoring of the middleware has been successful in terms of memory footprint. Reusability and configurability of a mixin-based implementation helps to deal with device heterogeneity.

As future work, we want to integrate new features like security, persistence or fault-tolerance. Here, other software engineering methods like aspect-oriented programming, multi-dimensional separation of concerns or feature-oriented domain modeling look promising. Another issue is the performance of mixin-based middleware, in combination with reusability, customization and extensibility.

Acknowledgments. We thank Helge Sichting for much help with this study. We acknowledge the generous support of METOP GmbH, Magdeburg.

References

1. D. Batory and S. O'Malley. The Design and Implementation of Hierarchical Software Systems with Reusable Components. *ACM Transactions on Software Engineering and Methodology*, 1(4), 1992.
2. D. Batory, J. N. Sarvela, and A. Rauschmayer. Scaling Step-Wise Refinement. In *Proc. of the 25th Int. Conference on Software Engineering*, 2003.

3. G. S. Blair et al. Reflection, Self-awareness and Self-healing in OpenORB. In *Proc. of the 1st Workshop on Self-healing Systems*, 2002.

4. B. Box et al. Simple Object Access Protocol 1.1. Technical report, W_3C, 2000. http://www.w3.org/TR/SOAP.

5. G. Bracha and W. Cook. Mixin-Based Inheritance. In *Proc. of ECOOP / OOPSLA*, 1990.

6. L. Capra, W. Emmerich, and C. Mascolo. CARISMA: Context-Aware Reflective Middleware System for Mobile Applications. *IEEE Transactions on Software Engineering*, 29(10), 2003.

7. R. Cardone, D. Batory, and C. Lin. Java Layers: Extending Java to Support Component-Based Programming. Technical Report CS-TR-00-11, Computer Sciences Department, University of Texas, 2000.

8. A. Colyer and A. Clement. Large-scale AOSD for middleware. In *Proc. of the 3rd Int. Conference on Aspect-Oriented Software Development*, 2004.

9. E. Eide et al. Dynamic CPU Management for Real-Time, Middleware-Based Systems. In *10th IEEE Real-Time and Embedded Technology and Applications Symposium (RTAS 2004)*, Toronto, Canada, 2004.

10. R. A. Engelen and K. A. Gallivan. The gSOAP Toolkit for Web Services and Peer-To-Peer Computing Networks. In *Proc. of IEEE CCGrid Conference*, 2002. http://www.cs.fsu.edu/~engelen/soap.html.

11. C. Gill et al. ORB Middleware Evolution for Networked Embedded Systems. In *Proc. of the 8th Int. Workshop on Object Oriented Real-time Dependable Systems (WORDS'03)*, Guadalajara, Mexico, 2003.

12. P. Grace, G. S. Blair, and S. Samuel. ReMMoC: A Reflective Middleware to Support Mobile Client Interoperability. In *Proc. of the Int. Symposium on Distributed Objects and Applications (DOA 2003)*, Catania, Italy, 2003.

13. G. Kiczales et al. Aspect-Oriented Programming. In *Proc. of ECOOP*, Berlin, Heidelberg, and New York, 1997.

14. F. Kon et al. Monitoring, Security, and Dynamic Configuration with the dynamicTAO Reflective ORB. In *Proc. of Middleware'2000*, New York, 2000.

15. T. Ledoux. OpenCorba: A Reflective Open Broker. In *Proc. of the 2nd Int. Conference on Meta-Level Architectures and Reflection*, 1999.

16. A. D. McKinnon et al. A Configurable Middleware Framework with Multiple Quality of Service Properties for Small Embedded Systems. In *Proc. of 2nd IEEE Int. Symposium on Network Computing and Applications*, Cambridge, MA, 2003.

17. S. M. Omohundro. The Sather Programming Language. *Dr. Dobb's Journal*, 18(11), 1993.

18. H. Ossher and P. Tarr. Multi-Dimensional Separation of Concerns and The Hyperspace Approach. In *Proc. of the Symposium on Software Architectures and Component Technology: The State of the Art in Software Development*, 2000.

19. D. L. Parnas. Designing Software for Ease of Extension and Contraction. *IEEE Transaction on Software Engineering*, SE-5(2), 1979.

20. M. Román, F. Kon, and R. Campbell. Reflective Middleware: From Your Desk to Your Hand. *IEEE Distributed Systems Online (Special Issue on Reflective Middleware)*, 2(5), 2001.

21. D. C. Schmidt et al. TAO: A Pattern-Oriented Object Request Broker for Distributed Real-time and Embedded Systems. *IEEE Distributed Systems Online*, 3(2), 2002.

22. Y. Smaragdakis and D. Batory. Mixin Layers: An Object-Oriented Implementation Technique for Refinements and Collabroation-Based Designs. *ACM Transactions on Software Engineering and Methodology*, 11(2), 2002.

23. B. Stroustrup. *The C++ Programming Language*. Addison-Wesley, 1997.

24. V. Subramonian et al. Middleware Specialization for Memory-Constrained Networked Embedded Systems. In *10th IEEE Real-Time and Embedded Technology and Applications Symposium (RTAS 2004)*, Toronto, Canada, 2004.

25. M. Weiser. The Computer for the 21st Century. *Scientific American*, Sep. 1991.

26. M. Weiser. Hot Topics: Ubiquitous Computing. *IEEE Computer*, 26(10), 1993.

27. C. Zhang and H.-A. Jacobsen. Refactoring Middleware with Aspects. *IEEE Transations on Parallel and Distributed Systems*, 14(11), 2003.

Extending Standard Java Runtime Systems for Resource Management

Walter Binder[1] and Jarle Hulaas[2]

[1] Artificial Intelligence Laboratory, EPFL, CH–1015 Lausanne, Switzerland
[2] Software Engineering Laboratory, EPFL, CH–1015 Lausanne, Switzerland
firstname.lastname@epfl.ch

Abstract. Resource management is a precondition to build reliable, extensible middleware and to host potentially untrusted user components. Resource accounting allows to charge users for the resource consumption of their deployed components, while resource control can limit the resource consumption of components in order to prevent denial-of-service attacks. In the approach presented here program transformations enable resource management in Java-based environments, even though the underlying runtime system may not expose information concerning the resource consumption of applications. In order to accurately monitor the resource utilization of Java applications, the application code as well as the libraries used by the application – in particular, the classes of the Java Development Kit (JDK) – have to be transformed for resource accounting. However, the JDK classes are tightly interwoven with the native code of the Java runtime system. These dependencies, which are not well documented, have to be respected in order to preserve the integrity of the Java platform. We discuss several hurdles we have encountered when rewriting the JDK classes for resource management, and we present our solutions to these problems. Performance evaluations complete this paper.

Keywords: Bytecode rewriting, Java, JDK, program transformations, resource management.

1 Introduction

Resource management (i.e., accounting and controlling physical resources like CPU and memory) is a useful, yet rather unexplored aspect of software. Increased security, reliability, performance, and context-awareness are some of the benefits that can be gained from a better understanding of resource management. For instance, accounting and controlling the resource consumption of applications and of individual software components is crucial in server environments that host components on behalf of various clients, in order to protect the host from malicious or badly programmed code. Resource accounting may also provide valuable feedback about actual usage by end-clients and thus enable precise billing and provisioning policies. Such information will currently be furnished in an ad-hoc way by the underlying operating system, but higher software layers would definitely benefit from receiving it through standardized APIs in order to

T. Gschwind and C. Mascolo (Eds.): SEM 2004, LNCS 3437, pp. 154–169, 2005.

enable portable and tightly integrated implementations of policies at the middleware level.

Java [9] and the Java Virtual Machine (JVM) [12] are being increasingly used as the programming language and deployment platform for such servers (Java 2 Enterprise Edition, Servlets, Java Server Pages, Enterprise Java Beans). Moreover, accounting and limiting the resource consumption of applications is a prerequisite to prevent denial-of-service (DoS) attacks in mobile agent systems and middleware that can be extended and customized by mobile code. Yet another interesting target domain is resource-constrained embedded systems, because software run on such platforms has to be aware of resource restrictions in order to prevent abnormal termination.

However, currently the Java language and standard Java runtime systems lack mechanisms for resource management that could be used to limit the resource consumption of hosted components or to charge the clients for the resource consumption of their deployed components. Prevailing approaches to provide resource management in Java-based platforms rely on a modified JVM, on native code libraries, or on program transformations. For instance, KaffeOS [1] and the MVM [6] are specialized JVMs supporting resource control. JRes [7] is a resource control library for Java, which uses native code for CPU control and rewrites the bytecode of Java programs for memory control.

Resource control with the aid of program transformations offers an important advantage over the other approaches, because it is independent of any particular JVM and underlying operating system. It works with standard Java runtime systems and may be integrated into existing middleware. Furthermore, this approach enables resource control within embedded systems based on modern Java processors, which provide a JVM implemented in hardware that cannot be easily modified [5]. In this approach the bytecode of 'legacy' applications is rewritten in order to make its resource consumption explicit. Thus, rewritten programs will unknowingly keep track of the number of executed bytecode instructions (CPU accounting) and update a memory account when objects are allocated or reclaimed by the garbage collector. These ideas were first implemented in the Java Resource Accounting Framework (J-RAF) [4], which has undergone a complete revision in order to provide far better reliability, programmability, and performance. Details concerning the new bytecode rewriting scheme of J-RAF2[1] can be found in [10]. The drawback of this approach is that we cannot account for the resource consumption of native code.

In this paper we focus on the solutions developed specifically for correctly and efficiently rewriting the Java runtime support, called the Java Development Kit (JDK). Typically, rewriting the bytecode of an application is not sufficient to account and control its resource consumption, because Java applications use the comprehensive APIs of the JDK. Therefore, resource-aware versions of the JDK classes are needed in order to monitor the total resource consumption of an application. Ideally, the same bytecode rewriting algorithm should be used to rewrite application classes as well as JDK classes. However, the JDK classes are tightly interwoven with native code of the Java runtime system, which causes subtle complications for the rewriting of JDK classes. In this paper we report on the difficulties we encountered with JDK rewriting and on our solutions

---

[1] http://www.jraf2.org/

to these problems. While we describe the problems and solutions in the context of CPU management, they apply for memory management in a similar way. Finally, we present benchmark results of different strategies for JDK rewriting on various Java runtime systems.

This paper is structured as follows: In the next section we explain the basic idea of our program transformations for CPU management. In section 3 we discuss the problems in applying these transformations to the JDK classes, and in section 4 we show the necessary refinements for JDK rewriting. Section 5 presents a tool that helped us extend certain JDK classes. In section 6 we discuss performance measurements of different program transformation strategies. Finally, section 7 concludes this paper.

2   Transformation for Resource Control

In our approach the bytecode of each Java method is rewritten to expose its CPU consumption.[2] Every thread has an associated `ThreadCPUAccount` that is updated while the thread is executing the rewritten code. In each basic block of code the number of executed bytecode instructions is added to a counter within the `ThreadCPUAccount`. Periodically, the counter is checked and if it exceeds a dynamically adjustable threshold, a method is invoked on the `ThreadCPUAccount` which reports the thread's CPU consumption to a user-defined CPU manager. As multiple `ThreadCPUAccounts` may be associated with the same CPU manager, the manager is able to aggregate the CPU consumption of a set of threads. For instance, a CPU manager may be responsible for a set of threads executing within a component (such as a Servlet or a mobile agent). The CPU manager may implement an application-specific accounting, scheduling, and controlling policy. For example, the CPU manager may log the reported CPU consumption, it may try to terminate threads that exceed their allowed CPU quota, or it may delay threads if their execution rate is too high. Because the task of executing scheduling policies is distributed among all threads in the system, we call this approach *self-accounting*. While the details and APIs of our self-accounting scheme are presented in [10, 2], in this paper we exclusively focus on the particularities of transforming the classes of standard Java runtime systems.

The code in table 1 illustrates how the `ThreadCPUAccount` could be bound to a thread using a thread-local variable (thread-local variables are bound to `Thread` instances, i.e., each thread has its own copy). The method `ThreadCPUAccount.getCurrentAccount()` returns the `ThreadCPUAccount` associated with the calling thread. The thread-local variable has to be set whenever a thread is created.

As each Java method has to access the `ThreadCPUAccount`, a simple transformation scheme may load the `ThreadCPUAccount` on method entry as shown in table 2.[3]

---

[2] The rewriting operation is normally performed statically, and this can happen either once for all (as would be expected in the case of standard classes like the JDK), or at load-time (for application-level classes).

[3] For the sake of easy readability, we show the transformation at the level of the Java language, whereas our implementation operates at the JVM bytecode level.

Table 1. Binding `ThreadCPUAccounts` to threads using thread-local variables

```
public class ThreadCPUAccount {
  private static final ThreadLocal currentAccount = new ThreadLocal();

  public static ThreadCPUAccount getCurrentAccount() {
    return (ThreadCPUAccount)currentAccount.get();
  }
  ...
}
```

Table 2. Simple rewriting scheme: The `ThreadCPUAccount` is loaded on method entry

```
void f() {
  ThreadCPUAccount cpu = ThreadCPUAccount.getCurrentAccount();
  ... // method code with accounting
  g();
  ...
}
```

Table 3. Optimized rewriting scheme: The `ThreadCPUAccount` is passed as extra argument

```
void f(ThreadCPUAccount cpu) {
  ... // method code with accounting
  g(cpu);
  ...
}
```

Here we only show the method entry as well as the exemplary invocation of a method g(), whereas the actual accounting code is not presented in this paper (see [10] for details).

Unfortunately, it turns out that an entry sequence as depicted in table 2 causes high overhead. Access to thread-local variables requires loading of the `Thread` object representing the currently executing thread. Thus, we opted for a different transformation scheme as illustrated in table 3. In this approach the `ThreadCPUAccount` is passed as additional argument to methods/constructors. This scheme works insofar as all invocation sites are updated to provide the additional actual argument. In the best case, the `ThreadCPUAccount.getCurrentAccount()` method will be invoked only once at program startup, and then the resulting account will flow through the extra arguments during the rest of the execution.

Because native code may invoke Java methods and we do not modify native code, we have to preserve a method with the same signature as before rewriting.[4] For this reason, we add wrapper methods as shown in table 4, which load the `ThreadCPUAccount`

---

[4] One example is the main() method, which by convention has to have exactly one argument, an array of strings containing the command-line arguments; the main() method will very likely be invoked at startup by native code, or by Java code making use of the reflection API, hence the invocation sites cannot be updated by our systematic scheme.

Table 4. Wrapper method with unmodified signature

```
void f() {
  ThreadCPUAccount cpu = ThreadCPUAccount.getCurrentAccount();
  ... // account for execution of wrapper
  f(cpu);
}
```

Table 5. Reverse wrapper for native method

```
void n(ThreadCPUAccount cpu) {
  ... // account for execution of reverse wrapper
  n();
}

native void n();
```

and pass it to the resource-aware methods that take the `ThreadCPUAccount` as extra argument. Compatibility with non-rewritten and non-rewritable code is thus ensured.

As we do not change native methods, they do not receive the additional `ThreadCPUAccount` argument. Because rewritten Java methods will invoke methods with the extra argument, we provide reverse wrappers for native methods, as depicted in table 5.

3   Applying the Transformation to JDK Classes

While the transformations presented in the previous section are conceptually simple and work well with application classes, they cannot be directly applied to JDK classes. In this section we summarize the difficulties we encountered when rewriting the JDK. In the following section we will elaborate solutions to these problems.

3.1   Thread Without `Thread` Object

The implementation of `ThreadCPUAccount.getCurrentAccount()` invokes `ThreadLocal.get()`, which calls `Thread.currentThread()`. During the bootstrapping of the JVM there is no `Thread` object associated with the thread that loads and links the initial JDK classes. If `Thread.currentThread()` is executed during the bootstrapping process, it will return `null`. Hence, at this initial stage thread-local variables must not be used. Consequently, if we use the `ThreadCPUAccount` implementation shown in the previous section and rewrite all JDK classes (including, for instance, the static initializers of `Object` and `Thread`) according to the scheme presented before, the bootstrapping of the JVM will fail.

3.2   Endless Recursion When Accessing Thread-Local Variables

Another problem is related to the implementation of the class `ThreadLocal`. If all JDK classes – including `ThreadLocal` – are rewritten accord-ing to the transformations given in the previous section, the execution of

`ThreadCPUAccount.getCurrentAccount()` will result in an endless recursion, since the wrappers of the `ThreadLocal` methods will invoke `ThreadCPUAccount.getCurrentAccount()` again.

3.3   Native Code Depending on a Fixed Call Sequence

In the JDK certain methods rely on a fixed invocation sequence. Examples include methods in `Class`, `ClassLoader`, `DriverManager`, `Runtime`, and `System`. These methods inspect the stack frame of the caller to determine whether an operation shall be permitted. If wrapper methods (or reverse wrappers for native methods) are added to the JDK, the additional stack frames due to the invocation of wrapper methods will violate the assumptions of the JDK programmer concerning the execution stack.

While in [13] the authors claim to have added wrapper methods to all JDK methods without any problems, we discovered the problem mentioned before during the execution of the SPEC JVM98 benchmarks [14]. The problem was not easy to detect, simple applications may execute successfully in a JDK with wrapper methods.

4   Solving the Difficulties of JDK Rewriting

In this section we refine the implementation of `ThreadCPUAccount.getCurrentAccount()` and the transformation rules for the rewriting of JDK classes.

4.1   Refined Implementation of `ThreadCPUAccount`

To solve the problems discussed in sections 3.1 and 3.2, we decided to avoid the JDK implementation of thread-local variables and to attach the `ThreadCPUAccount` directly to the `Thread` object. For this purpose, we add the field 'public `ThreadCPUAccount org_jraf2_cpuAccount;`' to the `Thread` class.[5] Moreover, we modify the `Thread` constructors in order to allocate a new instance of `ThreadCPUAccount` and to store it in the field `org_jraf2_cpuAccount`. Consequently, whenever a `Thread` is allocated, it will receive its own `ThreadCPUAccount` instance. For these modifications, we have developed a simple but convenient tool to patch and extend legacy code, which we present in section 5. Another advantage of this approach is that the access to the `org_jraf2_cpuAccount` variable is faster than using the JDK implementation of thread-local variables, because we avoid the lookup in a hashtable.

In table 6 we show some part of the code of the refined implementation of `ThreadCPUAccount`. If `Thread.currentThread()` returns `null` during the bootstrapping of the JVM, a default `ThreadCPUAccount` is returned. This simple check solves the problem outlined in section 3.1. Moreover, during bootstrapping `Thread.currentThread()` may return a `Thread`

---

[5] To ensure that malicious applications do not directly access the added public variable, we verify each class before rewriting to ensure that it does not refer to that variable. The methods of the reflection API can be modified as well in order to prevent access to the variable.

Table 6. Implementation of `ThreadCPUAccount` based on a modified `Thread` class

```
public class ThreadCPUAccount {
  private static final ThreadCPUAccount defaultCPU = new ThreadCPUAccount();

  public static ThreadCPUAccount getCurrentAccount() {
    Thread t = Thread.currentThread();
    if (t == null) return defaultCPU;
    ThreadCPUAccount cpu = t.org_jraf2_cpuAccount;
    return cpu == null ? defaultCPU : cpu;
  }
  ...
}
```

object which has not yet been completely initialized. In this case, a default `ThreadCPUAccount` is returned, too. To avoid an endless recursion when calling `ThreadCPUAccount.getCurrentAccount()` (see section 3.2 for details), we have to ensure that `Thread.currentThread()` does not receive a wrapper calling `ThreadCPUAccount.getCurrentAccount()`. Usually, this is not an issue, if `Thread.currentThread()` is implemented as a native method. For the same reason, the method `ThreadCPUAccount.getCurrentAccount()` itself is excluded from rewriting.

4.2   Analysis and Refined Rewriting of JDK Classes

In order not to violate assumptions regarding the structure of the call stack when a JDK method is invoked, we have to make sure that there are no extra stack frames of wrappers of JDK methods on the stack. A trivial solution is to rewrite the JDK classes according to the transformation shown in table 2. However, as we have mentioned before, such a rewriting scheme may cause high overhead on certain JVMs.

A first step towards a more efficient solution is to ensure that native JDK methods are always invoked directly. That is, reverse wrappers as depicted in table 5 are to be avoided for native JDK methods. For this purpose, we have developed a simple tool to analyze the JDK, which gives out a list of methods L that must not receive wrappers. This list is needed for the subsequent rewriting of JDK and of application classes, since invocations of methods in L must not pass the extra `ThreadCPUAccount` argument.

Obviously, L includes all native JDK methods. Additionally, we have to consider polymorphic call sites that may invoke native JDK methods. In this case, the extra `ThreadCPUAccount` argument must not be passed, since the target method may be native and lack a reverse wrapper. Hence, if a native method overwrites/implements a method m in a superclass/interface, m has to be included in L. We use the following simple marking algorithm to compute L.

1. Compute the class hierarchy of the JDK. For each class, store the class name, a reference to the superclass, references to implemented interfaces, and a list of the signatures and modifiers of all methods in the class.
2. Mark all native methods.
3. Propagate the marks upwards in the class hierarchy. Let m_c be a marked method, which is neither static nor private. Furthermore, let C be the class defining m_c, and A the set of ancestors of C, including direct and indirect superclasses as well as all

Table 7. Rewriting scheme for JDK methods: The code is duplicated

```
void f() {
  ThreadCPUAccount cpu = ThreadCPUAccount.getCurrentAccount();
  ... // method code with accounting
  g(cpu);
  ...
}

void f(ThreadCPUAccount cpu) {
  ... // method code with accounting
  g(cpu);
  ...
}
```

implemented interfaces. For each class or interface X in A, if X defines a method m_x with the same signature as m_c, which is neither static nor private, mark m_x.

4. All marked methods are collected in the list L.

The JDK methods in the list L are rewritten as follows:

- Native methods do not receive the reverse wrapper shown in table 5.
- Abstract methods are not modified; the signature extended with the extra argument is not added.
- The signature of Java methods is not touched either; they are transformed according to the simple rewriting scheme given in table 2.

So far, we have ensured that native JDK methods are always invoked directly. However, as we have mentioned in section 3.3, there are JDK methods which require that their callers are not invoked through wrappers either. To respect this restriction, the code of each JDK method not included in L is duplicated, as presented in table 7.[6] As there are no wrappers for JDK methods, the call sequence within the JDK remains unchanged. While the code is approximately duplicated (with respect to the rewriting scheme for application classes), the execution performance does not suffer significantly, because the `ThreadCPUAccount` is passed as argument whenever possible.

5   Extending Java Legacy Code

We have developed a simple tool called MergeClass, which allows to insert new functionality into compiled Java classfiles. With the aid of MergeClass it is possible to plant new features into standard JVMs and to experiment with the modified JVM. After the desired extension has been written in Java and has been compiled, MergeClass directly merges it into given classfiles. This approach is more favorable than resorting to low-level tools, such as disassemblers, assemblers, or decompilers, which would require to patch each class manually and separately. Moreover, many Java decompilers have problems to correctly decompile certain Java classfiles, e.g., obfuscated classes. Compared

---

[6] In this sample we assume that method g() is not in the list L. Otherwise, the extra argument must not be passed to g().

with tools for aspect-oriented programming, such as AspectJ [11], our MergeClass tool is simple and limited, but it is easy to use, it does not require to learn new language features, and it enables a very fast development and experimentation cycle.

5.1   The MergeClass Tool

The MergeClass tool takes 3 or 4 arguments. The first two arguments refer to existing Java classfiles. The first one is the class to be extended (usually legacy code), the second one is the extension to be merged into the first one (usually developed in Java and compiled with a standard Java compiler). The third argument specifies the output file to hold the resulting Java classfile. The fourth argument is optional, it defines a configuration file to parametrize the merging process.

MergeClass reads the original input classfile I_O and the extension input classfile I_E. In order to merge I_E into I_O, I_E has to fulfill several restrictions:

– I_E must extend one of the following 3 classes:
   1. `java.lang.Object`, allowing to merge simple extensions that are independent of I_O.
   2. The superclass of I_O, enabling the merging of classes with the same superclass.
   3. I_O, allowing to merge the most specific subclass into its superclass (if all constraints are met, this process may be iterated).
– I_E must not define more than 1 constructor. The constructor must not take any arguments. (Its signature has to be '( ) V'.)
– I_E must not have inner classes.

The resulting output class O has the same name, accessibility, and superclass as I_O. It implements the union of the interfaces implemented by I_O and I_E. O is final if I_E is final, i.e., the extensibility of I_E overrules the extensibility of I_O. (This feature may be used to 'open' a final legacy class by adding interfaces and making it extensible.)

If no special configuration file is defined, MergeClass first copies all members (fields, methods, and constructors) of I_O into an in-memory representation of O. Then it copies or merges all members of I_E into O with the following transformations or checks:

T1: All references to the name of I_E have to be replaced with a reference to the name of I_O.
T2: If I_E extends I_O and code in I_E invokes a private method in I_O (how this is possible will be explained at the end of this section), the `invokevirtual` bytecode instruction is replaced with an `invokespecial` bytecode instruction, as for private methods (in the resulting class) `invokespecial` has to be used.
C1: If there is a name clash (i.e., I_E and I_O define a field with the same name or a method with the same name and signature), an exception is thrown and no result classfile is created (as will be explained later, the optional configuration file can be used to resolve such name conflicts).

The static initializer and the constructor of I_E cannot be simply copied into O, but they have to be integrated with the code copied from I_O. More precisely, if I_O and I_E both define a static initializer, the code in the static initializer of I_E has to be appended to the code of the static initializer taken from I_O. In a similar way, if I_E defines a non-trivial constructor (i.e., a constructor that does more than just invoking the superclass constructor), the code of the constructor of I_E has to be appended to the code of each constructor taken from I_O. The following transformations are necessary to append code from I_E to code from I_O:

T3: `return` instructions in the code taken from I_O are replaced with `goto` instructions that jump to the begin of the code to be appended from I_E. Redundant `goto` instructions are removed.

T4: As the structure of the appended code remains unchanged, exception handlers in I_E are to be preserved.

T5: In the constructor of I_E the initial invocation of the superclass constructor is stripped off.

With the aid of a special configuration file, the merging process can be customized. The configuration file allows to deal with name clashes and to mark special methods in I_E whose code shall be merged into certain methods of I_O.

For each member in I_E (except for the constructor and static initializer), the configuration file may define one of the following properties:

– `DiscardInConflict`: If there is a name clash, the member in I_O will be preserved.

– `TakeInConflict`: If there is a name clash, the member in I_E will replace the member in I_O.

Moreover, for a void method M in I_E that takes no arguments, the property `InsertAtBegin(regular expression)` or `AppendAtEnd(regular expression)` may be defined. As a consequence, M will not be copied directly into O, but its code will be merged into all methods of I_O whose name match the given regular expression. If M is a static method, only static methods in I_O are considered for a match, otherwise only instance methods may match.

The code of M may be inserted in the beginning or at the end. If it is appended at the end, the transformations T1–T4 are applied. In addition, the following transformation is needed:

T6: If M is appended to a non-void method in I_O, the method result is stored in an otherwise unused local variable and each `return` instruction in the appended code is replaced with a code sequence to load the result onto the stack and to return it.

If the code of M is to be inserted at the beginning, the transformations T1, T2, and T4 have to be complemented with the following transformations (note that T3 is replaced with T7):

T7: `return` instructions in the code to be inserted from I_E are replaced with `goto` instructions that jump to the begin of the code taken from I_O. Redundant `goto` instructions are removed.

T8: All local variable indices in the code inserted from I_E are incremented accordingly in order to avoid clashes with local variables used in the code of I_O. For an instance method, the local variable 0 remains unchanged, since by default it holds the reference to `this`. This transformation ensures that the inserted code cannot mess up with the arguments passed to the method taken from I_O.

If multiple `InsertAtBegin` or `AppendAtEnd` expressions apply to a given method in I_O, the code merging happens in the order of the definition of the properties in the configuration file.

As mentioned before, it may be necessary that I_E references private or package-visible members in I_O. For this purpose, we offer a complementary tool, MakePublicExtensible, which takes as arguments the names of two Java classfiles, an input file and an output file. The output file is created by making the input class public and non-final, as well as making all its members public. Hence, the Java source of I_E may extend the class that results of applying MakePublicExtensible and access all of its members. The compilation of the Java source of I_E will succeed, because the accessibility and extensibility constraints have been removed. Afterwards, I_E is merged with the original I_O. Of course, in the merged class the code taken from I_E may access all members. The class resulting from applying MakePublicExtensible is discarded. It is only needed temporarily in order to be able to compile the sources of I_E.

5.2   Extending `Thread` Using MergeClass

Table 8 illustrates how the `Thread` extensions described in section 4 can be separately implemented, compiled, and injected into the `Thread` class using our MergeClass tool. MergeClass adds the field `org_jraf2_cpuAccount` to `java.lang.Thread`. Moreover, it appends the allocation of a `ThreadCPUAccount` object to each constructor in Thread.

Table 8. `Thread` extension

```
public class ThreadExtension extends java.lang.Thread {
  public ThreadCPUAccount org_jraf2_cpuAccount;

  // to be appended to each constructor:
  public ThreadExtension() {org_jraf2_cpuAccount = new ThreadCPUAccount();}
}
```

Using MergeClass we have been able to experiment with different strategies of maintaining accounting objects. We have implemented the thread extensions in pure Java and compiled them with a standard Java compiler. Furthermore, we were able to test the thread extensions with various versions of the JDK without any extra effort (apart from applying MergeClass). We also integrated some more elaborate features into the `Thread` class, for instance a mechanism that initializes the new `ThreadCPUAccount` with the CPU manager of the calling thread's `ThreadCPUAccount`. This ensures that a spawned thread will execute under the same CPU accounting policy as its creator thread. For details concerning CPU managers, see [10]. Moreover, the thread extensions can be easily adapted for other accounting objects, such as memory accounts (for details concerning memory accounting in Java, see [3]).

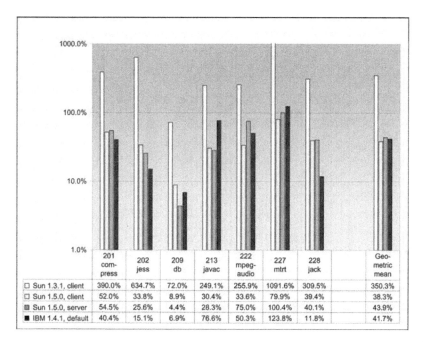

	201 com-press	202 jess	209 db	213 javac	222 mpeg-audio	227 mtrt	228 jack	Geo-metric mean
☐ Sun 1.3.1, client	390.0%	634.7%	72.0%	249.1%	255.9%	1091.6%	309.5%	350.3%
☐ Sun 1.5.0, client	52.0%	33.8%	8.9%	30.4%	33.6%	79.9%	39.4%	38.3%
▨ Sun 1.5.0, server	54.5%	25.6%	4.4%	28.3%	75.0%	100.4%	40.1%	43.9%
■ IBM 1.4.1, default	40.4%	15.1%	6.9%	76.6%	50.3%	123.8%	11.8%	41.7%

Fig. 1. Overhead of CPU accounting: JDK and benchmarks transformed with the simple scheme

6 Evaluation

In this section we present some benchmark results comparing the accounting overhead of different rewriting strategies on various JVMs. We ran the SPEC JVM98 benchmark suite [14] on a Linux RedHat 9 computer (Intel Pentium 4, 2.6 GHz, 512 MB RAM). For all settings, the entire JVM98 benchmark was run 10 times, and the final results were obtained by calculating the geometric means of the median of each sub-test. Here we present the measurements made with IBM's JDK 1.4.1 platform in its default execution mode, with Sun's JDK 1.3.1 in its 'client' mode, as well as with Sun's JDK 1.5.0 beta platform in its 'client' and 'server' modes. While IBM JDK 1.4.1 and Sun JDK 1.5.0 represent recent JVMs with state-of-the-art just-in-time compilers, we intentionally added an older JVM for comparison.

   The most significant setting we measured was the performance of a rewritten JVM98 application on top of a rewritten JDK. Figure 1 shows the relative overhead of the *simple* transformation scheme of table 2 applied to the JDK as well as to the benchmark classes. In the beginning of each method `Thread.currentThread()` is invoked. We expected this rewriting scheme to result in high overhead on certain JVMs (worst case). In particular, the older Sun JDK 1.3.1 performs badly in this setting, the overhead is up to 1090% for the mtrt benchmark, the geometric mean is about 350% overhead. Apparently, `Thread.currentThread()` is not implemented efficiently on this JVM. For the other JVMs, the average overhead is about 40% in this setting. Because of this big difference, we used a logarithmic scale in figure 1.

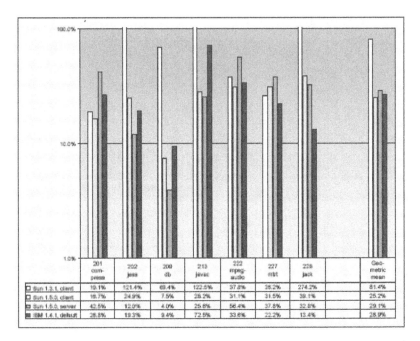

Fig. 2. Overhead of CPU accounting: JDK transformed with the simple scheme, benchmarks with the wrapper scheme

For the measurements in figure 2, the JDK classes were rewritten according to the *simple* transformation scheme (table 2), whereas the benchmark classes were transformed using the *wrapper* strategy of table 3. In this setting, Sun JDK 1.3.1 incurred an overhead of about 80%, whereas on the other JVMs we measured only 25–30% overhead.

For figure 3, the JDK classes were transformed based on the scheme of table 7 (*no wrappers*, code duplication), while the benchmark classes were rewritten according to the *wrapper* scheme of table 3. In this setting, all JVMs incur an overhead of 30–40%. For Sun JDK 1.3.1, this scheme gives the best results. Interestingly, for the other more recent JVMs, this scheme does not improve the performance, which can be explained as follows: On the one hand, the rewriting of the JDK classes significantly increases the code size and hence causes overheads during class loading and just-in-time compilation. On the other hand, the number of invocations of `Thread.currentThread()` is reduced. For recent JVMs with a rather fast implementation of `Thread.currentThread()` this rewriting scheme does not pay off, but for the older Sun JDK 1.3.1 the benefits of reducing the number of `Thread.currentThread()` invocations outweigh the overheads due to the increased code size.

We can conclude that current JDKs shall be transformed using the simple scheme, whereas older releases will perform better when rewritten with code duplication. For libraries other than the JDK and for application classes, the wrapper scheme performs best.

Note that we did not apply any optimization apart from passing `ThreadCPUAccount` objects as extra arguments. Currently, we are evaluating optimizations that reduce the number of accounting sites in the rewritten code. For

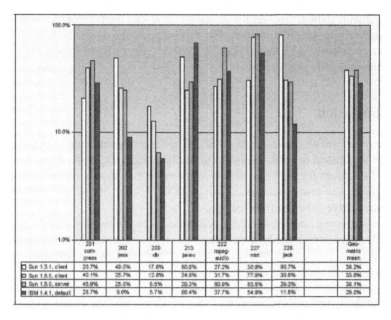

Fig. 3. Overhead of CPU accounting: JDK transformed with code duplication, benchmarks with the wrapper scheme

instance, we are working on control flow optimizations that increase the average size of basic blocks of code and therefore reduce the proportion of accounting instructions during the execution of rewritten programs. In particular, we are considering special cases of loop unrolling which do not result in a significant increase of the code size, but allow to remove accounting instructions from loops. Initial measurements of optimized CPU accounting, which are not presented in this paper due to space limitations, indicate that such optimizations allow to further reduce the overhead to about 20% and below on current standard JVMs.

The rewriting process itself takes only a very short time, although our tools have not yet been optimized to minimize the rewriting time. For example, rewriting the 20660 methods of the 2790 core classes of IBM's JDK 1.4.1 takes less than one minute on our test machine. The implementations of our tools are based on the bytecode engineering library BCEL [8], which provides an object representation for the individual bytecode instructions. Optimizing our tools for dynamic rewriting of classes during class loading may require resorting to a lower-level bytecode representation.

We have also considered using tools for aspect-oriented programming in order to define the sites where accounting is needed and to insert the accounting code there. However, in our approach accounting sites are ubiquitous, as they are based on the low-level concept of basic blocks of code. Most tools for aspect-oriented programming, such as AspectJ [11], allow to define only higher-level pointcuts, such as method invocations, the beginning of exception handlers, etc. With such tools it is not easily possible to express that accounting code is to be inserted into each basic block of code. Moreover, it would be difficult to specify our particular scheme of passing acocunting objects as extra arguments (which involves the creation of wrapper methods or the duplication of code) with current aspect languages. For our purpose, the direct manipulation of the JVM bytecode is the best suited approach, which allows us to implement low-level transformations and optimizations.

7   Conclusion

Program transformation techniques allow to transparently integrate resource management into Java-based systems, although current Java runtime systems do not support this feature. To account for the total resource consumption of an application component, it is not sufficient to rewrite its classes, but all used libraries, including middleware and JDK classes, have to be transformed, too.

In this paper we have outlined the difficulties of modifying the classes of standard JDKs. The native code of the Java runtime system relies on several low-level assumptions regarding the dependencies of Java methods in certain JDK classes. Thus, program transformations that are correct for pure Java may break native code in the runtime system. Unfortunately, these dependencies are not well documented, which complicates the task of defining transformation rules that work well with the Java class library.

Moreover, the transformed JDK classes may seem to work as desired even with large-scale benchmarks, while the transformation may have compromised the security model of Java. Such security malfunctions are hard to detect, as they cannot be perceived when running well behaving applications. We have experienced that a minor restructuring of the method call sequence completely breaks several security checks, which are based on stack introspection and assume a fixed call sequence. Consequently, modifications and updates of the JDK are highly error-prone.

In this paper we have presented program transformations for resource management, in particular focusing on CPU accounting, which are applicable to application classes as well as to the Java class library. We have developed different transformation schemes and evaluated their respective performance. The most elaborate scheme results in an overhead for CPU accounting of about 25–30% (without optimizations to reduce the number of accounting sites).

References

1. G. Back, W. Hsieh, and J. Lepreau. Processes in KaffeOS: Isolation, resource management, and sharing in Java. In *Proceedings of the Fourth Symposium on Operating Systems Design and Implementation (OSDI'2000)*, San Diego, CA, USA, Oct. 2000.
2. W. Binder and J. Hulaas. A portable CPU-management framework for Java. *IEEE Internet Computing*, 8(5):74–83, Sep./Oct. 2004.
3. W. Binder, J. Hulaas, and A. Villazón. Resource control in J-SEAL2. Technical Report Cahier du CUI No. 124, University of Geneva, Oct. 2000. ftp://cui.unige.ch/pub/tios/papers/TR-124-2000.pdf.
4. W. Binder, J. Hulaas, A. Villazón, and R. Vidal. Portable resource control in Java: The J-SEAL2 approach. In *ACM Conference on Object-Oriented Programming, Systems, Languages, and Applications (OOPSLA-2001)*, USA, Oct. 2001.

5. W. Binder and B. Lichtl. Using a secure mobile object kernel as operating system on embedded devices to support the dynamic upload of applications. *Lecture Notes in Computer Science*, 2535, 2002.

6. G. Czajkowski and L. Daynès. Multitasking without compromise: A virtual machine evolution. In *ACM Conference on Object-Oriented Programming, Systems, Languages, and Applications (OOPSLA'01)*, Tampa Bay, Florida, Oct. 2001.

7. G. Czajkowski and T. von Eicken. JRes: A resource accounting interface for Java. In *Proceedings of the 13th Conference on Object-Oriented Programming, Systems, Languages, and Applications (OOPSLA-98)*, volume 33, 10 of *ACM SIGPLAN Notices*, New York, USA, Oct. 1998.

8. M. Dahm. Byte code engineering. In *Java-Information-Tage 1999 (JIT'99)*, Sept. 1999. `http://jakarta.apache.org/bcel/`.

9. J. Gosling, B. Joy, G. L. Steele, and G. Bracha. *The Java language specification*. Java series. Addison-Wesley, Reading, MA, USA, second edition, 2000.

10. J. Hulaas and W. Binder. Program transformations for portable CPU accounting and control in Java. In *Proceedings of PEPM'04 (2004 ACM SIGPLAN Symposium on Partial Evaluation & Program Manipulation)*, pages 169–177, Verona, Italy, August 24–25 2004.

11. I. Kiselev. *Aspect-Oriented Programming with AspectJ*. Sams Publishing, Indianapolis, 2003.

12. T. Lindholm and F. Yellin. *The Java Virtual Machine Specification*. Addison-Wesley, Reading, MA, USA, second edition, 1999.

13. A. Rudys and D. S. Wallach. Enforcing Java run-time properties using bytecode rewriting. *Lecture Notes in Computer Science*, 2609:185–200, 2003.

14. The Standard Performance Evaluation Corporation. SPEC JVM98 Benchmarks. Web pages at `http://www.spec.org/osg/jvm98/`.

Modeling Distributed Applications for QoS Management*

Patrice Vienne, Jean-Louis Sourrouille, and Mathieu Maranzana

INSA Lyon, PRISMa, Bat. B. Pascal,
F-69621, Villeurbanne Cedex, France
{Patrice.Vienne, Jean-Louis.Sourrouille, Mathieu.Maranzana}@insa-lyon.fr

Abstract. To increase the total QoS (Quality of Service) provided by a system, run-time adaptation of application behavior to execution context is a promising way. This paper focuses on modeling of distributed applications in order to manage their QoS through a middleware. The model captures the information required to schedule application activities in order to improve QoS and share out resources. Since only applications hold the required knowledge for alternative execution or graceful degradation, they adapt themselves under the control of the middleware. To ease the design of applications, a virtual execution environment implements the proposed middleware and emulates the execution of applications from their model.

1 Introduction

Generally, computer systems provide services according to a best effort policy that proves to be satisfactory as long as the required resources are available. When resources are becoming scarce, a more effective policy should be implemented to improve the provided QoS (Quality of Service). It expects applications to provide resource requirements associated with a satisfaction indicator named utility. This paper focuses on modeling of distributed applications to manage their QoS through a middleware. Modeling depends on factors such as execution context (e.g., distributed), nature of applications (e.g., multimedia, real-time), resource management policy (e.g., reservation) or QoS optimization policy (e.g., simplex, heuristic). From the middleware point of view, this model specifies the application behavior and QoS features needed to achieve QoS management.

This work addresses reactive applications stimulated by events whose arrival law is unpredictable, running in environments in which resource use is fully controlled. Before any application activity, an admission control should check resource availability to guarantee end-to-end execution, from the initial stimulus to the reply (to cancel a running task is always expensive [2]). QoS management requires applications to supply degrees of freedom to adapt their behavior and tune resource consumption. To achieve tunability, applications provide the same

---

* This work was partly supported by the BQR fund of INSA Lyon.

T. Gschwind and C. Mascolo (Eds.): SEM 2004, LNCS 3437, pp. 170–184, 2005.

service with several m odes, e.g., normal, degraded (execution level in [5]). Each mode is associated with a utility, and mode selection aims to maximize the total utility of the system according to available resources.

In distributed contexts, the QoS Management System (QMS) architecture is generally based on a middleware relying on existing layers [4]. Our middleware, PMQDA (Plan-based M iddleware for Q oS m anagem ent of D istributed A pplications), manages resources and controls applications with the aim of optimizing their satisfaction. To enforce guarantees, unregistered applications can only use unscheduled resources (CPU with a low priority, free bandwidth, etc.). We assume that the underlying layers of PMQDA, including OS (Operating System) and communication layers, provide all the needed basic services such as CPU and bandwidth control, messaging, etc. PMQDA will use available platform services only, therefore issues related to changes in underlying layers are out of the scope of the study (other approaches in [19] or [14] that abstracts network protocols). Symmetrically, the way applications change their resource consumption is unknown: the PMQDA mechanisms apply whatever the application area.

The paper uses the UML [20] wherever possible due to its high expressive power that extension mechanisms increase even more. Moreover, UML is becoming a standard that most readers know. The paper is organized as follows: section 2 specifies the context of the work and discusses the major decisions; section 3 describes the application model; section 4 gives features about middleware implementation and virtual execution environment; finally, section 5 deals with related works.

2   Context of the Work and Choices

PMQDA manages the QoS of applications distributed on several nodes: an application is composed of "local applications" running on different computing nodes. Let's assume an application supplying three data transmission modes and running on two nodes (see table 1). The execution of local applications on each node should be synchronized in such a way that when data are compressed on node A, they are decompressed on node B using the same policy: related local applications should run in the same mode on all the nodes. According to the execution context and the required resources, PMQDA sets the running mode

Table 1. Application example

Mode	Node A	Node B
1	Acquisition, then Transmission	Reception, then Display
2	Acquisition, Compression-1, Transmission	Reception, Decompression-1, Display
3	Acquisition, Compression-2 (degrading), Transmission	Reception, Decompression-2, Display

for all the applications. In the above example, large bandwidth availability fits with mode 1, while narrow bandwidth and available CPU on both nodes fit with the modes 2 and 3 (3 using even less bandwidth).

The rest of the section discusses strategic choices and gives additional precisions to define more precisely the QoS management policy.

2.1   Intrusive/Non-intrusive Policy

The choice of an adaptation policy induces a major decision about architecture. When using a non-intrusive management policy, the execution environment (OS and middleware) controls adaptations independently of applications, while applications are involved in adaptation when using an intrusive policy.

Non-intrusive Policy. The OS, including communication layers, controls the adaptations. Any OS already manages the QoS, for instance allocating CPU time, hence only adding QoS management functions is needed [2]. As a great advantage, all the applications running in the environment automatically benefit from the same QoS services. When it is not possible to modify the OS, the QoS management functions are implemented on top of the OS and underlying layers using a middleware, which is easier to port.

Intrusive Policy. In fact, only the application has the necessary knowledge to set up alternative behaviors: it may downgrade a frame rate from 25 to 12fps to reduce resource consumption thus keeping a fair service, while an OS that would reduce equivalently the application resources would get an unacceptable result. This approach only deals with specifically developed software and requires applications to be finely described: operating modes, resource consumption, etc.

Most works propose a compromise in which applications export their resource needs and provide an interface to modify their behavior hence allowing control from the outside (e.g., [7, 12]). This approach has been chosen for it takes advantage of the two policies: a control system shared by all the applications to reduce development work as well as customized adaptation based on application knowledge. The QMS is implemented in a middleware and relies on the best effort standard services of usual OS. As an additional advantage, this architecture leads to a separation of concerns: the middleware deals with reusable QoS management functions while the application deals with target system specific functions. It would be neater not to export the application's characteristics to hide its implementation, but it would require the QMS to enter into endless negotiations such as "Who can give me memory? CPU time?".

2.2   Model of Execution

Numerous works about QoS deal with periodic multimedia applications. Practically, QoS management policies depend on the nature of applications.

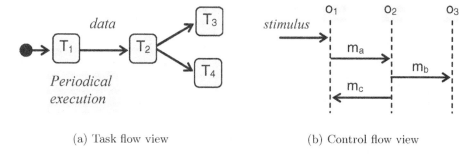

(a) Task flow view   (b) Control flow view

Fig. 1. Different points of view on systems

Periodic task flow (UML activity diagram Fig. 1(a)). A periodic task T_i produces data that in turn becomes inputs for the next tasks. Data availability automatically synchronizes the sequence of tasks. Constraints are generally associated with the delay between two tasks.

Aperiodic events (UML Sequence diagram Fig. 1(b)). A sequence of operations is a transaction with explicit synchronization. At event arrival, the corresponding sequence of operations executes in the given order until transaction is complete, i.e., all the outputs are produced. Time constraints are associated with the delay between input and output. A periodic system is a particular case of aperiodic system that is periodically stimulated by a clock. Our work focuses on systems subject to aperiodic events.

2.3   Resource Management

Two main policies are used to manage resources in QMS subject to aperiodic events: average load reservation and planning reservation.

Average Load Reservation. For each activity, an acceptable range of available CPU time within a period specifies the resource consumption (e.g., [6]). For instance the activity b_3 Fig. 2(a) requires [100ms..500ms] each second. The starting time of the activity within the period is unknown. The QMS deduces the percentage of free resource from the description of activities. When a new application asks for an admission, a new operational point is computed, sometimes analytically (e.g., solving a system of linear equations in [10]). The maximal delay to execute a sequence of activities is statically deduced from timing specifications.

The main advantage of this approach is its simplicity. It assumes that activities organize themselves automatically: wait and synchronization are not managed.

Planning Reservation. Each activity supplies its resource requirements in the worst case and its deadline. From these requirements, an exact planning is computed (e.g., [3]). Figure 2(b) shows an example with three activities (a_1, a_2,

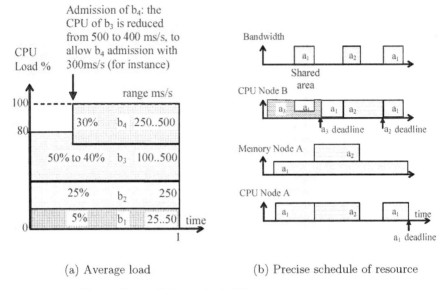

(a) Average load   (b) Precise schedule of resource

Fig. 2. Two policies to deal with resource reservation

a_3) running on two nodes with various requirements. The activity a_1 requires memory on node A from starting time to $a_1 deadline$, 150ms of CPU on node A, then bandwidth and CPU on both nodes A and B etc.

This approach is complex since the general optimization problem of utility without planning is already NP-Hard [15]. In practice, the goal is to reach a compromise between high quality and planning effort using a heuristic (e.g., [1]).

In spite of this drawback, we have chosen planning reservation, which takes into account synchronization and ensures end-to-end deadline: any admitted treatment is guaranteed to execute. In fact, the two approaches may be used together to share resources inside a planed area. For instance, on Fig. 2(b) the transmission between two nodes A and B does not consume the entire CPU time (shared area) and a_1 shares the CPU with a_3. We use this policy but under some conditions to avoid timing faults (no deadline within the shared range).

2.4   Application Control

The QMS controls applications using two main approaches.

Continuous. The average quantity of available resources for an application is continuously tuned with nearly immediate effect, for instance modifying a sample rate in the task flow on Fig. 1(a) (e.g., [5], feed-back adaptation in [6]).

Discrete. The quantity of available resources is modified only at predefined points of the program Fig. 3 (e.g., [8]). The execution of an application is a path

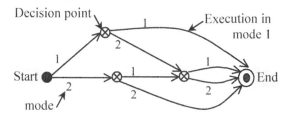

Fig. 3. Execution graph

in a graph whose nodes are decision points. At each decision point a mode is chosen and does not change until the next decision point.

Continuous control is suitable for periodic applications. Discrete control associated with planning reservation allows enforcing end-to-end deadlines for events whose arrival law is unpredictable: on Fig. 3, when the treatment starts, it is guaranteed to reach End through one path.

PMQDA is based on discrete control, which induces constraints on managed applications: at each decision point, an application must wait till the QMS communicates the next execution mode, hence a decision point is also a waiting point used by the QMS to enforce the schedule of applications.

3   Modeling the Application

The model of an application is its representation from the middleware point of view: its specification in terms of QoS. This model provides all the required information to handle the application QoS during execution.

Figure 4 shows a simplified static model of an application (same form as in [18]). An application is composed of a sequence of SchedulingUnits whose deadlines are computed from an origin (scheduling time) and an offset (the specified delay). A scheduling unit consists of a sequence of Activities. An activity is a treatment that can be executed in several Modes, each with a utility. Within a mode, an activity is a sequence of Steps, each specifying its resource requirements. A step runs on a unique node whereas an activity may be distributed. In the model, a LocalApplication stands for a logical node that will be associated with a physical node at run-time.

3.1   UML Model of an Application

Table 2 illustrates the model of an application starting (after initialization) on node A with the acquisition of N medical images on the physician request (nextacquisition Fig. 5). Each image is immediately transmitted on node B (with or without compression) and displayed. Finally, the set of images is analyzed on node B.

At the step level, a rendezvous (RdV) synchronizes the execution of two steps belonging to the same activity but to different local applications:

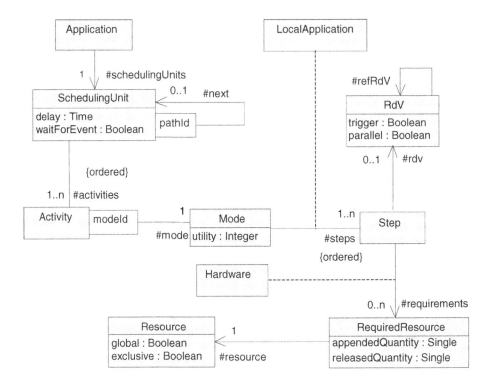

Fig. 4. Simplified static model of an application

Table 2. Example of an application with activities distributed on two nodes

Scheduling unit	Activity	Mode	Step	Node
Initialize	A_Initialization	1	Load local application	A
			Load local application	B
Sample (loop)	A_Asquisition	1	Acquisition	A
		1	Transmission1	A
			Reception1	B
	A_Transmission	2	Compression	A
			Transmission2	A
			Reception2	B
			Decompression	B
	A_Display	1	Display1	B
		2	Display2	B
Analyze	. . .	. . .	. . .	B

– A sequential rendezvous specifies that a step execution starts after the end of a previous one,
– A parallel rendezvous specifies that two steps start simultaneously (synchronous).

The model handles exclusive resources such as processor, and nonexclusive resources such as memory. In both cases, a resource is either bounded to a node or shared with several nodes (global). Moreover, a resource may be preserved through several steps, whether or not they belong to the same activity (or scheduling unit). For instance, memory must not be released before the end of the last step that uses it. In the model, resource persistence is specified by:

- appendedQuantity of additional resource to allocate at the beginning of the step,
- releasedQuantity of resource to release at the end of the step.

The remaining quantity, which has not yet been released, is kept for the following steps.

3.2 Execution Graph and Application Data Flow Control

The execution graph is a representation of a PMQDA application execution. Figures 5 and 6 present the execution graph of the application depicted in table 2 using UML activity diagrams and two representation levels:

- Scheduling units sequence on Fig. 5,
- Detailed steps sequence on Fig. 6.

The whole set of execution paths and the distribution on local applications figure on the execution graphs. Parallelization results in simultaneous execution of treatments on different nodes. At step level (Fig. 6), the rendezvous specifies the synchronization whereas at scheduling unit level (Fig. 5), the sequence depends on events and paths.

When a scheduling unit ends up with a wait for event, the following scheduling units are not scheduled (whatever the node) and their deadline origin will be set to the event arrival time. Consequently, an application cannot wait for an event within a scheduled treatment. In the sequence of scheduling units, the model represents alternatives using paths. When there are several paths, the application chooses at run-time. A path forbids the schedule of the following scheduling units, like the wait for event, although the deadline origin does not change.

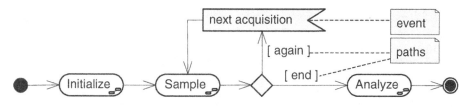

Fig. 5. Global execution graph for the application table 2

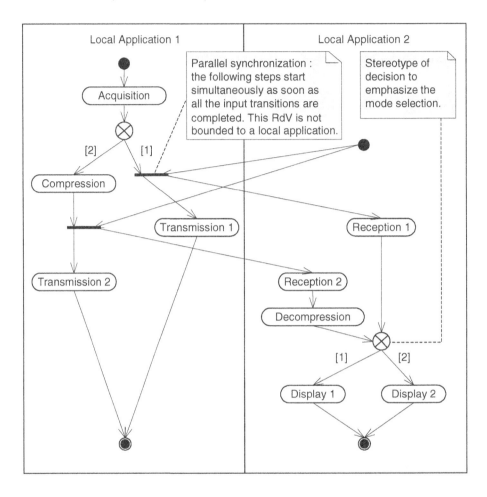

Fig. 6. Detailed execution graph for the scheduling unit *Sample* (The semantics of UML is slightly modified to handle one initial and final state for each local application)

4   Implementation

4.1   Software Architecture

PMQDA relies upon three components: Global Manager, Local Manager and Loader (Fig. 7). Loaders launch the applications and register their local part identified by a type (which application description?), an identifier (which instance?) and a role in the distributed application (which local application?). Each loader asks its local manager to admit a local application. In case of success (schedulable), the loader starts this local application (one loader per local application). Once admitted, the application directly communicates with its local manager. The LocalManager checks application sincerity (really used resources)

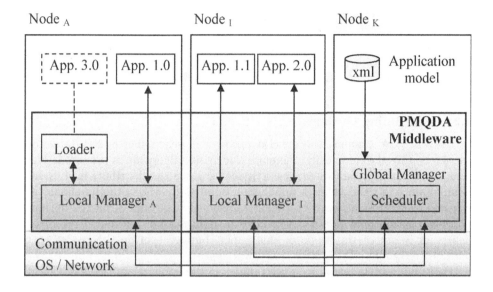

Fig. 7. PMQDA logical architecture (App. 1.0 means: instance identifier is 1 and local application is 0)

on its node and acts as an intermediary between applications and global manager. The GlobalManager schedules and controls the execution of the whole set of applications from their model. It selects the mode of activities in order to optimize the QoS. Resource monitoring exploits and relies on properties of the underlying layers that will finally supply the expected resource management.

After activation, an application executes its steps in the specified mode and at the specified time. It reports the end of each step, the arrival of an event and the selection of a path to its local manager, which forwards the information to the global manager.

At present, the global manager centralizes the scheduling task. This approach is preferable for distributed applications: as they require resources on several nodes, their scheduling affects the schedule of local resources on different nodes. Building the planning on a single node avoids any negotiation. In a decentralized approach, each local manager schedules its own resources, which decreases communication costs for applications running on a single node. On the other hand, this approach leads to heavy communication costs for multi-node applications. Assuming that a master node manages the negotiation, for each step it will ask each involved node for resource availability until an acceptable range be found, and then broadcast the decision (e.g., 1 to N negotiation protocol of ISO [13]). When ranges do not overlap, nodes may move already scheduled tasks, which increases the number of communications (Fig. 2(b), scheduling manually a_1, then a_2, and a_3 shows moving issues). Moreover and even more important, a solution is a path in a tree, and when backtracking is required to check another path (new mode choice or resource affectation), the communication costs may increase dramatically.

Anyway, as a great advantage of the middleware architecture, applications are not involved in this choice and the approach could be changed independently. We plan to test a mixed approach with resource credits for each local manager.

4.2   Scheduling Outlines

In the PMQDA context, the general problem of scheduling is NP-Hard and cannot be solved dynamically, therefore a heuristic algorithm is proposed. This solution is not as disadvantageous as it seems: since the distribution of events is unknown (e.g., end of step, application admission), the optimum should be assessed every time a new event occurs. Obviously, the sum of partial optimal policies is not optimal and in this context, no policy can be optimal. To compare heuristics is out of the scope of this paper, but we provide the reader with outlines to complete the system overview.

Paths and events introduce uncertainties in the application progress. Consequently, the schedule is computed from the current point to the next uncertainty. Thus, at the first scheduling time of the application described in table 2, Initialize and Sample are the only schedulable units because the next path is not specified yet (Sample again or Analyze). The remaining schedule is built similarly as soon as the uncertainty is removed.

To keep the maximal amount of available resources, and thus increase the admission chances, we schedule at the latest time and in the mode with the lowest utility [9]. As an advantage, when the system is stressed there is no need for degradation, i.e., schedule modification. As soon as a node is idle, the next ready step starts. When it is the beginning of an activity, it starts in the mode with the highest utility that is schedulable. With this policy, scheduling may only occur on admission request, uncertainty removal or end of step.

4.3   Integration in Development Process

An intrusive behavior adaptation policy requires the design of specific applications. First, the different operating modes must be designed. Second, the code has to be instrumented so that the application executes each step at the expected time.

Development Process. QoS management fulfills system requirements that have to be identified at the very beginning of the development. At the highest modeling level, the designer only needs to know the waiting points and paths that separate treatments (Fig. 5). Then, according to the available alternatives and the synchronization constraints, he/she builds the detailed model (Fig. 6). Treatments are split into activities according to modes, while activities are split into steps according to rendezvous and resource consumption changes. During the design phase, the code implementing the interactions between application and local manager is added. The API includes a few messages only (e.g., Register,

NextStep, EndOfApplication), sent through a proxy. It should be noted that QoS management uses its owns communication channels.

Each mode is assigned a utility value. Within an application, utility values are relative while they are absolute between applications: the level should depend on application importance, and designers must tune values in the application models. Resource consumption is estimated or measured from code, as in usual real-time applications. To declare too high resource needs may be a bad strategy since admission checks reject requests when resources are unavailable. To declare too low resources is risky since the local manager checks application sincerity.

Regarding the development process, our solution has two major advantages:

- A modeling offering several abstraction levels hence leading to an easier mastery of huge projects (scalability),
- The use of an UML standard tool with extension mechanisms such as stereo-type for decision points, tagged values for resource requirements or hardware characteristics (as in [18]). Afterwards, the model can easily be translated into PMQDA format (XML).

Virtual Execution Environment. In fact, to introduce the required tasks in the development process is less difficult than to split applications into activities and to design their alternatives. For this reason, we have implemented a virtual execution environment that emulates applications according to their model. Thus, the designer can test various node distributions offline, identify the resource availability issues and add alternatives to solve them. This simulation has been implemented using IBM-Rational Rose RealTime and its distributed communication layer (Connexis). The application model proves to be suitable for scheduling and emulation. The designer may watch the planning and the event trace in real-time on a separate node, while application models are displayed to check results.

Within a true time simulation context, the application prototype properties widely depend on underlying layers (OS, communication, etc.). This tool aims to bring out guidelines since only estimations of durations are available. A more precise adjustment in the target environment is still needed.

5   Related Works

Most QMS for distributed applications are implemented at the middleware level and rely on standard underlying layers (best effort). In this section, only the modeling aspect is taken into account among the numerous middlewares based on agents [5][12], layers [17], middlewares such as CORBA [14] or hierarchical services [6].

Two major categories of solutions are proposed to support QoS-aware applications [17]: reservation-based systems using resource reservation and admission control mechanisms, and adaptation-based systems attempting to adapt the system behavior to available resources. Since our approach mixes these two solutions, our modeling requirements are rather high.

Any model describes a point of view on a system, therefore a universal application model for QoS description should encompass all the points of view. The QoS Modeling Language (QML [11]) handles contracts but does not cope with dynamic aspects. The profile "Schedulability, Performance and Time" (SPT [18]) covers a broad area with special care to timing aspects. It is partitioned into a general resource modeling framework, including time and concurrency modeling, and analysis models including performance and schedulability analysis. Compared with PMQDA, the SPT does not provide the notions of adaptation and operating mode, and the execution model has only two levels (scenario and step) while PMQDA holds three levels and alternatives for the activities (Fig. 4). Any UML profile hence the SPT may be extended, but it deals with such a large area that it seems difficult to force users to learn much more than they need. In the terms of SPT, the proposed model is an analysis view [1] easy to translate into XMI-based UML interchange format. This way, we keep a customized and easy to learn representation while conforming to the standard with a few additional notions and a slightly different semantics (concurrency on activity diagrams).

To quantify utility is difficult. To avoid the issue, operating modes are ordered, then the utility is assigned the rank value: for instance a utility of 1 for a sampling rate of 16kHz, 2 for 24kHz, etc. [16]. Many works do not handle explicitly the utility and use the rank [10], the importance of the application or a feasible region in the multi-dimensional space of resources [6]. To ease QoS optimization, most works require the utility to vary in the same direction than resource use. This constraint is mandatory with one resource dimension, but is not necessary with several resources (see example Sect. 2). This constraint does not apply to PMQDA that scans the modes in the utility order until a valid one is found. The utility value represents a relative importance in case of admission conflict.

QoS models often have less parameters than PMQDA. For instance, in [10] application behavior is set through a consumption level without explicit utility. CPU time is assigned to periodical tasks via a simplex. Applications provide the QoS middleware with a vector of requests sorted in decreasing preference, while each request defines the CPU needs in a given time interval. In return, the application is informed about the admission controller's choice. This exchange is typical of intrusive policies. A finer description of the behavior in the form of a path to follow depending on the mode is given in [8]. They define flows with different QoS features (JPEG, MPEG...) and choose at run-time the best path available. In [7], the path is chosen from the outside of the application via a common adaptation interface. To improve and accelerate the search of an acceptable path, data may be stored in a convenient form quicker to use (performance base in [7], fault-tolerant plans in [3]).

---

[1] "An analysis view is a simplified version of the complete model and is extracted on the basis of a particular *analysis* or *domain viewpoint*".

To sum up, PMQDA has a set of features that make it different from other works: planning reservation, run-time admission check with a parameterized deadline, application guided specification of paths at run-time, and execution in synchronized operating modes on different nodes. Moreover, PMQDA deals with aperiodic multi-resource systems.

6 Conclusion

To manage QoS explicitly, we propose to adapt dynamically the behavior of applications to execution context, under the control of a middleware that schedules resource use. This approach applies to systems reacting to stimuli and ensures end-to-end deadline for scheduling units at application admission, at event arrival, and at path choice. Applications run in the mode with the greater utility that is schedulable (heuristic). When the system is overloaded, PMQDA selects alternatives execution modes and ensures that a distributed activity runs in the same mode on related nodes.

PMQDA controls applications based on their model. This model describes application resource requirements, operating modes, the context of each node or hardware (e.g., bandwidth, memory), etc. The model is written using a slightly extended UML, and abstraction levels make top-down modeling easier. However, to design applications with alternatives modes is not usual, and to aid designers we have developed a virtual environment that emulates the application from its model, and implements the middleware on top of OS and communication layers.

Currently we have mainly validated the application model, and future works will deal with the organization of the middleware (decentralization), and the scheduling to tune the compromise effort/result. Moreover, additional experiments are needed since the proposed QMS may a priori apply to areas such as fault tolerance and even load balancing providing that appropriate

References

1. T.F. Abdelzaher, E.M. Atkins, K.G. Shin, "QoS Negotiation in Real-Time Systems and its application to Automated Flight Control", *IEEE Trans. Computers*, Vol. 49(11), 2000, pp.1170-1183
2. T.F. Abdelzaher, Kang G. Shin, Nina Bhatti, "Performance Guarantees for Web Server End-Systems: A Control-Theoretical Approach", *IEEE Trans. Parallel and Distributed Systems*, Vol. 13(1), 2002, pp.80-96
3. E.M. Atkins , Tarek F. Abdelzaher , Kang G. Shin, "Planning and Resource Allocation for Hard Real-time, Fault-Tolerant Plan Execution", Proc. Int. Conf. on Autonomous Agents (Agents'99), ACM Press, 1999, pp.244-251
4. C. Aurrecoechea, Andrew T. Campbell, Linda Hauw, "A survey of QoS architectures", *Multimedia Systems*, Vol. 6, Springer-Verlag, 1998, pp.138-151
5. S. Brandt, G. Nutt, T. Berk, J. Mankovich, "A dynamic Quality Of Service Middleware Agent for Mediating Application Resource Usage", *RTSS*, 1998, pp.307-317
6. I. Cardei, Rakesh Jha, Mihaela Cardei, Allalaghatta Pavan, "Hierarchical Architecture for Real-Time Adaptive Resource Management", *Middleware 2000*, LNCS 1795, pp. 415-434

7. F. Chang, Vijay Karamcheti, "Automatic Configuration and Run-time Adaptation of Distributed Applications", *IEEE. High Performance Distributed Computing*, 2000, pp.11-20
8. S. Chatterjee, J. Sydir, B. Sabata, T. Lawrence, "Modeling Applications for Adaptive QoS-based Resource Management", *IEEE High-Assurance System Engineering Workshop*, 1997, pp.194-201
9. J.L. Contreras, J.L. Sourrouille, "A Framework for QoS management", *TOOLS'39*, IEEE press, 2001, pp.183-193
10. H. Domjan, T.R. Gross, "Extending a Best-Effort Operating System to provide QoS Processor management", *IWQoS 2001*, pp.92-106
11. S. Frolund, J. Koistinen, "Quality of Service Specification in distirbuted object systems", *Distributed Systems Engineering Journal*, Vol. 5(4), 1998, pp.179-202
12. J. Huang, Y. Wang, F. Cao, "On Developing Distributed Middleware Services for QoS- and Criticality-Based Resource Negotiation and Adaptation", *Journal of Time-Critical Computing Systems*, Kluwer, 1999, Vol. 16, pp.187-221
13. Information Technology - Quality of Service - Guide to Methods and Mechanisms - ISO/IEC 13243 Draft 1.0 — Project JTC1 21.57, 15/10/1997
14. D.A. Karr, C. Rodrigues, Y. Krishnamurthy, I. Pyarali, D.C. Schmidt, "Application of the QuO Quality-of-Service Framework to a Distributed Video Application", *Distributed Objects and Applications (DOA)*, 2001, pp.299-308
15. C. Lee, D Siewiorek, "An Approach for Quality of Service Management", CMU-CS-98-165
16. C. Lee, John Lehoczky, Ragunathan (Raj) Rajkumar, Dan Siewiorek, "On Quality of Service Optimization with Discrete QoS Options", *RTAS*, 1999, 276-286
17. Li, K. Nahrstedt, "QualProbes: Middleware QoS Profiling Services for Configuring Adaptive Applications", *Middleware 2000*, LNCS 1795, pp.256-272
18. "Schedulability, Performance and Time", Final adopted specification, 2002
19. R.E. Schantz, J.P. Loyall, C. Rodrigues, D.C. Schmidt, Y. Krishnamurthy, I. Pyarali, "Flexible and Adaptive QoS Control for Distributed Real-Time and Embedded Middleware", *Middleware 2003*, LNCS 2672, pp.374-393
20. "Unified Modeling Language Specification", OMG, Version 1.5, 2003

Accuracy of Performance Prediction for EJB Applications: A Statistical Analysis

Yan Liu and Ian Gorton

National ICT Australia,
1430, NSW, Australia
{jenny.liu, ian.gorton}@nicta.com.au

Abstract. A challenging software engineering problem is the design and implementation of component-based (CB) applications that can meet specified performance requirements. Our PPCB approach has been developed to facilitate performance prediction of CB applications built using black-box component infrastructures such as J2EE. Such deployment scenarios are problematic for traditional performance modeling approaches, which typically focus on modeling application component performance and neglect the complex influence of the specific component technology that hosts the application. In this paper, an overview of the PPCB modeling approach is given. Example results from predicting the performance of a J2EE application are presented. These results are then statistically analyzed to quantify the uncertainty in the predicted results. The contribution of the paper is the presentation of concrete measures of the confidence an architect can have in the performance predictions produced by the PPCB.

1 Introduction

Distributed component-based technologies such as the Java 2 Enterprise Edition (J2EE) and .NET have become important infrastructure technologies for building multi-tier applications. The overall performance of such component-based applications depends on a number of factors. These include the implementation of the supporting component container, the architectural decisions taken in the design of components, application-specific deployment configurations, and the specific application client behavior [6]. It is consequently challenging for software architects to design a system with a priori confidence that it will perform well enough to meet its requirements.

Consequently, architects are forced develop prototypes to evaluate the performance of an application design [2,6,11]. For complex applications, this can be time-consuming and expensive. We believe that the process of predicting the performance of a component-based system based on an architecture-level design could significantly reduce the engineering costs and risks of a deployed system failing to meet performance requirements.

In related research, performance modeling has proved a useful approach [1, 3,4,14,17,20,24] . A performance model can represent the underlying architecture as well as application behavior in terms of its performance characteristics. A common

T. Gschwind and C. Mascolo (Eds.): SEM 2004, LNCS 3437, pp. 185–198, 2005.
© Springer-Verlag Berlin Heidelberg 2005

practice is to build a prototype and use this to obtain measures for the values of parameters in the model [12]. However, for a complex application, this is expensive and time-consuming.

Therefore, we propose using *benchmarking* to overcome these difficulties. Benchmarking is the process of running a specific program or workload on a machine or system and measuring the resulting performance [21]. In PPCB (Performance Prediction of Component Based systems), benchmarking is used to provide values for certain parameters in the performance model that is used for prediction. However, the abstraction inherent in the performance model and approximations in the benchmarking measurements introduce uncertainty in to the resulting predictions.

The major contribution of this paper beyond that of [15] is the use of statistical methods to analyze the predicted performance for an application. This provides statistical evidence of the accuracy of the results of the PPCB. The results of the analysis reveal a high level of accuracy in the predictions. To the best of our knowledge, this is the first time such high levels of confidence in performance predictions of applications executing on black-box based component infrastructures have been published.

The structure of this paper is as follows. Section 2 gives an overview of the PPCB approach. Section 3 presents the example application on which we conduct performance prediction using PPCB, along with some sample performance prediction results. Section 4 details the statistical analysis, and Section 5 discusses related work.

2   PPCB Overview

The essence of our framework shown in Figure 1 is combining performance modeling and benchmarking techniques. This enables performance prediction at the design level of software applications that are based on specific component technology. A comprehensive description of the performance model is beyond the scope of this paper, and can be found in [15,16]. Given a component technology, such as an implementation of Enterprise JavaBeans (EJB), the approach has the following steps:

1. **Modeling.** We establish a general model P for the chosen technology, by identifying the main components of the system, and noting where queuing delays occur. This abstracts details of the infrastructure components and their communication.
2. **Calibrating.** The model has to be calibrated for a specific architecture before it can be used to predict performance, so we must develop the function f^A, which is the function used to calibrate the generic performance model P to specific architecture A. An architectural choice can be mapped to a set of infrastructure components and their communication pattern [4]. The operations of service components can be further aggregated into computing modules. Calibrating the performance model means deriving mathematical models with parameters characterizing those computing modules.
3. **Characterizing.** The purpose of characterizing an application is to determine the load that an application places on the underlying component infrastructure when the application takes the form of architecture A. For a given application, we can determine how often each component is executed. This depends on their business

logic, which tells us how often methods are called, and what operations are performed by which computing modules.

4. **Benchmarking.** The above produces a performance prediction for the designed system in the form of an equation with parameters. Some of the parameters represent observable or tunable features of the configuration, but other parameters reflect internal details of the black-box middleware platform that hosts the application components. We therefore implement a simple application, with minimal business logic and a simple architecture, on the target middleware platform, and measure its performance. Solving the performance model corresponding to the simple application allows us to determine the required parameter values, which we describe as the performance profile of the platform.

5. **Populating.** The parameters of the middleware platform profile can be substituted into the performance model of the designed application, giving the required quantitative prediction of performance of that application.

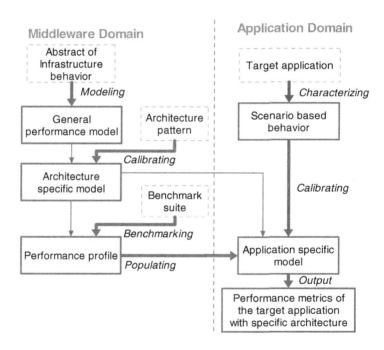

Fig. 1. The performance prediction framework

The PPCB approach provides a solution to overcome the difficulties in populating the performance profile of component infrastructure, or middleware. Instead of prototyping the system and measuring it, the explicit parameter values of the performance model are obtained by benchmarking a simple application. These benchmark results can then be applied to any applications that execute of the benchmarked middleware platform.

3 Example Results

The PPCB approach has been applied to predict the performance of a J2EE application, *Stock-Online*. In this section, we briefly describe the benchmark design and how benchmarking can be integrated with the performance model of an infrastructure to predict the overall performance of an EJB-based application. The predicted results are summarized and they are used in the next section for statistical validation.

3.1 Predicting Stock-Online Performance

Stock-Online [5] is a simulation of an on-line stock-broking system. It supports six business transactions and enables users to buy and sell stocks, inquire about the up-to-date prices of particular stocks, and get a holding statement detailing the stocks they currently own. There are four database tables to store details for accounts, stock items, holdings and transaction history.

We have implemented Stock-Online with EJB components. Three distinct implementations have been created that employ very different component architectures. These are:

1. One architecture solution uses Container Managed Persistence (CMP) entity beans, applying the standard EJB design pattern of a session bean as a façade to entity beans. A single session bean implements all transaction methods. Four entity beans, one each for the database tables, manage the database access. Transactions are container managed. We refer this architecture as CMP.
2. The second architecture optimizes the access mechanism to persistent data in the CMP architecture for business scenarios with intensive read-only operations. This architecture is implemented using the Read-Mostly (RM) EJB design pattern [19]. Read-only and read-write operations are separated into two entity beans, which are mapped to the same database data. Read-only operations have direct access to cached data inside the container, thus reducing the overhead of access to the database. The synchronization of cache data and persistent data is managed by the container.
3. The third architecture leverages an Optimistic Concurrency Control [13] (OCC) algorithm. A container that supports OCC does not hold a lock for any persistent data. The ACID transaction properties are managed by the database system. This increases the concurrency of the application when there is no confliction of two simultaneously running transactions.

The deployment environment for each of these solutions is identical. It consists of a commercial J2EE application server as the container for Stock-Online and a commercial relational database for persistence. The clients, J2EE container and database each execute on separate machines. The client requests are from web server hosted components under a full, sustained request load. Given this scenario, it is desirable for an architect to determine the level of performance that the system can provide under load without building its solution.

Basically, we have developed a queuing network model of the J2EE application server infrastructure and calibrated it for the three different component architectures. The approach to characterize an application behavior from scenarios is developed and presented in [15,16]. This produces a performance prediction for the designed system in the form of an equation with parameters, which we describe as the performance profile of the platform. These parameters capture the performance characteristics of the internal behavior of an EJB container. The parameters and the descriptions are listed in Table 1 below. Importantly, the performance profile and its value are obtained by benchmarking without access to the implementation and deployment of Stock-Online.

Table 1. Performance profile of an EJB container

T_{SINIT}	The service time of the container's initialization process
T_s	The service time of a session bean's operation, which doesn't include the time waiting for replies from nested beans' operations
T_o	$T_o = T_{SINIT} + T_s$
T_1	The service time for the container to access the entity data in its cache
T_2	The service time of the container to active/passivate an entity bean instance to secondary storage
T_{create}	The service time of the container to create an entity bean object
T_{remove}	The service time of the container to remove an entity bean object
T_{load}	The service time to load an entity data into the container
T_{store}	The service time to store updates of an entity data
T_{insert}	The service time to insert a new record of an entity into the database
T_{delete}	The service time to remove a record of an entity from the database

3.2 Benchmark Design

Component technologies leverage many standard services (e.g. security, transactions) to support application development. The benchmark scenario is thus designed to exercise the key elements of a component infrastructure involved in the application execution.

We have designed and implemented a benchmark suite for modeling the performance of EJB-based applications. The benchmark suite consists of four modules, namely a workload generator, benchmark application, monitoring utility and profiling toolkit in Figure 2.

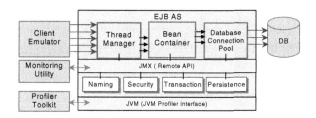

Fig. 2. A benchmark suite for EJB technologies

The benchmark clients simulate active requests from proxy applications, such as servlets executing in a web server. Under heavy workloads, this kind of proxy client has an ignorable interval between two successive requests 1. Its population in a steady state is consequently bounded[1.] Hence the benchmark client spawns a fixed number of threads for each test. Each thread submits a new service request immediately after the results are returned from the previous request to the application server. The 'thinking time' of the client is thus effectively zero. The benchmark also uses some utility programs to collect the measurement of black-box metrics, such as response time and throughput.

The implementation of the benchmark application involves a session bean object *Agent* and an entity bean object *Record*. Container managed persistence (CMP) is used for entity beans and transactions are container-managed. The example collaboration diagram in Fig 3 shows the benchmark application scenario for *read /write* and *get Records*.

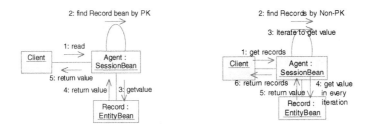

Fig. 3. Benchmark application events

A monitoring utility is implemented using the Java Management Extensions (JMX) API. It collects performance metrics for the application server and the EJB container at runtime, for example the number of active server threads, active database connections and the hit ratio of the entity bean cache.

A profiling toolkit *OptimizeIt* [18] is also employed. *OptimizeIt* obtains profiling data from the Java virtual machine, and helps in tracing the execution path and collecting statistics such as the percentage of time spent on a method invocation, from which we can estimate the percentage of time spent on a key subsystems of the J2EE server infrastructure. Profiling tools are necessary for COTS component-based systems, as instrumentation of the source code is not possible.

3.3 Predicted Performance

The explicit parameter values for the performance profile are obtained by solving the performance model using the inputs measured from benchmarking. Then the popu-lated performance profile provides inputs for predicting the performance of Stock-Online. This relationship is shown in Figure 4. Detailed solutions are is presented in [15, 16].

---

[1] A web server has configuration parameters to limit the active workload. For example, Apache uses *MaxClient* to control the maximum number of workers, thus the concurrent requests to the application server are bounded.

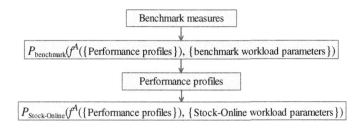

Fig. 4. Dataflow of the Stock-Online performance prediction

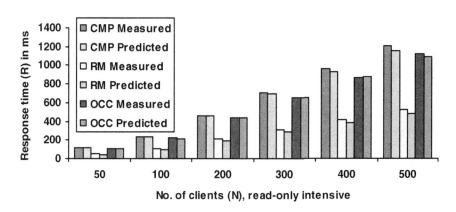

Fig. 5. Stock-Online Performance (*Read-only intensive* business model)

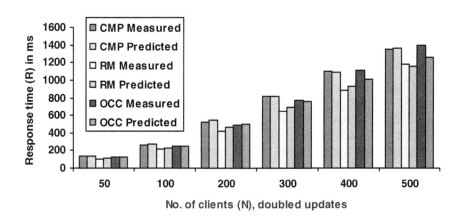

Fig. 6. Stock-Online Performance (*Doubled updates* business model)

In order to assess the accuracy of the model's predictions, we have implemented and measured the performance of Stock-Online for each of the three different implementations (i.e. CMP, RM and OCC). Below, we present two sample sets of results that are used for subsequent analysis:

- Figures 5 and 6 compare actual versus predicted performance of Stock-Online for a single J2EE server configuration (in this case, utilizing 20 threads). The aim is to infer how accurate the future predictions are based on the measured samples. The predicted client response time for the three architecture models under different workload with the same server configuration is shown.
- Figures 7, 8 and 9 compare the predicted and measured optimal response times as the J2EE thread pool setting is varied, under a stable client workload.

4 Statistical Analysis

As can be seen in Figure 5 to Figure 9, the predicted performance, while close, is not 100% accurate. Hence we need to assess the effectiveness of the overall approach. Hence, similarly to [9, 10], two appropriate statistical methods are used:

- Statistical intervals for the first data set.
- Linear correlation analysis for the second data set

4.1 Statistical Intervals

Statistical intervals can be used to quantify the uncertainty in the sample data [8,23]. We use *tolerance intervals* to estimate the boundary of the prediction error. A tolerance interval covers a fixed proportion of the population with a stated confidence [8]. The prediction error is defined as:

$$Error = \left| \frac{Predicted - Measured}{Measured} \right|$$

We calculated the statistical intervals as follows:

Step 1: Use *Shapior-Wilk* normality test to determine if the original distribution of *Error* is a normal distribution. We use the *shapiro.test* function in the S-Plus[22] library MASS. IF it is normal distribution, then DO Step 3.

Step 2: Transform the original data using the *BoxCox* function. The *BoxCox* function in S-Plus library MASS computes the profile likelihood function for the largest linear model to be considered as a guide in choosing a value for λ, which will then remain fixed [22].

$$y^{(\lambda)} = \begin{cases} (y^{\lambda} - 1)/\lambda & \lambda \neq 0 \\ \log y & \lambda = 0 \end{cases} \tag{1}$$

Step 3: The statistical software *SInt* [8] is used to calculate the tolerance interval for the (transformed) normal distribution of *Error*. As we are interested in the upper bound of the *Error* given a confidence level, only a one-side tolerance interval is considered.

The statistical intervals of prediction error can be also calculated as distribution-free intervals. [8] shows that a distribution-free interval (if one exists) will generally be longer than a corresponding interval based on a particular distribution.

The original statistical error metrics are listed in Table 2, 3 4 for the three architecture models CMP, RM and OCC respectively. The statistical results, for example the statistical intervals of the CMP model in Table2, can be interpreted as:

90% of CMP model prediction error will not exceed roughly 14.75% and we have 95% confidence level that this upper bound is correct.

This gives a concrete measure of the confidence an architect can have in the predictions produced by the performance modeling and benchmarking approaches we have developed for black box component-based applications. The statistical intervals show that the accuracy of the RM and OCC models are a little lower than the CMP model. One reason is that both the RM and OCC models do not cover the overhead of invalidating an entity bean cache element involved in conflicting transactions. This is mainly due to a technical limitation. These parameters depends on the internal implementation of the EJB container, and currently the monitoring and profiling tool can not identify the operations involved in these functions and their associated performance metrics. According to [17] however, a prediction error under 30% is still acceptable for capacity planning of a system.

Table 2. Statistical intervals for the CMP model

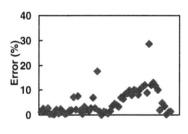

Original distribution of *Error*

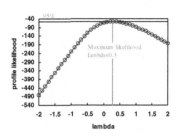

boxcox outputs

Statistical intervals	Value
Sample size	$N=61$
Sample mean	$\bar{x} = 4.97$
Sample standard deviation	$s = 5.19$
Percentile of the population	$p = 90\%$
Confidence level	$\gamma = 0.95$
Upper-bound of Error	$UB = 14.75$

Table 3. Statistical intervals for the RM model

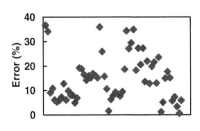

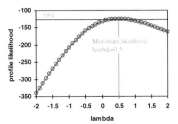

Original distribution of *Error*   *boxcox* outputs

Statistical intervals	Value	
Sample size	$N=61$	$N=61$
Sample mean	$\bar{x} = 14.72$	$\bar{x} = 14.72$
Sample standard deviation	$s = 9.31$	$s = 9.31$
Percentile of the population	$p = 80\%$	$p = 50\%$
Confidence level	$\gamma = 0.95$	$\gamma = 0.95$
Upper-bound of Error	UB = 25.15	UB = 15.21

Table 4. Statistical intervals for the OCC model

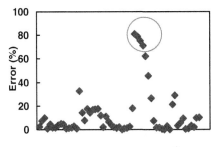

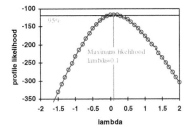

Original distribution of *Error²*   *boxcox* outputs

Statistical intervals	Value	
Sample size	$N=61$	$N=61$
Sample mean	$\bar{x} = 13.05$	$\bar{x} = 13.05$
Sample standard deviation	$s = 20.40$	$s = 20.40$
Percentile of the population	$p = 80\%$	$p = 68\%$
Confidence level	$\gamma = 0.95$	$\gamma = 0.95$
Upper-bound of Error	UB = 26.16	UB = 14.66

---

[2] The high *Error* in the circled samples is due to the ratio of transactions rolled back is high when the ratio of updating transaction increases. The overhead of rolling back transaction is not covered in the model.

4.2 Linear Correlation

Linear correlation analysis can measure the strength of the linear relationship between two variables. The thread pool size for an EJB container is an important tuning option. Our model can be used to predict the performance under different settings of the

Table 5. Linear correlation between predited and measured response time

Model	Correlation Coefficient R	Coefficient of determination R^2	p-value
CMP	0.9919	0.9837	0
RM	0.9981	0.9962	0
OCC	0.9984	0.9769	0

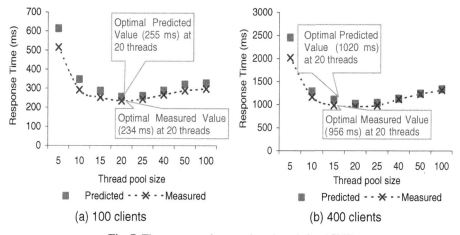

Fig. 7. The response time vs. thread pool size (*CMP*)

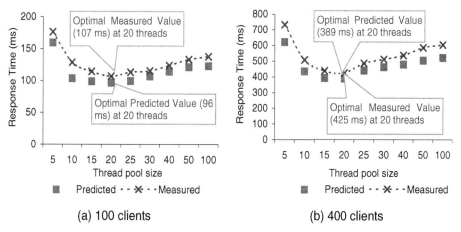

Fig. 8. The response time vs. thread pool size (*RM*)

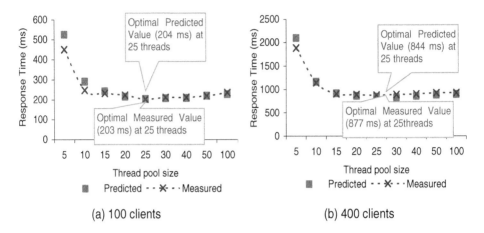

(a) 100 clients   (b) 400 clients

Fig. 9. The response time vs. thread pool size (*OCC*)

thread pool size, and consequently be used to find the optimal value with the best performance under a given workload. The linear relationship between predicted and measured response time is assessed to indicate the accuracy of the predicted optimal value. The calculation is shown in Table 5. The correlation coefficients of the three models indicate a good linear relationship between predicted and measured response time under the various settings of thread pool size. The statistical results can be interpreted as, for example in the CMP model, approximately 98.37% of the variation in the values of predicted response time is accounted for by a linear relationship with measured response time and the confidence level is 95%.

5   Future Work and Conclusions

In the Prediction-Enabled Component Technology (PECB) framework, the quality of the reasoning framework is evaluated by statistical intervals [9,10]. The accuracy of the prediction model is higher than ours, however, their performance model is developed for a white-box system and detailed measurements for each component can be easily discovered through source code instrumentation. This is not possible in our example of using a black-box COTS component technology. However, we hope our models may influence component technology vendors to expose APIs that allow the measurements of important parameters required for performance prediction.

In this paper, we statistically evaluate our PPCB approach for predicting the performance of black-box CB applications. The results demonstrate that 80% of the prediction error is within upper bound of 27% with a confidence level of 95%. This provides statistical evidence to the architects that our approach is accurate enough for predicting the performance for different architectures at the design level.

While these results are encouraging, and to our knowledge, the first that focus on black-box components that have been presented in the literature, they are of course based on a small sample. More evidence is required that the approach is broadly applicable and scalable. To this end we are working to:

- Enhance the PPCB approach to cover additional architectural features such as asynchronous messaging, widely varying message sizes and complex distributed transactions.
- Test the approach on more complex applications.
- Design software engineering tools that hide the complexity of the modeling and analysis steps in PPCB from an architect.

Acknowledgements

National ICT Australia is funded through the Australian Government's *BackingAustralia's Ability* initiative, in part through the Australian Research Council. We would also like to thank Professor Weber from the University of Sydney for his advise on statistical models.

References

1. Balsamo, S., Personè, V.D. N. Inverardi, P.: A Review on queueing network models with finite capacity queues for software architectures performance prediction, Performance Evaluation, Volume/Issue: vol 51/2-4, (2002) 269 – 288.
2. Cecchet, E., Marguerite, J., Zwaenepoel, W.: Performance and scalability of EJB applications, Conference on Object Oriented Programming, Systems, Languages and Applications (2002) 246-261.
3. Chen, S.; Liu, Y.; Gorton, I.; Liu, A.: Performance Prediction of Component Based System, Journal of Systems and Software, In Press (2004).
4. Gomaa, H., Menascé, D.A.: Design and performance modeling of component interconnection patterns for distributed software architectures, Proc. Workshop on Software and Performance (2000) 117-126.
5. Gorton, I.: Enterprise Transaction Processing Systems, Addison-Wesley (2000).
6. Gorton, I., Liu, A.: Performance evaluation of alternative component architectures for EJB applications, IEEE Internet Computing, vol.7, no. 3, (2003) 18-23.
7. Gorton, I., Liu, A., Brebner, P.: Rigorous evaluation of COTS middleware technology, IEEE Computer, vol. 36, no.3 (2003) 50-55.
8. Hahn, G. J.; Meeker, W.Q.: Statistical Intervals: a guide for practitioners, New York: John Wiley & Sons, 1991
9. Hissam, S. A., Moreno, G., Stafford, J., Wallman, K.: Packaging predictable assembly, Component Deployment: IFIP/ACM Working Conference, LNCS 2370 (2002) 108-224.
10. Hissam, S. A., Hudak, J., Ivers, J., Klein, M., Larsson, M., Moreno, G., Northrop, L., Plakosh, D., Stafford, J., Wallnau, K., Wood, W.: Predictable Assembly of Substation Automation Systems: An Experiment Report, Second Edition, CMU/SEI-2002-TR-031, ESC-TR-2002-031 (2002).
11. Juse, K.S., Kounev, S., Buchmann, A.: PetStore-WS: measuring the performance implications of web services, Proceedings of the International Conference of the Computer Measurement Group (2003).

12. Kounev, S., Buchmann, A.: Performance modeling of distributed E-Business applications using queuing petri nets, Proc. of IEEE Int'l Symp on Performance Analysis of Systems and Software (2003).
13. Kung, H. T. and Robinson, J. T.: On optimistic methods for concurrency control, ACM Transactions on Database Systems, vol. 6, No. 2, (1981) 213 - 226.
14. Lazowska, E., Zahorjan, J., Graham, S., Sevcik, K.: Quantitative System Performance, Prentice Hall (1984).
15. Liu, Y.; Fekete, A.; Gorton, I.: Predicting the performance of middleware-based applications at the design level, 4th International Workshop on Performance and Software Engineering (2004) 166-170.
16. Liu, Y.: A Framework to Predict the Performance of Component-based Applications, PhD Thesis, University of Sydney, Australia (2004).
17. Menascé, D., Almeida, V.A.F.: Scaling for E-Business: Technologies, Models, Performance, and Capacity Planning. Prentice-Hall, 2000.
18. OptimizeIt Suite, http://www.borland.com/optimizeit/
19. Rakatine, D.: The Seppuku Pattern, 2002. http://www.theserverside.com/patterns/thread.tss?thread_id=11280
20. Rolia, J. A., Sevik, K.C.: The method of layers, IEEE Transaction on Software Engineering, vol. 21, no. 8. (1995) 689-700.
21. Saavedra, R. H., Smith, A. J.: Analysis of benchmark characteristics and benchmark performance prediction, ACM Transactions on Computer System, vol. 14, no. 4, (1996) 344-384.
22. Venables, W. N.; Ripley, B. D.; Modern Applied Statistics with S-Plus, Springer, (2002).
23. Walpole, R. E., Myers, R. H.: Probability and Statistics for Engineers and Scientists, Fifth Edition, Macmillan Publishing Company (1993).
24. Woodside, C.M., Neilson, J.E., Petriu, D.C., Majumdar, S.: The Stochastic Rendezvous Network Model for Performa of Synchronous Client-Server-Like Distributed Software, IEEE Transactions on Computers, vol. 44, no. 1, January (1995) 20-34.

A Proposal for Evolution Driven Middleware Architecture for eBusiness Process Execution

Yuji Sakata and Shigeyuki Matsuda

NTT Data Corporation, Research and Development Headquarters,
21-2, Shinkawa 1-chome, Chuou-ku, Tokyo 104-0033, Japan

Abstract. Abstract. This paper proposes the EDMA (Evolution Driven Middleware Architecture) for eBusiness process execution. EDMA is a middleware architecture which is adaptable for eBusiness evolution based on workflow management system and web services technologies. In order to build the highly adaptable architecture, we pay attention to an evolutionary model of eBusiness. We show characteristic phases of the eBusiness evolution and illustrate that EDMA is so adaptable that middleware implementing EDMA need not be replaced but instead be added with components to comply with the phases of the eBusiness evolution. In addition, we introduce our implementation of a workflow engine and researches related to EDMA.

1 Introduction

Recently, eBusiness, a business transaction by means of Internet technologies, has been a significant factor in increasing the benefits of businesses and their partners. Specifically, performing complex and various transactions electronically brings great benefit to current businesses. Therefore, a technology for communicating various partners over the Internet and executing a process of business transactions automatically has become necessary. Nowadays, web services have been common technologies for communicating various partners over the Internet. A Web service is a software system designed to support interoperable machine-to-machine interaction over a network. It has an interface described in a machine-processable format (specifically, Web Services Definition Language), and other systems interact with the web service in a manner prescribed by its description using SOAP[1]-messages, typically conveyed using HTTP with an XML serialization in conjunction with other Web-related standards [1]. Because of its interoperability, web services technologies bring about an effective solution to the method of communicating with the partners which implement their eBusiness software using various platforms (.Net and J2EE) or languages (C++, Java, Perl and so on). On the other hand, many standards for describing the process of business transaction (hereafter, we will call the definition described by these standards the 'process definition') are proposed [3], for example, BPEL4WS [4], WS-CDF [5] and BPML [6]. Each standard should not be compared with the others among these overlapping standards only by their process modeling

T. Gschwind and C. Mascolo (Eds.): SEM 2004, LNCS 3437, pp. 199–213, 2005.

paradigm. They are compared advantageously relative to business models. Besides, each process definition is typically required to be interpreted and executed by its specific run-time middleware. Therefore, if a company tries to improve its business model, it may be required to replace all of its middleware. The total replacement of the middleware will prevent the company from agilely improving the business model. In this paper, we propose an evolution driven middleware architecture (hereafter, we will call it EDMA). As explained above, adaptability to a business evolution is a crucial requirement for a process execution middleware. In order to build a highly adaptable architecture, we pay attention to an evolutionary model of eBusiness. The rest of this paper is structured as follows. In section 2, we start with specifying the five characteristic phases of a typical evolutionary eBusiness model. In section 3, we abstract the requirements for each phase and derive the architectural features from the requirements. Moreover, we designate the architecture of the middleware and illustrate how the usage of the designated architecture simplifies upgrading the middleware to correspond to the eBusiness evolution. Then, we introduce the workflow engine which implements the designated architecture in section 4. Finally, we will discuss related works in section 5 and conclude this paper in section 6.

2   Business Use - EDI Like Purchasing

In this section, using a typical eBusiness case, we explain the characteristic phases of eBusiness evolution. Because we study a process execution middleware independent of any business domain, these phases are abstracted by focusing on the evolution of the static structure or the generation procedure of business process, which is a set of one or more linked activities and exchanged business documents between business partners which collectively realize a business objective or policy goal. Please note the concrete behavior of each activities executed by the business process, for example ordering, confirmation and catalogue-distributing, is ignored in the context of this model.

2.1   Description - A Purchase Transaction

Company A is a large manufacturer of computers. It purchases components of computers from a number of component manufacturers, which have already set up mutual trading relationship. Company X is one of these component manufacturers and is also doing business with many other customers providing its components. Note that this case is based on binary transactions to make the explanation simple. Company A already has several internal systems supporting the purchase of components, including a system for the approval of purchase, an ordering system and a payment system. Additionally, company A and company X are connected with each other by a proprietary VAN (Value Added Networks) and are utilizing EDI for their transactions. Currently, buyers in company A who want to purchase components (hereafter, we may call them just the 'buyers') must utilize their internal systems and proprietary EDI applications manually following a business process defined by company A. Because the cost for using

EDI is relatively high, Company A desires to introduce eBusiness technologies into its purchase transactions.

2.2   Five Phases for eBusiness Evolution

In this clause, we show five phases through which eBusiness applied to the purchase transaction of company A is going to evolve. We show a brief description of each phase in 'description' section. Then, we explain the motivation and limitation for shifting from the previous phase, stopping at the phase and shifting to the next phase in 'motivation/limitation' section. This explanation is information that indicates whether and how long each phase exists in a given business domain.

Phase I: Static Transaction with Specific Partners

Description. 'Static transaction with specific partners' phase is the phase in which a fixed business process for the purchase transaction with specific partners is automated by a process execution middleware. Company A and company X have beforehand agreed on the format of exchanged documents and the order of exchange. The left part of Fig. 1 depicts the transaction model in this phase. The middleware is responsible for managing the business process and interacting with both internal systems and systems of a component manufacturer.

Motivation/Limitation

- A primary motivation for shifting to this phase is increasing the efficiency of a regular business process such as a purchase transaction. Automated processing is very efficient because it is much cheaper than making system-dependent documents by hand and also is more accurate.
- Phase I means that automating process will start only with specific component manufacturers that will be integrated. This is the case where numerous agreements with each component manufacturer are required to realize the process automation because of the diversity among the manufacturers' systems and the procedures of transactions. Therefore, this phase may be skipped when the interfaces among manufactures are very similar or have already been standardized.

Phase II: Static Transaction Among Participants

Description. 'Static transaction phase among participants' phase is the phase in which company A is able to integrate with multiple components manufacturers. Moreover, each components manufacturer integrates with multiple computer manufacturers. The right part of Fig. 1 depicts the transaction model of this phase.

Motivation/Limitation

- In the previous phase, company A must agree with each specific partner on how to interact with its systems because of the diversity. However, in

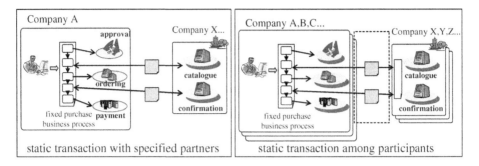

Fig. 1. The evolution of static transaction

the case where numerous manufacturers want to join transactions, every manufacturer is hardly able to maintain the methods of interaction with all transacting partners. In such an environment, organizational autonomy, which means that 'the organization cannot be controlled by another through (some) interactions' [7], is essential. Therefore, a primary motivation for shifting from the previous phase is further increasing the efficiency of regular business transaction according to fixing (or establishing) the way to integrate a business process with partner's systems.

– In this phase, buyers are supposed to select manually from which manufacturer they purchase components because information used in order to select the adequate manufacturer automatically is not sufficient (note that bulk transaction history data and data mining technology to analyze the bulk data may be required for serious selection).

Phase III: Role-Based-Dynamic Transaction

Description. 'Role' is a unit of characteristic and expected transaction behavior as a partner. 'Role-based-dynamic transaction' phase is the phase in which company A automatically selects transacting components manufacturer at the start of executing a business process using the information. The left part of Fig. 2 depicts the transaction model of this phase.

Motivation/Limitation

– A primary motivation for shifting to this phase is not an increase in the efficiency of executing business process but an optimization of its business transaction itself. In previous phases, the manufacturer from which buyers purchase components is selected statically or manually. However, information that is used to select the component manufacturer such as a components' price, a possible time limit of delivery and so on would be much and complex. Moreover, such information is likely to change dynamically. Therefore, selecting a partner at the start of a transaction would mean realizing more adequate transaction.

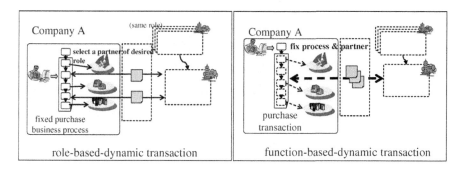

Fig. 2. The evolution of dynamic transaction

- In this phase, the smallest dynamically changing unit is 'role', for example, 'component-seller', 'component-buyer', 'settlement gateway' and so on.

Phase IV: Function-Based-Dynamic Transaction

Description. 'Function' is an atomic procedure executed by internal or external systems. 'Function-based-dynamic transaction' phase is the phase in which company A automatically composes its business process and selects a transacting partner to achieve an optimal transaction using the information at the start of a transaction to achieve requirements for it. The right part of Fig. 2 depicts the transaction model of this phase.

Motivation/Limitation

- A primary motivation for shifting to this phase is the optimization of transaction more effectively according to fixing of adequate business process using dynamic information just at the start of a transaction. When eBusiness evolves to be more open, it is not easy that all manufactures in an industry agree on the fixed business processes for a specific kind of transaction. Namely, semantically identical business processes for the transaction may be provided by different manufacturers. Therefore, in the paradigm of the previous phase, the company A should prepare various business processes in advance to have a potentially better choice available. It is, however, hard to maintain. Therefore, composing a business process from requirements of a transaction is required.
- In this phase, the smallest dynamically changing unit is 'function'.
- In this phase, company A fixes a complete business process at the start of a transaction. However, if the transaction takes for a long term, the optimal business process may change and differ from the one at the start of its transaction - it is the problem in some cases.

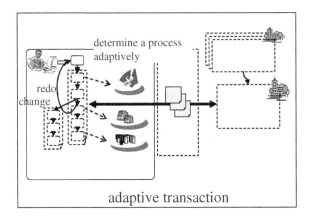

Fig. 3. Adaptive transaction

Phase V: Adaptive Transaction

Description. 'Adaptive transaction' phase is the phase in which the process execution middleware determines the subsequent adequate functions and processes after every execution of a function according to the situation of that instance. Fig. 3 depicts the transaction model of this phase.

Motivation/Limitation. A primary motivation for shifting to this phase is a further effective optimization of transaction by enabling company A to re-evaluate the optimal process while in progress of executing the current determined process. This 'step by step' approach of executing the process enables company A to select the optimal decision. Moreover, it helps to execute a process which cannot

Table 1. The charasteristic of eBusiness phase from the viewpoint of business

Time→

	I	II	III	IV	V
eBusiness phase	static transaction with specified partners	static transaction among participants	role-based-dynamic transaction	function-based-dynamic transaction	adaptive transaction
the primary motivation	the increasing in the efficiency of regular business processes		the optimization of business		
the model of interaction with partners	specified	static	dynamic		adaptive
the smallest dynamically-changing unit	no change		role	function	

be determined completely at the start time and handle an accidental error that occurs during the execution of the process.

2.3   The Phases Through eBusiness Evolution

Table 1 summarizes requirements on each phase of the eBusiness evolution based on the discussion above.

Five phases are mainly distinguished by how to select partners interacting with and the smallest dynamically-changing unit.

3   Evolution Driven Middleware Architecture for eBusiness Process Execution

In this section, we discuss about suitable architecture of the process execution middleware in each phase.

3.1   Architectural Requirements of Middleware for eBusiness Process Execution

At first, we abstract the considerable requirements and their solutions for each phase. Subsequently, we find the functional components that the process execution middleware consists of. Table 2 shows a summary of the architectural requirement and solution for each business phase. The details will be explained below.

Conventionally, Phase I and II are distinguished as a static integration and phase III, IV and V are distinguished as a dynamic integration. In phase I, a process execution middleware is required at least to interact with both internal/partner's systems implemented by various technologies and to enact the workflow for a transaction. SOAP [1], which is a technology of standard messaging, is certain to help to integrate all systems independent of their implementation. Besides, the middleware must consist of a workflow engine (defined in [9]). Moreover, the centralized control of a workflow by a stand-alone workflow engine is adequate as the execution model of business process in view of increasing efficiency due to the manageability. In phase II, choreography, that is, an explicit description of the interface (typically described by WSDL [10]) of functions and their executing order among organizations, is required. Since the organization should not control behind the interfaces of others, distributed workflow engine would be deployed at each organization. Accordingly, workflow distilling, which allows an organization to derive the fragment of its own workflow description from the choreography of a joined transaction, is required. In phase III, a primary requirement would be how to pick up the optimal partner among possible partners in desired 'role' automatically and how to execute a business process with picked partners. What information is effective and how this is evaluated in order to select an optimal partner is application-dependent. Therefore, only the semantics must to be specified for meta-data to express a transaction condition formally (for example, price, time limit of delivering and quality of or partners of transactions). The process execution middleware must interpret the formal requirement

Table 2. The architectural requirement and solution for each eBusiness phase

Time→

eBusiness phase	I	II	III	IV	V
considerable requirement(s)	1. automation of process 2.implementation independency	organizational autonomy	optimal partner detection	optimal workflow determination	adaptiveness
technological solution(s)	1. workflow management 2. standard messaging (SOAP)	1.chereography 2.Concrete interface (WSDL) 3. workflow distilling	1. semantics for static property 2. registry (UDDI)	1. semantics for dynamic systems 2. process composition	policy
usage model and characteristic functions of process execution middleware	typically called 'static' integration		typically called 'dynamic' integration		
	stand-alone		distributed		
			dynamic binding	dynamic binding and workflow	adaptive binding and workflow
process execution model in a transaction					
	⬭ function ▊ middleware ▢ organization ⌐ ⌐ same role set				

of the organization and find an adequate partner from a database storing formal representations of possible partners. In phase IV, instead of selecting an optimal partner playing a role, the way to fix optimal partners and the way to compose a process are needed. It means that the formalized model for the dynamics of a system is required. Situation Calculus [8] is one of such formalized models. The characteristic of the middleware of phase V is the adaptiveness of executing a business process, which means that the process execution middleware can determine the subsequent function in the resultant situation in order to meet the desired requirements of the organization. We regard policy as a significant technology to achieve this characteristic. In the context of this paper, policy means 'information which influences the behavior of an object' [11]. Policy controls not just a transaction but always influences all of the behavior of an application.

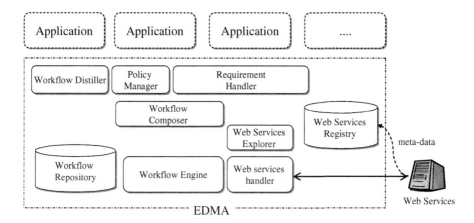

Fig. 4. Evolution driven middleware architecture

3.2   EDMA

We propose EDMA (Evolution Driven Middleware Architecture). The architecture is architecture for integrating internal systems and those in other organizations. This architecture has the characteristics that a suitable addition of components enables the middleware to fit eBusiness evolution explained above. The EDMA, which is depicted in Fig. 4, consists of the following components.

Workflow Engine. Workflow Engine is the component which controls an instance of the given pre-defined workflow definition.

Workflow Repository. This is the components which stores available workflows for transactions. Storing available workflows increases reusability of workflows.

Web Services Handler. This is the component which interacts with internal and external systems by means of Web services. This component is responsible for transmitting SOAP message and transforming implementation-independent SOAP message into data dependent of EDMA implementation.

Workflow Distiller. This component is responsible for 'distilling' a workflow template which is an abstract workflow that enables the workflow engine to interpret from a given choreography. The distilled workflow is stored in the workflow repository. Application may add detail function to the distilled template.

Web Services Registry. This is the registry which stores the meta-data of available web services and enables Web Services Discoverer and Web Services Composer to search and find web services fulfilling given conditions. This may comply with UDDI (Universal Description, Discovery and Integration) specification [12] as a way to discover meta-data of web services.

Web Services Discoverer. This component is a client of web services registry. It searches for web services satisfying meta-data from Requirement Handler.

Requirement Handler. This is a module for interpreting a request from a human requestor.

Workflow Composer. This is a component for composing a workflow to satisfy a request from Requirement Handler using web services retrieved from Web Services Registry.

Policy Manager. This component is used in phase V. It forces the application to observe defined policies.

3.3   The Usage Model of EDMA

We show the adaptability of EDMA, that is, we illustrate that the middleware implementing EDMA need not be replaced and it only needs additional components to go through eBusiness evolution.

Fig. 5 depicts collaborations between components in each phase to execute a transaction. In Fig. 5, filled squares are required components. An arrow means an interaction with components and application. Moreover, numerals appended to the arrow means the order of interaction in a transaction. Note that components are gradually added to the middleware as eBusiness evolves through the phases. In phase I, application invokes Workflow Engine by a pre-defined workflow definition, which may be read from Workflow Repository. Workflow

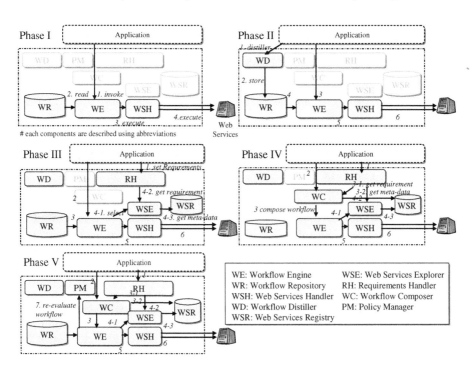

Fig. 5. Collaboration between components in each phase

Engine executes the workflow and web services by means of Web Services Handler. In phase II, the workflow definition is distilled from choreography among participants of a transaction. It proves the confirmation to executing a whole transaction that each participant distills its workflow from a total description of the choreography. In phase III and IV, application does not fix all details of the workflow definition but set its requirements to Requirements Handler. Web Services Explorer and Workflow Composer fixes at the start time of a transaction using data stored in Web Services Registry. In phase V, the executed workflow is re-evaluated whether an application observes policies after every execution of a function and updated.

4   An Implementation and a Related Research of the EDMA

In this section, we introduce the implemented framework and our on-going research related to EDMA. ΣServ is the framework which fulfills EDMA and achieves Phase I of eBusiness evolution. Shortly, it mainly consists of Workflow Engine, Workflow Repository and Web Services Handler. Besides, ΣServ has some additional components to have quality for industry use (for example, reliable messaging, data format conversion and various legacy system supports). Hereafter, we explain the details of ΣServ. ΣServ is middleware that executes a business process where the processing procedure is decided beforehand, that is, it achieves static service integration. Moreover, it conforms to the Web service. Moreover, this middleware runs on Java. ΣServ consists of four functions.

1. ΣServ FlowManager: This is a Workflow Engine that controls the business process. The business process is executed according to the processing procedure for deciding beforehand. It corresponds with Workflow Engine and Workflow Repository. Besides, it is based on eCo-Flow [13]
2. ΣServ TrustMessage: This is a component to connect between the middleware with web services. Moreover, reliable transmitting of messages is en-

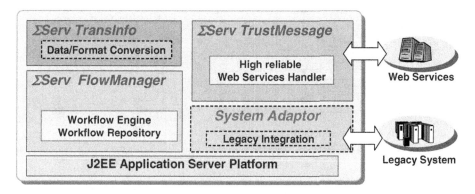

Fig. 6. ΣServ framework

abled. This conforms to the specification of SOAP and ebXML Messaging Service Specification [14].It corresponds with Web Services Handler.

3. ΣServ TransInfo: This component has a function of data conversion and the format conversion.

4. System Adaptors: The system that integrates might not necessarily conform to the Web service, and integrates with the legacy system. Accordingly, ΣServ implements adaptors to connect it with the system of non-Web service.

4.1   On-going Researches

We are now implementing the prototype for IV based on ΣServ. Here, we introduce our research for web services composer.which plays an important role to realize the middleware for phase IV.

Workflow Distiller. We have studied a method for extracting the UML activity diagram which a specific partner must execute from the whole business process among business partners describing as a single process using UML activity diagram with swimlane (Fig 7). The distilled workflow is stored in the workflow repository.

Workflow Composer. We have proposed a method for composing a workflow definition regarding the state change of an application [15]. This method is overviewed as follows. Beforehand, every web service is formally defined as what state of an application its function can affect and what state it will change the original state of the application into as a function axiom and the axiom is stored in Web Services Registry as meta-data of web services. Then, the current state and the desired state are formalized as a requirements sentence. This formalization is achieved by means of Situation Calculus [8].Workflow Composer inferred the adequate workflow from the function axioms and the requirement sentence.

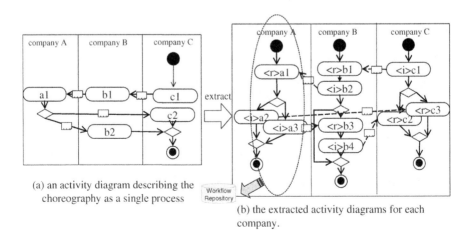

(a) an activity diagram describing the choreography as a single process

(b) the extracted activity diagrams for each company.

Fig. 7. The function of workflow distiller

5   Related Works and Discussion

Currently, there are many efforts on academic or industry research about the methodology for managing software evolution, enterprise application or component technologies. They are related to our proposal, so we show these works as follows. Gnatz proposed a process framework, which is modularly structured and defines the concept of process patterns in order to correspond to change and evolution of development processing [16]. Shortly, this study focuses not on re-usable run-time modules but on the development process. Hartwich proposed the architecture for enterprise application where the evolution of the application is mainly a matter of reconfiguration in [17]. Levi demonstrated CBDi (component-based development and integration) for mapping a business architecture to a component-based software architecture in [18]. Rausch outlined a well-founded common system model for componentware that copes with the behavioral aspects using explicit requirements/assurance-contracts formalization in [19]. The framework proposed in [20] is an eBusiness middleware comprising RDF-based languages to model processes, services, and service composition, and supporting technologies to generate executable workflow models. This research does not mention the suitable framework complying with eBusiness evolution. Here, we discuss the suitability of our proposed model for eBusiness evolution. The model of Phase I and II has already been adopted. In the early period of eBusiness, companies that have adopted the model early realized inter-company transactions over the Internet by means of various methods and rules which they fixed independently. This period corresponds to Phase I. Now, a typical successful example of Phase II is RosettaNet [21]. RosettaNet standardized business processes and a dictionary that is used for business documents. The standards of RosettaNet are widely adopted by Information Technology, Electronic Components and so on. The evolution into phase III and subsequent phases will arise in the future. Based on ΣServ and our research, we are going to implement a prototype system for phases III and IV. Technically, the shift to these phases will be possible. However, in these phases, it is important how participants joining a transaction will negotiate a contract and will manage trust between them, because determining a business process dynamically requires estimating the risk based on the trust in the participants. As for phase V, it is still unclear whether the 'step by step' approach of executing the process in this phase is adequate for future eBusiness, but we think this approach will have a fairly large demand. For example, this approach will be needed in a case where environment around a company changes considerably as time goes by and a case where the result of an activity is non-deterministic and subsequent activities are affected by that result. This approach can be used in B2C domain, for example for reserving a flight or a hotel during a trip. The shift to this phase will probably occur in the eBusiness domain as well. Our proposal of the middleware architecture is a starting point for realizing adaptable middleware for eBusiness process execution. The functional requirements of a transaction are not all we must discuss as to middleware architecture. As eBusiness evolves, non-functional requirements would be more significant. Therefore, concerning our proposal, we should also consider requirements about security, trust and the quality of services.

6   Conclusion

This paper proposes EDMA (Evolution Driven Middleware Architecture) for eBusiness process execution. The feature of EDMA is adaptable architecture considering eBusiness evolution. Therefore, EDMA is so adaptable that the middleware implementing EDMA need not be replaced but be added with components to go through eBusiness evolution.

References

1. Martin Gudgin et al, "SOAP Version 1.2 Messaging Framework", http://www.w3.org/TR/soap12-part1/, June 2003.
2. David Booth et al, gWeb Services Architectureh, http://www.w3.org/TR/2003/ WD-ws-arch-20030808, August 2003.
3. David Hollingsworth, "The workflow reference model: 10 years on", The Workflow Handbook 2004, Future Strategies Inc., 2004, accessible from http:// www.wfmc.org/standards/docs/ Ref_Model_10_years_on_Hollingsworth.pdf.
4. Tony Andrews et al, "Business Process Execution Language for Web Services (BPEL4WS) Version 1.1", http://www-106.ibm.com/developerworks/library/ws-bpel/, May 2003.
5. Nickolaos Kavantzas et al, "Web Services Choreography Description Language (WS-CDF) Version 1.0", http://www.w3.org/TR/ws-cdl-10/, April 2004.
6. Assaf Arkin, "Business Process Modeling Language(BPML)", http://www.bpmi.org/bpml_prop.esp, November 2002.
7. Jari Veijalainen et al, "Research Issues in Workflow Systems", Proceedings of 8th ERCIM Database Research Group Workshop, October 1995, accessible from http://www.ercim.org/publication/ws-proceedings/8th-EDRG/veijal.ps.
8. Raymond Reiter, gKnowledge in Actionh, ISBN: 0262182181, MIT Press, 2001.
9. Workflow Management Coalition, "Workflow Management Coalition Terminology and Glossary", WFMC-TC-1011 in WfMC public documents, Feb. 1999, accessible from http://www.wfmc.org/standards/docs/TC-1011_term_glossary_v3.pdf.
10. Roberto Chinnici et al., "Web Services Description Language Version 2.0 Part 1: Core Language", http://www.w3.org/TR/wsdl20/, March 2004.
11. M. Sloman et al, "An Architecture for Managing Distributed Systems", Proc. 4th IEEE Workshop on Future Trends of Distributed Computing Systems, 40–46, 1999.
12. Tom Bellwood et al, "UDDI Version 3.0", UDDI.org, July 2002.
13. T. Hatashima et al, "Web Services Processing Platform - eCo-Flow", SAINT 2002, Workshop, Jan. 2002, pp. 186-195.
14. Ian Jones et al, gebXML Message Service Specification Version 2.0h, OASIS ebXML Messaging Services TC, Feb. 2002.
15. Yuji Sakata et al, "A Method for Composing Process of Non-deterministic Web Services", Proceedings of 2004 IEEE International Conference on Web Services (in press), July 2004.
16. Michael Gnatz et al., "Towards a Living Software Development Process Based on Process Patterns", Proceedings of the Eight European Workshop on Software Process Technology number2077, 2001.

17. Christph Hartwich, "An Enterprise Application Architecture for Reconfigurable Distributed Process Topologies", the Proc. of the 23nd Intl. Conf. on Distributed Computing Systems Workshops, 2003.
18. Keith Levi and Ali Arsanjani, gA Goal-driven Approach to ENTERPRISE COMPONENT IDENTIFICATION AND SPECIFICATIONh, COMMUNICATIONS OF THE ACM Vol. 45 No. 10 p45, Oct. 2002.
19. Andreas Rausch, "Software Evolution in Componentware using Requirements/Assurances Contracts, ICSE 2000, 2000.
20. Lerina Aversano et al., gIntroducing eServices in Business Process Modelsh, the fourteenth International Conference on Software Engineering and Knowledge Engineering, July 2002.
21. RosettaNet: http://www.rosettanet.org/

Experience with Lightweight Distributed Component Technologies in Business Intelligence Systems*

Leticia Duboc[1], Tony Wicks[1], and Wolfgang Emmerich[2]

[1] Searchspace Ltd., 80-110 New Oxford Street,
London, WC1A 1HB, U.K
{l.duboc, t.wicks}@searchspace.com
[2] Dept. of Computer Science,
University College London,
WC1E 6BT, U.K
w.emmerich@cs.ucl.ac.uk

Abstract. Business Intelligence (BI) systems address the demands of large scale enterprises for operational analytics, management information and decision support tasks. Building such applications presents many challenges. They must support complex and changing data models, have fast turnarounds, present an up-to-date and accurate view of information and provide extensibility mechanisms for new analyses.

Widely adopted distributed object systems, such as J2EE can be heavyweight and inflexible when applied to the described scenario. This paper presents our experience when developing a data analysis system that applies a combination of lightweight distributed component technologies available for Java.

These technologies are combined in an event-based architecture that anticipates constant changes to analysis algorithms in short time frames and provides the ability to maintain correlated analyses in a consistent state. The resulting architecture is extensible, easy to deploy, highly configurable and has a very flexible data model. We compare this approach with existing distributed object systems and evaluate its suitability to provide business intelligence.

1 Introduction

BI encompasses a wide variety of tools and applications that can extract better business understanding from raw, typically transactional, data. This variety incorporates query and reporting tools, OLAP servers, data mining and data integration tools [3]. While traditional BI solutions are appropriate for many tasks, they are best aimed at the dimensions of a problem that remain relatively static. Operational analytics tools, instead, seek to better extract meaningful

---

* This work is partially supported by tti Ltd. through KTP 3528.

T. Gschwind and C. Mascolo (Eds.): SEM 2004, LNCS 3437, pp. 214–229, 2005.
© Springer-Verlag Berlin Heidelberg 2005

information based on self-tuning and learning, resource conservation and dynamic expansion to the true dimensionality of the problem [2]. They should support complex data models, be extensible accumulate new analysis and allow for scalability.

We are interested in systems that will be capable of handling volumes in excess of 100 million transactions per day, accumulated over months or years. Scalability is often achieved by distributing computational tasks across a number of processors executing in parallel. This number can be increased to accommodate growing volumes, if the distributed software architecture has been chosen carefully. In enterprise settings, such software architectures are often implemented using distributed component technologies. Nevertheless, widely adopted distributed object systems, such as architectures based on the Java 2 Enterprise Edition (J2EE), can be inappropriate when applied to data intensive analysis scenarios [17].

The main contribution of this paper is an account of our experience when architecting PLUS, which is such an experimental environment to devise algorithms to be deployed in Searchspace's operational analytics solution. We initially investigated J2EE technologies, most notably the Enterprise Java Bean component model (EJB) [17] and the Java Messaging Service (JMS) [18]. Instead we present reasons why these technologies do not do justice to the data-intensive problem domain and instead present a solution that uses more lightweight technologies. The main technologies used in this work were:

- Hibernate, an open source object/relational mapping toolkit for storing plain old Java objects (POJOs) to a database [20].
- Java Management Extensions (JMX), which provides management capabilities for a service-driven network [12].
- XDoclet, a meta-data template engine that parses the source code and generate artifacts such as configuration files and support code [21].

This paper is organized as following: Section 2 discuss some of the common used tools and techniques for data analysis. Section 3 presents PLUS, the real world system described in this paper, and its requirements. The following section discusses the inadequacy of J2EE for the problem described. Section 5 briefly introduces the software architecture that we have built using lightweight distributed component technologies. General observations and lessons learned are drawn in section 6. We then conclude the paper in Section 7.

2 Background

Extracting meaningful information from large data sets is challenging. Selection of suitable analysis approaches is non-trivial and comprises iterative processes of experimentation and testing. For numerous reasons, a single analysis algorithm will usually be split into a sequence of dependent steps. These steps reduce algorithmic complexity, allow intermediate results to be available for other purposes, such as user interrogation, and enable new analysis streams to use derived data that may already be available in the system. Additionally, division of algorithms has benefits in terms of system scalability and performance.

Layering analyses in this way introduces dependencies between algorithms and additional complexity in terms of managing dependencies associated with the data being processed. The challenge is therefore to create mechanisms that can manage these dependencies such that a system provides guaranteed, consistent results arising from changes to transactional, reference or other system data feeds. These features are necessary to force results to be re-calculated whenever analysis algorithms are changed and, more importantly, must be correctly managed to allow deployment into operational data changing environments.

A common approach is to use purpose built analytic tools, such as IDL [16] and MATLAB [22], which enable users to perform ad-hoc analysis. These tools, however, do not provide means to deploy an analysis in an operational environment. To reproduce a result with such tools, the analyst is forced to repeat the whole process. Further they are not designed to scale to the type of environment we are interested in. Vendor specific approaches have other degrees of limitation. For instance, BusinessObjects is an analytical tool for summarization, visualization and reporting, not designed to be used as a framework to generate analysis that can be deployed operationally [5].

An alternative approach is to create analyses that can be deployed operationally. Commonly, this would include database stored procedures and OLAP [23] tools, which are efficient and powerful query mechanisms. Nevertheless, those solutions, by themselves, do not provide a means for distribution, sampling and parallelism. In addition, they may introduce portability problems.

3   Problem Statement

PLUS is a data analysis environment that is used to extract meaningful information from large amounts of transactional data. The system comprises data loading, transformation and analysis. Report generation and information navigation (e.g. drill-down capabilities) are performed by an external system, the integration of which is beyond the scope of this paper. PLUS provides an environment for data analysts to create, test, execute and store analysis algorithms. Once defined and tested in PLUS, analyses can be deployed operationally in a business environment.

PLUS is currently used in the banking/finance domain in applications such as money laudering and fraud prevention. To date PLUS has been applied to analyze two million transactions over a historical period of two years, comprising over twenty gigabytes of data.

¿From an analytic point of view, PLUS is an experimental framework for the development of analysis algorithms. Based on data held within the system, or externally in a file, the analyst defines algorithms that are deployed into the PLUS framework. Analyses can be divided in logical stages, having intermediate results persisted for user consultation. Algorithms are stored by PLUS, so they can be re-executed whenever required. As an example, the analyst can produce from

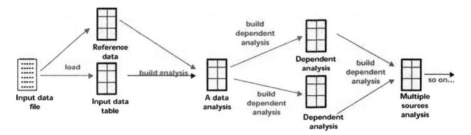

Fig. 1. Dependent Analysis

transactional data, summary information that may be reused by later analyses. If new transactional data is added or a stage's algorithm is modified, the system automatically updates itself, maintaining a consistent state. Figure 1 illustrates those dependencies. Note that analyses can also be dependent on multiple previous results.

From an operational point of view, PLUS deals with large amounts of transactional data. Sampling capabilities allow analysis strategies to be tested before being applied to the whole set of data. PLUS also provides a means to split analyses into logical and operational units of work. Analyses can be executed in parallel based on predefined analytical criterias. Dependencies are self-managed using inversion of control. Each analysis know its own dependency and this information is used by PLUS to compose individual components, so that changes can propagate through the system. Further, PLUS provides instrumentation through a web interface. Analysis parameters can be modified and their execution controlled.

We now introduce the main requirements for PLUS that led to the selection of the lightweight technologies described in this paper.

Support a Complex and Changing Data Model: BI systems often maintain months or even years of detailed transactions. Analyzing such large volumes of data to identify trends, patterns and exceptions is a very complex process. PLUS required a rich data model that allowed algorithms to take advantage of object-oriented features, simplifing the analysis process. In addition, the data model had to be independent of the underlying database schema, offering a level of abstraction and simplifying its implementation.

Support for Experimentation: When dealing with large amounts of data, it may not be clear from the outset how best to extract meaningful information. Analysts often try many different approaches in order to derive a comprehensive set of algorithms capable of obtaining relevant information from the data.

PLUS architecture had to provide an efficient means for experimentation. Such features included support for fast development, deployment and test of analyses. The task of defining analysis algorithms had to be reduced to a minimum, ideally being tool-supported. The analyst should be able to concentrate on the business logic and leave other time-consuming, non-core requirements to be addressed automatically by the system.

Ability to Incorporate New Analyses: To experiment efficiently with data analysis strategies, analysts had to be able to extend the system to support new algorithms with minimum effort. It was also a requirement that newly created analyses could be easily deployed and immediately incorporated, without affecting the running of the overall system.

Repeatable Process and Fast Turnaround: In general, BI systems deal with very large amounts of data. Testing analysis algorithms against the whole data is, most of the time, inefficient and unnecessary. The system had to offer sampling capabilities and a means to store algorithms that, once tested and tuned, could be applied to the whole data.

Maintaining Consistent and Accurate View of Data: Loading new data and changing algorithms will, almost certainly, impact subsequent analyses. Immediately reflecting those changes is crucial, as BI systems should maintain a consistent and accurate view of information. Given the complexity dependencies may assume, manual update would be time consuming and error-prone.

PLUS had as a requirement to offer a means to automatically update dependent analyses in face of changes. It is important, however, to bare in mind that PLUS provides an environment for experimentation. Tests cannot impact already deployed analyses. PLUS had therefore to allow the deactivation of dependent analyses, while others are under test.

Execution Control: Control over execution should offer, at a minimum, the ability to start, stop, restart, resume and change analysis properties.

Scalability and Performance: Support for scalability is not unique to BI systems. However, it is of significant importance, considering the large amount of calculations performed by algorithms. It was therefore a requirement that PLUS could accommodate new analyses and update existing ones with minimum impact on the system performance.

The requirements above demand a flexible, loosely coupled architecture that can be easily extended. A component-based architecture comes as a natural choice, allowing data analyses to be encapsulated by loosely coupled components that can be plugged into the system with relatively little effort.

4   Business Intelligence Systems with J2EE?

Initial investigations of the implementation considered the J2EE specification and, in particular EJB and JMS. At the time, like other Java developers, we went through a learning curve. Currently, many of the issues we faced are well documented in literature [19]. Our experience is summarized here:

– We considered using Entity Beans with container managed persistence for the persistence layer in order to achieve data independence from the database schema. This approach did not work because Entity Beans were designed to be stateful distributed components, not lightweight domain objects. In addition, despite the support for relationships, EJBs impose restrictions on the object format. Need for rich data models is not unique to BI systems and for all such cases EJB container-managed persistence represents according to [19] is limited by "tight coupling, obscure development models, integrated concerns and sheer weight". PLUS had as a requirement the ability to persist any Java object, so it could take advantage of OO/Java features, like inheritance and polymorphism. The use of EJB container-managed persistence was therefore discarded.

- The structure of database tables often does not match the structure of the logical entities they represent. Sometimes, even when objects differ from their exterior design, internally they still need to take advantage of the database structure to increase performance and achieve scalability. Examples include logically separated entities that map to the same denormalized table, a single entity that maps to multiple tables and given table (e.g. address) that is referenced by other tables (e.g. order and customer) with no explicitly relationship. CMP Entity Beans cannot naturally handle such cases [17].

- EJB QL allows additional finder methods to be defined in the Entity Bean home interface, associating each one of them with an EJB QL query in the deployment descriptor. This constraint means that the query logic had to be defined in the entity bean. For PLUS, which have different analyses using the same domain objects, the logic should be in the analysis class instead of in the entity bean. This approach does not only simplify the entity bean, but also makes analysis objects self-contained, providing a better understanding of the encapsulated algorithm.

- The EJB specification does not include management capabilities, despite the fact that it is implemented by some vendors. Using vendor specific features is not desirable, as it compromises the portability of the solution.

- JMS supports asynchronous communication between distributed components. It is integrated with the EJB specification through message beans that are invoked when messages arrive on a queue. We considered implementing a publish/subscribe mechanism to maintain system concistency, using JMS and Message Beans. We concluded that the result would have been too heavyweight. JMS is intended for asynchronous communication between distributed components. Therefore, messages usually carry heavy payloads and have a significant deployment overhead for queues and their persistent storage. We did not need these heavyweight mechanisms as all we required was to trigger re-execution of dependent analyses.

One can argue that EJB could be integrated with JMX for management purposes and with a flexible object persistence mechanism, such as Hibernate or Oracle TopLink, for the data modelling [15, 20]. For PLUS, however, JMX and Hibernate themselves are sufficient to address the system requirements, as explained in Section 5.2.

5   Implementing BI with Lightweight Technologies

5.1   Overview of Technologies

Selecting the appropriate set of technologies to implement an architecture that then fulfils the requirements is a challenging task, particularly since there is a complex inter-dependency between the use of particular forms of infrastructure and the architectures that they induce [8]. This section describes the technologies used in PLUS, along with the reason they have been chosen.

JMX: Java Management Extensions (JMX) provide the flexibility, interoperability, and dynamic management capabilities that are required for a service-driven network [12]. This work uses the JBoss implementation of the JMX specification. JBoss [10] is, itself, built around JMX. Our BI system architecture takes advantage of JMX, by implementing data analysis algorithms as JMX services.
JMX is particularly useful in the BI setting because:

- systems need to maintain an up-to-date and accurate view of information. Services can benefit from the JMX event-mechanism to re-calculate analyses if other services modify data they are dependent upon.
- analysis services can be hot-deployed into the JMX Server, being instantaneously recognized and incorporated into the system.
- the JMX instrumentation mechanisms allow a fine-grained control over execution and configuration of services.

Hibernate: Hibernate is an open-source object/relational mapping toolkit with facilities for data retrieval and update, transaction management and database connection pooling [20]. Hibernate was chosen in the PLUS architecture for the following reasons:

- BI systems usually have a complex and evolving data model. Unlike EJB, Hibernate provides a very flexible O/R mapping, designed to naturally persist objects following the common OO/Java idiom.
- PLUS strives for flexibility, giving the analyst the option to run analyses as simple standalone applications. Unlike the EJB persistence mechanisms, Hibernate can run from outside an application server, as it does not impose as many requirements on the objects to be persisted.
- Hibernate can be managed via a JMX Standard MBean, providing a convenient means to modify database related properties through the JMX console.
- Hibernate provides tools for code, mapping files and database schema generation. Shifting effort from labour intensive tasks, not only lets the analyst focus on business related problems, but also gives support for experimentation.

XDoclet: XDoclet, officially termed a "Javadoc metadata templating engine", parses metadata in Java source files and generates artifacts such as XML descriptors and/or source code [21]. XDoclet is a natural choice when using Hibernate, as mapping files and database creation scripts can be automatically generated from tags in the Java object to be persisted.

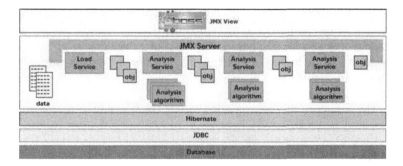

Fig. 2. System overview

Sun has announced metadata/annotations in J2SE 1.5. This new feature provides the ability to associate additional data alongside Java classes, interfaces, methods, and fields. This additional data, or annotation, can be discovered at runtime using the Java reflection API [6]. For PLUS, the ability to query metadata at runtime would mean that some properties files would not have to be generated. J2SE 1.5 metadata, however, does not replace XDoclet as a code generator.

5.2   PLUS Architecture

Analyses dependent nature and support for experimentation and demand a flexible and loosely coupled architecture. A natural choice is to implement analysis stages as independent components that can be easily assembled. Communication is achieved through events, in a similar approach to SEDA [14], which consists of a network of event-driven stages connected by explicit queues. It combines aspects of threads and event-based programming models to manage concurrency, I/O, scheduling, and resource management needs of Internet services. The main distinction between both approaches is that while SEDA intends to support a massive amount of concurrent user connections, PLUS focuses on data processing.

Easy of deployment, extensibility and management of components is achieved by layering PLUS on top of JBoss implementation of JMX. Components are represented by JMX services that can be dynamically deployed, being immediately incorporated to the overall system. PLUS services are generic components deployed with a set of analysis algorithms. As JMX services, components are exposed by JBoss JMX console for instrumentation.

Hibernate is placed between the JDBC layer and JMX services. It provides a level of abstraction, allowing POJOs to be persisted in the database. Free from constraints in input and output objects, analyses can take advantage of a rich data model and OO features like inheritance and polymorphism. The use of Hibernate is, however, not enforced. Analyses can have access to the underlying JDBC layer if desired. Fig. 2 gives an overview of PLUS architecture.

Services and Notification: In comparison with other distributed technologies which often lead to complex interfaces between components, message or event orientation creates a small number of simplified programming interfaces [9] [11]. This interfaces can be widely applied as the are not dependent on underlying functionality and comprise simple message or event handlers, which allow simple system re-configuration [7].

Given the amounts of data handled by PLUS, passing analysis results in messages would be prohibitively expensive. In addition, analysis results are by themselves useful information, which should be persisted. Hence, there is no need for direct interaction between components. Analyses algorithms have knowledge about their input and output data format, but are completely unaware of how the input data has been produced. Simple events that informs of changes in the input data are more appropriate than complex messages.

PLUS implements events through the JMX publish/subscribe mechanism. Once notified, the service can update its analysis accordingly and inform other services that are dependent on its results. Updated analysis results are therefore communicated through the system in an asynchronous way, maintaining correlated analyses in a consistent state.

To receive notifications, a service needs to register as a listener of other services that affect data it is dependent on. This includes already deployed services and others that may be deployed in the future. The assembly of components is implemented through inversion of control. Services have knowledge of the tables/hibernate objects they are dependent on. PLUS uses this information to assemble components as publishers and subscribers. In addition, a newly deployed service registers with the MBeanServer to be informed about the future deployment of services that can change its input data. This mechanism guarantees that dependencies are self-updated whenever a new service is deployed into the system.

Furthermore, PLUS architecture provides a mechanism to avoid unnecessary work when a notification is received. A service can recognise the changes in the input data and update only the affected database rows or persistent objects in the result. The ability to automatically maintain a consistent state offers a significant support for experimentation. Hence, users do not have to worry about downstream analyses that might be affected by the newly incorporated algorithm.

Definition of Analysis Algorithms: As an experimental environment, PLUS should provide a fast turnaround. Users must be able to quickly develop new analysis strategies and understand existing ones. Code generation plays an important role in rapid development and transparency. It can be used to avoid code duplication and transparent models [19].

PLUS adopts a code-centric approach for the implementation of data loading and analysis algorithms. This method requires from the analyst the implementation of a single Java task class. Each task encapsulates one analysis algorithm. Tasks read data from an input source (e.g. file or tables), perform the required computations and persist the results. The analyst embeds related meta-data in

```
/**
 * @task.input input-entity="BranchVolFin"
 *             control-entities="AnalysisFin.productId"
 *
 * @task.output.java name="DistinctBranchVolFin"
 *                   fields="batch:long:6,
 *                   productId:long:10,
 *                   transactionType:long:7,
 *                   analysisType:String:20,
 *                   score:double:10"
 */
public class DistinctBranchVolFinTask extends ServiceTask {
  ...
}
```

Fig. 3. Meta-data in task code

the javadoc comments of the class source code using XDoclet tags. Meta-data represent relevant information about the task, such as analysis specific properties, output data format and dependencies. Automatic generation of code and support file encourages experimentation by considerably reducing the amount of work done by the analyst.

To illustrate, Fig. 3 shows the XDoclet meta-data in a task's code. In this example, the task is dependent on the data in the `BranchVolFin` table and generates its result in the `DistinctBranchVolFin` table. The output data format is explicitly defined in the `task.output.java` tag. The `control-entities` tag is an example of an analysis specific property.

XDoclet is used to automatically generate properties and configuration files, Hibernate persistent classes, mapping files and even database tables. Most of the code/file generation process did not have to be developed, as it came for free with Hibernate and its integration with JMX. Fig. 4 illustrates part of the output Hibernate object that XDoclet derived from the tags in Fig. 3. The Hibernate object is simply a javabean object with XDoclet tags defining the format of the columns in the database. The Hibernate mapping file is an XML document that maps fields in the Java class to columns in the database. Tables themselves are automatically created when analyses are deployed into the PLUS framework.

One can argue that code generation, as used in PLUS, combines concerns that should be logically separated, such as code and database schema design. Coupling code and configuration is certainly a downside. We have however opted for this approach because, as an experimental environment, PLUS should provide a fast turnaround. Having output object definitions as XDoclets tags in the task code, helps not only in the generation of Hibernate code and database schema, but also gives a better understanding of the analysis logic itself.

PLUS does not enforce any restriction in the way data is retrieved, processed and stored by analysis tasks. Analysts may choose to use, for example, the Hibernate query language or direct JDBC. It is worth mentioning that, given the complexity of data in BI systems, Hibernate will provide many advantages. The very powerful object/relational mapping offered by Hibernate allows the task to take advantage of object-oriented features, like inheritance, association, composition and collections. The use of Hibernate also offers an abstraction

```
public class DistinctBranchVolFin {          <?xml version="1.0"?>
                                             <!DOCTYPE hibernate-mapping PUBLIC
    /** Independent Identifier **/            "-//Hibernate/Hibernate Mapping DTD
    private long id;                          2.0//EN" "hibernate-mapping-2.0.dtd">

    /** Batch id for this load **/           <hibernate-mapping  schema="tdb">
    private long batch;                        <class name="DistinctBranchVolFinTask"
                                                      table="DistinctBranchVolFin"
    /** Output Fields **/                            schema="tdb"
    private long productId;                          dynamic-update="false"
    private double score;                            dynamic-insert="false">

    /**                                          <id name="id"
     * @hibernate.id column="ID"                      column="ID"
     *              type="long"                        type="long"
     *              length="10"                        length="10">
     *              generator-class="native"      <generator class="native"/>
     */                                          </id>
    public long getId() {                        ...
      return id;                               </class>
    } ...                                      </hibernate-mapping>
```

Fig. 4. Generated Hibernate Object

layer, simplifying the task code, and other facilities, like transaction management, database connection pooling, programmatic as well as declarative queries and declarative entity relationship management. As an example, consider distinct Hibernate objects representing credit and debit card transactions. Having both extending from a common card transaction object, an analysis can take advantage of polymorphism to easily derive all card transactions in a given retailer chain during the summer sales.

Experiments have shown that there is a small performance penalty for using Hibernate. Nevertheless, specially in cases where the performance is constrained by the analytical work, this penalty is not the overriding factor when opting for one or the other approach. In an experiment, an analysis processing 10,000 rows took 123.47 seconds with JDBC and 140.19 seconds with Hibernate.

Execution and Instrumentation of Analysis: Scheduling and ordering of events is an important concern when using a staged event-driven approach. In approaches like SEDA [14], stages are responsible for defining their own scheduling policy for incoming events. Examples of policies are FIFO (First In, First Out) and SRTP (Shortest Remaining Process Time). PLUS uses events to maintain a consistent state between correlated analyses. The framework is not designed to support a large number of concurrent user connections, not having fairness in response time as a major concern. For this reason, PLUS uses a simple FIFO policy, having events processed in the order they arrive.

The event-based model is combined with thread level concurrency to enhance performance. Despite encapsulating a single algorithm, many task instances can be run simultaneously for different subsets of the data. The criteria for splitting the work to be done into tasks is data analysis specific, since the algorithm has to be consistent with the data set. For example, in a summary algorithm that requires the month of a given transaction, it is reasonable to partition the calculations according to the months, but not to days.

To handle the large amount of calculations required, PLUS uses a worker / task / controller architecture [13]. Workers are thread objects that execute

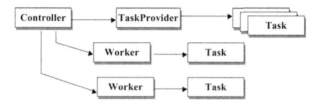

Fig. 5. Worker/Task/Controller Architecture

tasks. The number of workers, as well as other properties, can be dynamically set and controlled through the JBoss JMX console. The analysis work is split into several tasks, which are stored in a task provider and individually supplied to workers. The controller creates and manages the execution of workers. It is also the controller's responsibility to respond to instrumentation requests (start, pause, resume, complete, fail) sent through the JMX console. Fig. 5 illustrates this architecture.

Tasks are themselves Hibernate objects that are persisted in the database, as a "to do" list. Every time a task is completed, its Hibernate representation is removed from the persistent storage. Duplicate tasks are not persisted, so work is not unnecessarily executed. Adding this persistent nature to tasks only required an auto-generated mapping file and database table. This approach adds robustness to the solution, allowing the system to restart from where it has been paused and recover in case of a failure.

Instrumentation of components is yet another feature provided for free with JMX. Public methods of a service are automatically exposed through the JMX console, offering the data analyst fine control over the execution. Users can monitor task's execution, set analysis specific properties, stop, start, restart, resume and change the level of parallelism of services. Futhermore, the Hibernate integration with JMX provides the ability to modify the JDBC datasource properties, include/exclude mapping files and other features.

Scalability and Performance: Event based systems present a range of possibilities for increased performance, data redistribution and operation. Implementations can move to more performant realizations that use clustering, partitioning or other methods to bring system capabilities benefits. Having the system composed by self-contained components allows the use of clustered compute resources that are available with most application servers. In our case, we can use the JBoss clustering mechanism and apply it to the MBeans that execute services in order to exploit real parallel execution (as opposed to interleaved concurrency on the same CPU).

6   Lessons Learned

PLUS architecture evolved over time. This work involved investigation of technologies, experimentation with different designs and close interaction with analysts. Our experience is summarized below:

1. Persuasive industry driven technologies are not always the best solution. Market leaders like Sun, BEA, Oracle and IBM are aggressively pushing the use of "golden hammer" [4] [19] technologies like EJB. For PLUS, and systems with similar characteristics, full J2EE solutions represent a high-overhead with little benefits. Our experience with PLUS has shown that it is possible to leverage benefits from lightweight open source projects and industry standard mechanisms for component interoperability and communication. Hibernate, in particular, has proven to be able to handle complex data models required by BI systems.

2. Having dependencies directly handled by the system removes the need for scheduling, improving maintainability and management. Our previous experience in coordinating dependent components through scheduling mechanisms have proved to be error-prone and hard to configure and maintain. Analysts were required to have an overall knowledge of the complete system, so they could manually update dependencies when adding or removing components. PLUS makes use of hot-deploy and inversion of control to assemble components into a publish/subscribe model. Through information provided by the components themselves, PLUS is able to automatically update dependencies whenever they are added or removed from the system. This approach requires less knowledge to deploy a module, as analysts only have to be aware of the algorithm being developed and its input data format.

3. JMX provides a flexible approach for internal, and potentially external, management. JMX instrumentation has added significant support for experimentation, as it allows changes to the system configuration at runtime. This feature also provides means for future optimizations, such as automatic resource allocation for stages. In addition, as JMX is an open standard, PLUS can be directly integrated with external management systems, such as Tivoli [1], and operational environments.

4. A fundamental lesson learned was the importance of an optimal configuration. A staged event-based architecture potentially increases the performance of the system. However, the potential latency caused by both the granularity of the tasks and the sizes of the data chunks processed by stages could yield very poor performance. If stages were fully executed one after the other, the time to completion would comprise the sum of individual stages execution times. PLUS logically splits analyses into units of work, firing events when individual units have been completed. This approach enables dependent components to start execution before previous stages have been completed, creating a pipeline effect. Maximizing the throughput of this pipeline requires a careful design of analysis algorithms and eventing strategies.

    Consider an example where the input data represents transactions on a given retailer chain. A transaction has, among others, the following fields: "batch identifier", "month of the purchase" and "product identifier". For this example, assume that the two first fields coincide. Events informing changes in the transactional data are based on the "batch identifier". An over-simplified analysis defines the number of products purchased by month. The experiment started with 884,321 transactions, 10 batches and 100 different products. An

extra batch of 124,479 rows was added to the input table, forcing the analysis
to be recalculated. The following settings were tested:

- First, the analysis partitioned the work to be done in parallel tasks according to "month of purchase". This is a sensible choice, since the batch
coincides with the month of the transaction. The addition of a new batch
generated a single task that processed only the added batch. In this case,
the analysis completed in 10 seconds.
- In a second run, the work was split according to the "product identifier".
This is not an appropriate selection, as the algorithm is based on months,
not products. Having tasks selecting the input data by product identifier
unnecessarily recalculates the number of purchase for every month. This
setting generated 100 tasks, one for each product identifier, and took 126
seconds to run.
- In a third experiment, the work was divided according to both "product
identifier" and "month of purchase". This can be a reasonable choice if
the analysis component wants to take advantage of parallel execution
of tasks. In this case, again 100 tasks were instantiated, but the work
was only performed in the added batch. However, for this small sample
of data, 100 tasks were still an unnecessarily large number. Setting the
task to use a "modulo 10 function" on the product identifier creates 10
tasks which complete in 8 seconds.

There is a need for careful design of both architecture and analysis algorithms to maximize process usage and gain scalability. As illustrated by the
example, selection of tasks split criteria will be analysis dependent. Initial
setting usually follow guidelines and final tuning can be done through experimentation.

5. Although we talk about PLUS as a single system, it is actually a framework
composed of four independent sub-projects. The adoption of sub-projects
has improved the development as their external use has helped to generalize requirements. Further, this approach has considerably improved PLUS
configuration management.
6. As to any tool, PLUS has been carefully designed to provide information
and encouragement for the data analyst. We believe that part of the system
success was the tight interaction of developers and analysts operating as
users.

7   Conclusion

This paper has described PLUS, a data analysis environment to extract meaningful information from large amounts of data. PLUS can be classified as a BI
system and more broadly as a data-intensive application. In such systems, the
data process may be split into a sequence of dependent steps. These steps reduce
complexity and allow intermediate results to be available for other purposes.

PLUS uses an event-based architecture where large amounts of data are processed by dependent stages. Having stages defined by loosely coupled and self-
contained components allows for modularity, extensibility and scalability. Stages

can be added and redefined for optimal configuration. Performance is improved by in-process threading mechanisms within stages, having tasks parallel executed in different subsets of the data.

Dependencies in the proposed architecture are handled through a publish / subscribe event mechanism. Staged execution is triggered by events produced by previous phases, freeing the system from providing scheduling mechanisms. Furthermore, dependencies are self-managed, having stages automatically assembled through inversion of control.

Instrumentation also plays an important role in PLUS. Finding the optimal configuration may prove to be challenging. The ability to experiment, by controlling the execution of stages and tuning of data process specific properties, is a valuable feature for complex data analysis systems.

The proposed architecture caters for experimentation, allowing the system to accommodate changes either in short periods or over time. Finally, the realization of the design through the implementation of a real-world system has proven the adequacy of lightweight technologies to large scale data processing applications.

Acknowledgments

The authors would like to acknowledge Dave Martin, Nicola Harris and Alok Rana for their support in both development and review of this work.

References

1. Tivoli: Intelligent management software for the on demand world. Technical report, http://www-306.ibm.com/software/tivoli/.
2. Searchspace: Enabling the Intelligent Enterprise. Technical report, April 2003.
3. Software Scoops - Insights on Software. Technical report, August 2004.
4. William J. Brown, Raphael C. Malveau, Hays W. McCormick, III, and Thomas J. Mowbray. *AntiPatterns: refactoring software, architectures, and projects in crisis.* John Wiley & Sons, Inc., 1998.
5. Business Objects. Businessobjects query and analysis. Technical report, http://www.businessobjects.com/.
6. Calvin Austin. J2SE 1.5 in a Nutshell. Technical report, http://java.sun.com/developer/technicalArticles/releases/j2se15, 2004.
7. G. Cugola, E. Di Nitto, and A. Fuggetta. Exploiting an event-based infrastructure to develop complex distributed systems. In *Proceedings of the 20th international conference on Software engineering*, pages 261–270. IEEE Computer Society, 1998.
8. E. di Nitto and D. Rosenblum. Exploiting ADLs to Specify Architectural Styles Induced by Middleware Infrastructures. In *"Proc. of the 21st Int. Conf. on Software Engineering, Los Angeles, Cal."*, pages 13–22. ACM Press, 1999.
9. Lyman Do, Prabhu Ram, and Pamela Drew. The need for distributed asynchronous transactions. In *Proceedings of the 1999 ACM SIGMOD international conference on Management of data*, pages 534–535. ACM Press, 1999.
10. Marc Fleury, Scott Stark, and The JBoss Group. *JBoss Administration and Development.* John Wiley and Sons, Inc., 2002.

11. Ann Wollrath Samuel C. Kendall Jim Waldo, Geoff Wyant. Events in an rpc based distributed system. In *USENIX 1995 Technical Conference on UNIX and Advanced Computing Systems*, Mountain View, California, USA, 01 1995. USENIX, Sun Microsystems Laboratories.

12. Juha Lindfors, Marce Fleury, and The JBoss Group. *JMX: Managing J2EE with Java Management Extensions*. SAMS, 2002.

13. Anoop Mangat and Iain McLaren. Personal Communication, August 2000.

14. Matt Welsh and David E. Culler and Eric A. Brewer. SEDA: An Architecture for Well-Conditioned, Scalable Internet Services. In *Symposium on Operating Systems Principles*, pages 230–243, 2001.

15. Kirk Pepperdine. Oracle9iAS/TopLink By Example. Technical report, http://otn.oracle.com/oramag/webcolumns/2003/techarticles.

16. Research System Inc. The interactive data language. Technical report, http://www.rsinc.com/idl/.

17. P G Sarang, Kyle Gabhart, Andre Tost, Tim McAllister, Rahim Adatia, Matjaz Juric, Ted Osborne, Faiz Arni, Jeremiah Lott, Vaidyanathan Nagarajan, Craig A. Berry, Dan O'Connor, John Griffin, Aaron Mulder, and Dave Young. *EJB Professional*. Wrox Press Inc, 2001.

18. Sun Microsystems. Java message service specification 1.1. Technical report, http://java.sun.com/products/jms/docs.html.

19. Bruce A. Tate and Justin Getland. *Better, Faster, Lighter Java*. O'Reilly Media Inc., 2004.

20. Hibernate Team. Hibernate reference documentation 2.1.4. Technical report, http://www.hibernate.org/hib_docs/reference/en/html/.

21. XDoclet Team. Xdoclet: Attribute oriented programming. Technical report, http://xdoclet.sourceforge.net/xdoclet/index.html.

22. The MathWorks. Matlab tutorial. Technical report, http://www.math.ufl.edu/help/matlab-tutorial.

23. The OLAP Council. Olap and olap server definitions'. Technical report, http://www.olapcouncil.org/research/glossary.htm.

Integration of Component-Based Development-Deployment Support for J2EE Middleware

Adirake Pimruang, Kazuhiro Fujieda, and Koichiro Ochimizu

Japan Advanced Institute of Science and Technology, School of Information Science,
1-1 Asahidai, Tatsunokuchi, Ishikawa, Japan
{p-adirak, fujieda, ochimizu}@jaist.ac.jp

Abstract. From the widely use of component middleware, developers can reuse existing components not only developed by in-house development but also provided by other organizations. Some components developed in an organization can be deployed in other organizations via the Internet. Developers need to handle the dependency information between such components in both of development and deployment phases. We propose a system called J2DEP to generate and manage such information in the development phase, and to automate the deployment of components. J2DEP copes with configuration management systems to manage components and the information. It manages the dependency information between in-house components and third vendor components, and provides a consistent set of components in the release and deployment phases.

1   Introduction

The middleware, architecture for the development and deployment of software components, is now widely used in business (e.g. J2EE [1], Microsoft .NET [2] and CORBA [3]). Each component encapsulates part of a software system implementing a specific service or a set of services to support business requirements. To build large business systems, developers need several functionalities from the existing components. They can reuse their own in-house developed components or purchase components from third-party vendors to construct applications in middleware technology. Reuse of existing components can reduce time and cost of software development [4].

Each component can be provided by in-house development or come from other organizations distributed in different locations. These organizations generally publish their components to their release sites as binary units to avoid source code release [5]. Developers can integrate these binary components to develop new components or applications [6]. They, however, could not acquire the dependency information of third vendor components. They need to resolve component dependencies manually when they adopt the third vendor's components. In deployment phase, it is also troublesome and consumes time to deploy the proper

T. Gschwind and C. Mascolo (Eds.): SEM 2004, LNCS 3437, pp. 230–244, 2005.
© Springer-Verlag Berlin Heidelberg 2005

versions of components without their dependency information. Another problem occurs when the version of a component is changed. Version conflicts appear in the deployment phase because the effect of the change cannot be traced [7].

Current software configuration management (SCM) systems do not well provide to enable component-based development and component reuse [8]. Different organizations can provide several versions of components in which their dependency information is not explicitly described [9]. They cannot properly manage the evolution of components developed by third-party organization. Each third party organization develops its components and releases them in its own release policy. For example, some organizations may release sources of their components in their SCM repositories, and others may release binary components in their HTTP server. SCM systems cannot help us to manage the dependency information of components released with different policies.

The software deployment including following activities: obtaining components, these dependents, packaging, and releasing, should be done in automatic ways [10]. To realize automatic deployment, developers generally defines dependency information of components in the release phase. Then, deployers use a deployment tool to obtain components from the release site according to the information. In component-based development, component identification starts from the design phase [11]. Developers implicitly or explicitly use the information in the development phase and redefine it again in the release phase.

What we need is the SCM system that supports component-based development. SCM must support managing component relationships and the change of component versions by different organizations. This means such a system must help developers to adopt components based on different release policies, to generate the dependency information in the development phase and manage both sources and them in SCM repositories. With this system, the deployment process can be performed automatically. Developers can use the dependency information of components to obtain the correct versions of components to be assembled and deployed in developers' middleware in the build and test phase. Also, deployers can get correct versions of components to deploy in user middleware in component the installation phase.

In this paper, we propose J2DEP (J2EE DEvelopment-dePloyment support), which supports configuration management addressing both in development and deployment phases. J2DEP helps developers to create or generate dependency information from imported components and manages sources and dependency information inside a CVS repository to support the development process. Moreover, J2DEP can also publish the binary components to release sites by using FTP/HTTP servers. In the development process, J2DEP helps developers to import remote components, which is developed by different organizations, to its development environment by getting source files from the repository or binary components from the release site. Then, it generates the dependency metadata from imported components and control metadata files in the repository. The dependency metadata mainly represents the component details (e.g. name, version and type) and the method to obtain the component from a repository or a release site. Finally, in the deployment phase, J2DEP helps developers to get components from release sites, assemble relating components into application components and to install them and the dependency information to the target platform.

The paper is further structured as follows. We introduce the background of this research in Sect. 2 and give an example scenario that motivates this research in Sect. 3 We outline the overview and approach of J2DEP system in Sect. 4. In Sect. 5, we give the implementation details of J2DEP system in development-deployment phase support. We show related works in Sect. 6 and give a conclusion in Sect. 7.

2   Background

J2DEP intends to support both of component development and deployment phases. In this section, we would like to discuss about related works and motivation of this research.

2.1   Component Development-Deployment

To realize the problem raised in the development process in middleware, we would like to show the development roles and tasks in J2EE. J2EE development-deployment roles consist of the following main three ones [1].

Application Component Provider. An application component provider provides the building blocks of a J2EE application. A provider can develop components and package binary files into an application component. A component from provider may have dependencies on other components. In J2EE, there are two methods to handle such dependencies.

Package dependent components into a new component: The dependencies can be reduced by grouping the related components into a new component. However, this method reduces the degree of component reusability because dependent components become a part of the new component.

Do not package dependent components: This method can maximize the reusability of each component. We have to leave a room for application assemblers to pick and select components to compose J2EE applications.

The problem raised in this role is about the dependencies. In the development phase, generally, developers do not manage the dependency information and its changes of their components in their repositories. Moreover, dependency information in the development phase is often reduced in the release phase because some components may be a part of another component. In this case, the same components may have different dependency metadata in the repository and the release site.

Application Assembler. An application assembler groups a set of components developed by application component providers and to assemble them into a J2EE application. An application assembler is responsible for providing assembly instructions describing external dependencies of the application that the deployer must resolve in deployment phase.

To support application assembler automatically, the assemblers need to use dependency information to obtain related component and to generate deployment descriptor about external dependencies.

Deployer. A deployer installs components and applications into a J2EE server. He has to resolve all the external dependencies declared by the application component provider and the application assembler to configure them. The application component provider should define dependency information of components properly in the development phase.

2.2   Software Configuration Management (SCM)

Software configuration management concept is to manage charges of software artifacts. The most of SCM systems including RCS [12] and CVS [13] can manage only text file. While component-based development, developer has to deal with both component sources in text format and binary components. So we need a method to manage changes in binary components on local SCM systems (SCM systems of in-house development) when developers want to reuse them.

2.3   Software Deployment

The software deployment life cycle is evolving these activities: package, release, configure, assembler, install, update, remove and adapt [14]. The most of deployment tools can support component development and can manipulate the component dependencies. Some tools can support component development among distributed organizations. SRM [15], Software Dock [14], RPM [16] can manage multiple version of component. But these tools do not connect the deployment process with SCM. TWICS [10] resolves this shortcoming by supporting to get components from SCM repository (third vendor repository or in-house repository) to release and get the component from component publisher to a local SCM repository (source repository of in-house development).

However, deployment tools we mentioned above do not connect the development and deployment phases properly. The component dependencies are generally defined in the release phase. By reuse concept, related components have been defined in the design phase. The developer needs the dependencies defined in the deployment phase especially in the build and test phases, so the dependencies should be defined in the development phase rather than in the release phase.

3   Example Scenario

To clarify the issues of component development-deployment in middleware, we consider the relationship of components developed by different organizations shown in Fig. 1. The rectangle boxes represent components developed by each organization displayed in oval shapes. The arrows show the dependencies among

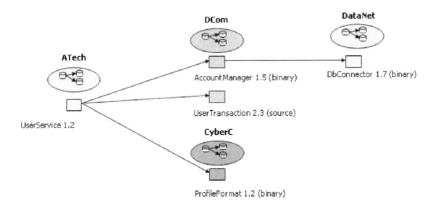

Fig. 1. Example scenario of component-based development

the components. The text below each rectangle box shows its component name, version and release type respectively.

The first issue is that each organization may develop several versions of components and each component may depend on other components. Developers have no support to document the dependency information properly. They need to resolve dependencies manually whenever they get the sources from their repository to put into the development environment. For example, the dependencies of UserService 1.2 on AccountManager1.5, UserTransaction 2.3, DbConnector 1.7 and ProfileFormat 1.2, are not provided in development phase. The dependency information in the release phase cannot be documented properly because it is not defined in the development phase. As the result, we cannot guarantee the consistency throughout the deployment phase.

The second issue is that the some dependencies may be reduced in release phase because developer may combine some components with another component. For example, the dependencies of UserService 1.2 are AccountManager1.5, UserTransaction 2.3, DbConnector 1.7 and ProfileFormat 1.2 in development phase. In release phase, the developer can combine AccountManager 1.5 and DbConnector 1.7 with UserService 1.2. The dependencies of the resulting UserService 1.2 become only UserTransaction 2.3 and ProfileFormat 1.2. The component dependencies in the development phase and the deployment phase can be different.

The third issue is that each organization may develop and publish the components based on different release policies. They may publish the component sources their repository, the binary components in their release server or attach the component sources with the binary components. Developers need not only the dependency information but also the methods to obtain the components. For example, to develop UserService, ATech needs to define the relations to AccountManager, UserTransaction and ProfileFormat. ATech needs to define also the methods to get binary versions of AccountManager and ProfileFormat from corresponding release sites and to get the component sources of UserTransaction from the repository. As the result, the component developer and deployer need the method to handle with different release policies.

To summarize the problem raised in component development-deployment process, current systems come into these shortcomings:

1. Dependency information defined in the development phase cannot be used in the release and deployment phases automatically.
2. Dependencies in the development phase and the deployment phase can be different because to combine components with another component can reduce the dependency information.
3. SCM systems cannot import sources or binary versions of components developed by different organizations into local development environment automatically and cannot manage the dependency information of each component.

We need a system to manage interrelated components in the development phase and to deploy consistent sets of components to middleware automatically.

4   Approach

The J2DEP research project addresses support to component development-deployment process. This system integrates the functionalities of the configuration management, component development and component deployment together.

The key insight of this research is to manage the evolution of third vendor components inside local configuration management. Rather than to bring and control all versions of third vendor components in the local configuration management, J2DEP supports developers to import the external components to development space mentioned below and generate the dependency information as **dependency metadata**. Then, J2DEP keeps and manages the dependency metadata in the local configuration management instead.

4.1   Development Space

Developers can use J2DEP to import third vendor components into the development spaces shown in Fig. 2 and to generate dependency metadata.

A development space is a directory structure to store source files, dependency metadata and dependent components imported by developer corresponding to dependency metadata. In a development phase, a developer can use J2DEP to import third-vendor components into his development space, and then he can control both the sources and the metadata in his local SCM. The details of the development space are shown in Fig. 6 in Sect. 5.

4.2   Dependency Metadata

Dependency Metadata mainly describes details of dependent components (component name, version, vendor, component type, and package type) and the method to obtain components either from source repositories or release sites.

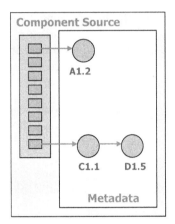

Fig. 2. An example of development space

```
<dependency_component>
  <name>ProfileFormat</name>
  <version>1.2</version>
  <vendor>CyberC</vendor>
  <type>Application Jar</type>
  <packagetype>binary</packagetype>
  <!-- binary package location-->
  <location>www.cyberc.com/release/profileFormat.jar</location>
</dependency_component>
```

Fig. 3. Dependency metadata from a release site

```
<dependency_component>
  <name>UserTransaction</name>
  <version>2.3</version>
  <vendor>DCom</vendor>
  <type>Session Bean</type>
  <packagetype>source</packagetype>
  <!-- source location-->
<location>cvshost.dcom.com</location>
  <cvsroot>/work/cvsroot</cvsroot>
  <authentication>pserver</authentication>
  <tag>UserTransaction-2.3</tag>
</dependency_component>
```

Fig. 4. Dependency metadata from a source repository

A developer can define the relationship among any combination of sources and
binary components with dependency metadata.

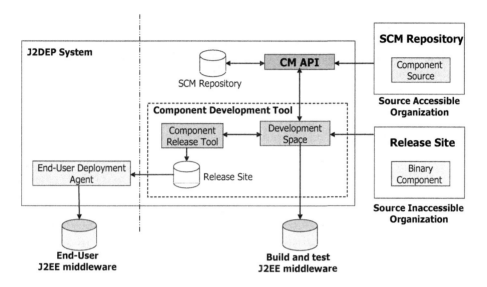

Fig. 5. J2DEP architecture

J2DEP supports to generate two kinds of metadata depending on the release policy of each component:

- Metadata of a component from a release site, shown in Fig. 3. It consists of component details and URL to download the component
- Metadata of a component from a source repository, shown in Fig.4. It consists of component details, the repository location, the authentication type and the tag name for checking out the component sources.

4.3   J2DEP Architecture

In Fig. 5, we show the overall J2DEP architecture. The development space is where developers place the component sources, dependencies and perform their development. They can use J2DEP to import dependent components by getting sources from organizations that allow accessing the sources in their repositories or by downloading the binary components from the organizations that publish only binary versions. After they fill out the component information to J2DEP, J2DEP will generate dependency metadata into their development space.

J2DEP connects development space with configuration management API (CM API) to manage versions of component sources and their dependencies and connects with release sites to publish components with dependency metadata. To support consistency of component versions in the deployment phase, J2DEP uses the dependency metadata defined in the development phase.

There are two kinds of middleware deployed components.

– Build and test middleware is for developers to deploy the components obtained from the repository and their dependencies. Developers can build binary components and deploy them with dependencies. They are used in the testing phase.
– User middleware is for end-users who deploy only binary components to operate their business requirements and have no relation to the component development process. Deployer can obtain binary components from release sites to deploy in user middleware.

4.4   Main Functionality

The J2DEP architecture consists of two main parts Component Development Support Tool and End-User Deployment Agent.

Component Development Support Tool. This tool supports to generate dependency information for each component and connect a development space with CM API, build and test middleware and release sites.

End-User Deployment Agent. This tool supports in the deployment phase to assemble related components to an application component and deploy it in end-users middleware. End-User Deployment Agent will also record the deployed component data to manage dependencies of components on end-user middleware.

5   Implementation

J2DEP supports various kinds of J2EE components based on the architecture described in Sect. 4. J2DEP prototype integrates the development spaces with CVS to manage sources and dependency metadata, HTTP/FTP servers to publish binary components and JBOSS middleware as a platform to deploy J2EE components.

In this section, we show the implementation details of Component Development Support Tool and End-User Deployment Agent. At first, we discuss about Component Development Support. We show how J2DEP supports to create the development spaces, import the related component, generate the dependency metadata, build component, deploy components with dependencies into the middleware in development sites and release the components to the release site. Then, we show how End-User Deployment Agent can support deployers.

5.1   Component Development Support Tool

Development Space Structure. J2DEP supports to build a development space, to create components, to obtain components from the source repository and to import the dependency information of them. In the prototype system, we use the same structure of the development space and the project metadata as

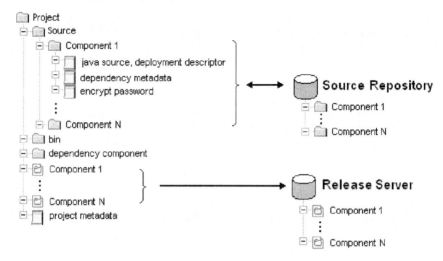

Fig. 6. Development space, source repository and release site

Eclipse [17] JDT (Java development tools), so that the developers can continue development with Eclipse easily. The development space structure (as illustrated in Fig. 6) consists of several locations for the following artifacts:

Source Directory. Component source files, dependency metadata and the encrypted user name and password to connect a source repository or a release site of dependent components.

Binary Directory. Compiled versions of Java sources.

Dependent Component Directory. Binary versions of dependent components imported by developers to the development space.

Binary Version of Component. Components built from corresponding sources in the source directory.

Project Metadata. Information about the components in the development space.

Development Space Initialization. Developers can start developing components by initializing a development space. J2DEP helps to create a new development space shown in Fig. 6. They can also open an existing development space from a project metadata file. Then, all components of the development space defined in the project metadata will be opened by the J2DEP tool.

J2DEP connects the development space with a CVS repository shown in Fig. 4. Developers can create new components or pull existing components from source repository to the development space. To create a new component, J2DEP supports to prepare source files and a deployment descriptor for a J2EE component. To pull an existing component from a repository, developers have to inform

J2DEP about the component name and version to check out the component by CVS tagging. J2DEP supports to check out sources, dependency metadata and encrypt user name and password file from source repository. Then, J2DEP will get dependent components corresponding to dependency metadata and put into Dependent component directory to prepare for the build and test process in the development phase.

Once, the developers create or check out components into the development space, they can continue development by using normal configuration management procedures (e.g. using CVS).

Dependent Component Import Tool. J2DEP helps developers to import the dependent components from either in-house or third vendor developments to the development spaces. The dependent components can be component sources from the SCM repositories or binary components from the release sites.

Developer has to select the methods to import the component from the repositories or the release sites. To import the dependent components, J2DEP supports the developers to import by three methods (1) downloading from release sites (2) checking out from repositories (3) copying from the local computer. J2DEP will import the components into Dependent Component Directory. Developers need to inform J2DEP about the component details and the connection details shown in Fig. 7 and Fig. 8.

After developers fill out the form, J2DEP generates the dependency metadata, like in Fig. 3 and Fig. 4, for the imported components. For the user name and the password to connect a repository or a release server, J2DEP will encrypt them and generate a new file separated from dependency metadata.

Notice that, the developers need to add the next level dependencies manually, when the component does not include any metadata (e.g. the component is not built by J2DEP).

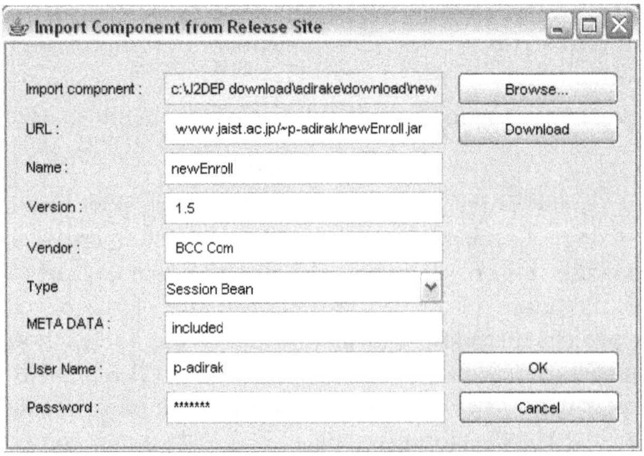

Fig. 7. The import tool for binary components from release sites

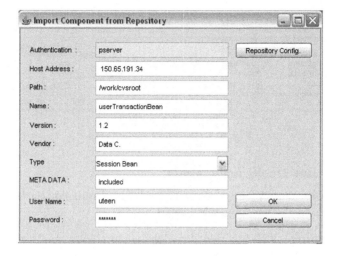

Fig. 8. The import tool for component sources from repositories

Component Packaging and Developer Site Deployment Support. When a developers finish developing by using the normal configuration management procedures, J2DEP supports to build the Java source files and package the compiled sources into a binary component automatically.

J2DEP supports to generate the default J2EE deployment descriptor and assemble the related components in Component Dependency Directory of the development space into a single J2EE module. They can deploy or redeploy a J2EE module to their middleware server to perform the testing phase. They can use this tool to undeploy components and their dependencies from middleware.

Component Release Tool. After developers finish testing the components in their development space, they can release the binary components to release sites. J2DEP supports developers to connect to FTP/HTTP servers and to upload the binary versions of components. Developers or end-users can download the components from the release sites by Developer Deployment Support or End-User Deployment Agent.

In the release phase, the developers need to select components and combine them into a new component for releasing. If they select a component to be included in other component package, the dependency on the component is removed. For example in Fig. 9, the dependency metadata between UserWeb-Component and transactionBean is removed because transactionBean becomes a part of UserWebComponent.

The developers also need to specify the release policy for each component that contains sources. If they do not want to release component sources, they have to inform J2DEP about the location to upload the binary component.

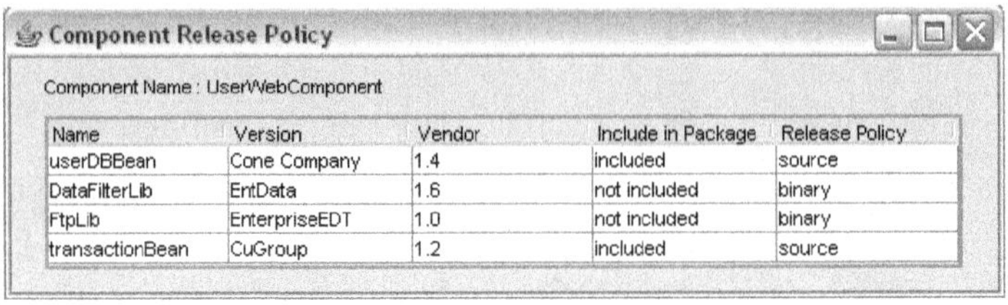
Component Release Policy

Component Name : UserWebComponent

Name	Version	Vendor	Include in Package	Release Policy
userDBBean	Cone Company	1.4	included	source
DataFilterLib	EntData	1.6	not included	binary
FtpLib	EnterpriseEDT	1.0	not included	binary
transactionBean	CuGroup	1.2	included	source

Fig. 9. Component release tool

5.2 End-User Deployment Agent

End-User Deployment Agent supports to deploy and undeploy the binary version of components to the end-user middleware.

Deploy Support. This function downloads components and their dependent components to middleware. To deploy components, the deployers have to inform the component name, version and location to download each component to End-User Deployment Agent. After finishing downloading components, End-User Deployment Agent generates the J2EE default deployment descriptor and assemble every component into an application. Then, it records the components that they have already deployed into a log file. When deployers want to deploy again, the existing components in middleware are not downloaded again.

Undeploy Support. This function removes components and their external dependencies. To maintain the consistency of the components in middleware, End-User Deployment Agent can remove only the components that are not shared by other components

6 Related Works

J2DEP is built to connect component development and deployment processes. There are several tools to support these processes. We discuss some integrated development environments (IDEs) such as Eclipse [17], NetBeansIDE [18] and JBuider [19]. We also discuss RPM [16] and TWICS [10] for component deployment support.

We compare the functionalities of each tool in development-deployment process in Table 1. These IDEs support the development process of Java including J2EE applications. They can support J2EE development by several kinds of plugins. Developers can use these tools to create various kinds of J2EE components, manage the component sources in their repositories, and test them. Although these tools provide the interface to connect the development environment with an SCM repository, the dependencies of components are not well resolved and managed in the repository. Developers have to manage the dependency information in the local configuration management manually.

Table 1. Functionalities of J2DEP and related tools

	IDEs	RPM	TWICS	J2DEP
Connect the tool with the development space	○	×	$\triangle_2$	$\triangle_4$
Generate dependency information	×	$\triangle_1$	$\triangle_3$	○
Connect the tool with SCM	○	×	○	○
Manage dependency information in SCM	×	×	○	○
Component release support	×	○	○	○
Deploy components to the development space	○	○	○	○
Deploy components to end-users' sites	×	○	○	○
Deploy components with dependencies	×	×	$\triangle_2$	○

○= supported, ×= not supported, $\triangle$= partially supported
$\triangle_1$ Generate the dependency but no detail about the component location.
$\triangle_2$ Support only components built by TWICS.
$\triangle_3$ Generate the dependency information only in the release phase.
$\triangle_4$ The target space must be the same as Eclipse development space in the development phase.

7   Conclusion

In this research, we proposed J2DEP, the integration of component-based development-deployment and software configuration management in middleware. This system is designed to support managing the interrelation of in-house components and third vendor components. J2DEP links between component development and component deployment. The dependency metadata defined in the development phase and component sources can be managed in local configuration management. J2DEP uses dependency metadata to support the build and release processes for developers. J2DEP also helps a developer or a deployer to deploy consistent sets of components in either developer site or user site.

Currently, J2DEP lacks some features for the component development-deployment support. For example, developers have to merge different versions of dependency metadata manually. We need to implement these features. In the current prototype, J2DEP is a tool separated from the other development tools. In the future, it would be advantage to implement J2DEP as the other development tool plug-ins, for example, Eclipse or NetBeanIDE. This would allow developers to gain the benefit from all infra-structure provided by the other tools.

References

1. Inderjeet, S., Stearns, B., Johnson, M.: Designing Enterprise Applications With the J2Ee Platform. Addison-Wesley (2002)
2. Corporation, M.: Microsoft .NET technical resources. `http://www.microsoft.com/net/technical/` (2004)

3. Object Management Group, Inc.: Common Object Request Broker Architecture: Core Specification. formal/04-03-12 edn. (2004)
4. Whitehead, K.: Component Based Development: Principles and Planning for Business Systems. Addison-Wesley (2002)
5. Cervantes, H., Hall, R.S.: Autonomous adaptation to dynamic availability using a service-oriented component model. In: Proceedings of 26th International Conference on Software Engineering (ICSE'04). (2004) 614–623
6. Szyperski, C., Gruntz, D., Murer, S.: Component Software: Beyond Object-Oriented Programming. 2nd edn. Addison-Wesley (2002)
7. Schmidt, D.C., Vinoski, S.: The corba component model: Part 1, evolving towards component middleware. C/C++ Users Journal (2004)
8. Weber, D.W.: Requirements for an scm architecture to enable component-based development. In: Proceedings of the 10th International Workshop on SCM. (2001)
9. Edwards, S.H., Gibson, D.S., Weide, B.W., , Zhupanov, S.: Software component relationships. In: the 8th Annual Workshop on Institutionalizing Software Reuse. (1997)
10. Sowrirajan, S., van der Hoek, A.: Managing the evolution of distributed and interrelated components. In: Proceedings of the 11th International Workshop on SCM. LNCS 2649, Springer-Verlag (2003) 217–230
11. Larsson, M., Crnkovic, I.: Configuration management for component-based systems. In: Proceedings of the 10th International Workshop on SCM. (2001)
12. Free Software Foundation, Inc.: RCS. `http://www.gnu.org/software/rcs/rcs.html` (2003)
13. Cederqvist, P., et al.: Version management with CVS for cvs 1.11.17. http://www.cvshome.org/docs/manual/ (2004)
14. Hall, R.S., Heimbigner, D., Wolf, A.L.: A cooperative approach to support software deployment using the software dock. In: Proceedings of the 21st International Conference on Software Engineering (ICSE'99). (1999) 174–183
15. van der Hoek, A., Hall, R.S., Heimbigner, D., Wolf, A.L.: Software release management. In: Proceedings of the 6th European Software Engineering Conference (held jointly with the 5th ACM SIGSOFT international symposium on Foundations of Software Engineering). (1997) 159–175
16. The RPM community: www.rpm.org homepage. `http://www.rpm.org/` (2002)
17. Eclipse Foundation: eclipse.org. `http://www.eclipse.org/` (2004)
18. netBeans.org: NetBeans IDE. `http://www.netbeans.org/products/ide/` (2004)
19. Borland Software Corporation: Borland JBuilder. `http://www.borland.com/jbuilder/` (2004)

Author Index

Lecture Notes in Computer Science

For information about Vols. 1–3358

please contact your bookseller or Springer

Vol. 3409: N. Guelfi, G. Reggio, A. Romanovsky (Eds.), Scientific Engineering of Distributed Java Applications. X, 127 pages. 2005.

Vol. 3408: D.E. Losada, J.M. Fernández-Luna (Eds.), Advances in Information Retrieval. XVII, 572 pages. 2005.

Vol. 3407: Z. Liu, K. Araki (Eds.), Theoretical Aspects of Computing - ICTAC 2004. XIV, 562 pages. 2005.

Vol. 3406: A. Gelbukh (Ed.), Computational Linguistics and Intelligent Text Processing. XVII, 829 pages. 2005.

Vol. 3404: V. Diekert, B. Durand (Eds.), STACS 2005. XVI, 706 pages. 2005.

Vol. 3403: B. Ganter, R. Godin (Eds.), Formal Concept Analysis. XI, 419 pages. 2005. (Subseries LNAI).

Vol. 3401: Z. Li, L.G. Vulkov, J. Waśniewski (Eds.), Numerical Analysis and Its Applications. XIII, 630 pages. 2005.

Vol. 3399: Y. Zhang, K. Tanaka, J.X. Yu, S. Wang, M. Li (Eds.), Web Technologies Research and Development - APWeb 2005. XXII, 1082 pages. 2005.

Vol. 3398: D.-K. Baik (Ed.), Systems Modeling and Simulation: Theory and Applications. XIV, 733 pages. 2005. (Subseries LNAI).

Vol. 3397: T.G. Kim (Ed.), Artificial Intelligence and Simulation. XV, 711 pages. 2005. (Subseries LNAI).

Vol. 3396: R.M. van Eijk, M.-P. Huget, F. Dignum (Eds.), Agent Communication. X, 261 pages. 2005. (Subseries LNAI).

Vol. 3395: J. Grabowski, B. Nielsen (Eds.), Formal Approaches to Software Testing. X, 225 pages. 2005.

Vol. 3394: D. Kudenko, D. Kazakov, E. Alonso (Eds.), Adaptive Agents and Multi-Agent Systems III. VIII, 313 pages. 2005. (Subseries LNAI).

Vol. 3393: H.-J. Kreowski, U. Montanari, F. Orejas, G. Rozenberg, G. Taentzer (Eds.), Formal Methods in Software and Systems Modeling. XXVII, 413 pages. 2005.

Vol. 3392: D. Seipel, M. Hanus, U. Geske, O. Bartenstein (Eds.), Applications of Declarative Programming and Knowledge Management. X, 309 pages. 2005. (Subseries LNAI).

Vol. 3391: C. Kim (Ed.), Information Networking. XVII, 936 pages. 2005.

Vol. 3390: R. Choren, A. Garcia, C. Lucena, A. Romanovsky (Eds.), Software Engineering for Multi-Agent Systems III. XII, 291 pages. 2005.

Vol. 3389: P. Van Roy (Ed.), Multiparadigm Programming in Mozart/OZ. XV, 329 pages. 2005.

Vol. 3388: J. Lagergren (Ed.), Comparative Genomics. VII, 133 pages. 2005. (Subseries LNBI).

Vol. 3387: J. Cardoso, A. Sheth (Eds.), Semantic Web Services and Web Process Composition. VIII, 147 pages. 2005.

Vol. 3386: S. Vaudenay (Ed.), Public Key Cryptography - PKC 2005. IX, 436 pages. 2005.

Vol. 3385: R. Cousot (Ed.), Verification, Model Checking, and Abstract Interpretation. XII, 483 pages. 2005.

Vol. 3383: J. Pach (Ed.), Graph Drawing. XII, 536 pages. 2005.

Vol. 3382: J. Odell, P. Giorgini, J.P. Müller (Eds.), Agent-Oriented Software Engineering V. X, 239 pages. 2005.

Vol. 3381: P. Vojtáš, M. Bieliková, B. Charron-Bost, O. Sýkora (Eds.), SOFSEM 2005: Theory and Practice of Computer Science. XV, 448 pages. 2005.

Vol. 3380: C. Priami, Transactions on Computational Systems Biology I. IX, 111 pages. 2005. (Subseries LNBI).

Vol. 3379: M. Hemmje, C. Niederee, T. Risse (Eds.), From Integrated Publication and Information Systems to Information and Knowledge Environments. XXIV, 321 pages. 2005.

Vol. 3378: J. Kilian (Ed.), Theory of Cryptography. XII, 621 pages. 2005.

Vol. 3377: B. Goethals, A. Siebes (Eds.), Knowledge Discovery in Inductive Databases. VII, 190 pages. 2005.

Vol. 3376: A. Menezes (Ed.), Topics in Cryptology – CT-RSA 2005. X, 385 pages. 2005.

Vol. 3375: M.A. Marsan, G. Bianchi, M. Listanti, M. Meo (Eds.), Quality of Service in Multiservice IP Networks. XIII, 656 pages. 2005.

Vol. 3374: D. Weyns, H.V.D. Parunak, F. Michel (Eds.), Environments for Multi-Agent Systems. X, 279 pages. 2005. (Subseries LNAI).

Vol. 3372: C. Bussler, V. Tannen, I. Fundulaki (Eds.), Semantic Web and Databases. X, 227 pages. 2005.

Vol. 3371: M.W. Barley, N. Kasabov (Eds.), Intelligent Agents and Multi-Agent Systems. X, 329 pages. 2005. (Subseries LNAI).

Vol. 3370: A. Konagaya, K. Satou (Eds.), Grid Computing in Life Science. X, 188 pages. 2005. (Subseries LNBI).

Vol. 3369: V.R. Benjamins, P. Casanovas, J. Breuker, A. Gangemi (Eds.), Law and the Semantic Web. XII, 249 pages. 2005. (Subseries LNAI).

Vol. 3368: L. Paletta, J.K. Tsotsos, E. Rome, G.W. Humphreys (Eds.), Attention and Performance in Computational Vision. VIII, 231 pages. 2005.

Vol. 3367: W.S. Ng, B.C. Ooi, A. Ouksel, C. Sartori (Eds.), Databases, Information Systems, and Peer-to-Peer Computing. X, 231 pages. 2005.

Vol. 3366: I. Rahwan, P. Moraitis, C. Reed (Eds.), Argumentation in Multi-Agent Systems. XII, 263 pages. 2005. (Subseries LNAI).

Vol. 3365: G. Mauri, G. Păun, M.J. Pérez-Jiménez, G. Rozenberg, A. Salomaa (Eds.), Membrane Computing. IX, 415 pages. 2005.

Vol. 3363: T. Eiter, L. Libkin (Eds.), Database Theory - ICDT 2005. XI, 413 pages. 2004.

Vol. 3362: G. Barthe, L. Burdy, M. Huisman, J.-L. Lanet, T. Muntean (Eds.), Construction and Analysis of Safe, Secure, and Interoperable Smart Devices. IX, 257 pages. 2005.

Vol. 3361: S. Bengio, H. Bourlard (Eds.), Machine Learning for Multimodal Interaction. XII, 362 pages. 2005.

Vol. 3360: S. Spaccapietra, E. Bertino, S. Jajodia, R. King, D. McLeod, M.E. Orlowska, L. Strous (Eds.), Journal on Data Semantics II. XI, 223 pages. 2005.

Vol. 3359: G. Grieser, Y. Tanaka (Eds.), Intuitive Human Interfaces for Organizing and Accessing Intellectual Assets. XIV, 257 pages. 2005. (Subseries LNAI).